36935

305.8
NEU

Neuhaus, Richard
John

Dispensations

$16,95

DATE DUE

Books by Richard John Neuhaus

Against the World for the World (editor)
Christian Faith and Public Policy
Freedom for Ministry
In Defense of People
Dispensations
Movement and Revolution (with Peter Berger)
Theology and the Kingdom of God (editor)
Time Toward Home
To Empower People (with Peter Berger)
The Naked Public Square

The Encounter Series (editor)

Virtue: Public and Private
Unsecular America

DISPENSATIONS

*The Future of South Africa
as South Africans See It*

by RICHARD JOHN NEUHAUS

GRAND RAPIDS, MICHIGAN
WILLIAM B. EERDMANS PUBLISHING COMPANY

Library of Congress Cataloging-in-Publication Data

Neuhaus, Richard John.
   Dispensations : the future of South Africa as South Africans see it.

   Includes bibliographical references.
   1. South Africa — Politics and government — 1978-   — Public opinion.
2. South Africa — Race relations — Public opinion.
3. Race relations — Religious aspects — Christianity — Public opinion.
4. Public opinion — South Africa.   I. Title.
DT779.952.N48   1986   305.8'00968   86-2150

ISBN 0-8028-3627-5

to
Robert Louis Wilken
    by the Sea of Galilee

CONTENTS

A WORD TO THE READER

A LMOST nobody is neutral about South Africa. Some Americans and Europeans view it mainly in geopolitical terms, believing it is strategically critical to the West. Others look at it economically and call it "the Persian Gulf of minerals." Yet others say it is the last hope for civilization and freedom in a continent that is otherwise dying. But most of us, it is fair to say, have a different understanding of South Africa. Most Westerners think of South Africa first as the land of apartheid in which a white racist minority brutally oppresses a black population more than five times its size.

This book is about the people of South Africa—black and white and, as they say, coloured and Indian. It is about economics and politics and revolution, to be sure, but chiefly it is about these people and how they view their future together—or apart. It is not the last word on South Africa, but it is their word.

Any book that comes out of talking with people has a certain bias. People who are trained in talking tend to be overrepresented. There are perhaps too many politicians and clergy and journalists and academics here and too few "little people" who also have a deep stake in the future of South Africa. But I hope the reader will recognize their presence on every page: the innumerable blacks who have been coercively uprooted and removed to a stark subsistence in their tribal "homelands," the Afrikaner shopkeepers with their deep forebodings about a changing order they no longer understand, the coloured clerk who aspires to be white but takes out insurance on the future by calling herself black, the Indian who sweeps floors and knows that he is marginal to a population group that is supposed to be rich. These too, these very importantly, are the people of South Africa.

The inevitable bias is also a strength, however. In these pages we meet the kind of people who are shaping the future, or who want to shape it. These are the people who have thought long about South Africa and its place in the world. They have many and often conflicting things to say about race and justice and nationhood and the prospect of peaceful change. Some are convinced that time has run out for South Africa. Others believe this is a time of new beginnings and high promise. Most are profoundly uncertain. This book is an exploration into the fears and visions of South Africans today.

My interest in South Africa dates from the 1960s. It was part of an interest in Africa itself, and that was undoubtedly related to my work in the civil rights movement and my years as pastor of a large black parish in Brooklyn, New York. My research and writing over the years also converge with the critical questions posed by South Africa today. More particularly, South Africa is a case study in the dialectic between "covenant" and "contract" in political theory, as that dialectic is examined in my *Time Toward Home.* My understanding of the engagement of religion in social change was set forth in *Christian Faith and Public Policy,* and the intensity of that engagement could hardly be more dramatic than it is in South Africa. Also, the reader will find threaded through the conversations in this book a concern about the nature and legitimacy of democratic governance, as that concern is also developed in my *The Naked Public Square: Religion and Democracy in America.*

In short, my interest in South Africa is far from being accidental. It is closely tied to practical and theoretical questions that have much broader application. I hope the reader too will discover in this book unexpected connections. South Africa is important in itself, of course, and eminently deserving of our close attention. But the debate about the future of South Africa is in many ways a debate about the future of our life together on this small earth—about relations between rich and poor, between races and ideologies, indeed about the meaning of freedom, peace, and justice in a deeply disordered world. Much of the debate is about oddities, wrongs, and fears peculiar to South African society. But those who have ears to hear the voices in these pages will be left with no doubt that South Africans talking about themselves are in fact talking about all of us, the kind of people we think we are and the kind of people we sometimes hope and sometimes fear we may really be.

I first visited South Africa in 1971, and in these pages I allude occasionally to conversations from that period. My most recent visit was in August 1985. The present book, however, comes chiefly out of hundreds of conversations with South Africans during the crucial months of the debate over "the new dispensation" in 1983. Developments in South Africa are, as they say in the news business, fast-breaking. This is especially the case in the past year when many politicians and media leaders "discovered" South Africa and made it an issue of overriding urgency in international and domestic politics.

It may therefore be thought that there is a certain temerity in publishing any book on South Africa at this moment. Significant changes will almost certainly outpace the progress of this manuscript on its way through the printer to the bookstore. However, in almost fifteen years of watching and talking with South Africans on all sides of that country's contentions I am deeply impressed by the continuity of the arguments, interests, and visions in conflict. The unrest (as it is called) of 1984–85 may have brought everything to a head; it may be that time has indeed run out and the denouement of the South African drama is now upon us. But, as the reader will soon see, it may also be that this period will be looked back upon as a violent spasm that momentarily contorted the continuing realities of South Africa's turmoil.

Finally, this book is not designed to compete with the many specialized and scholarly works on South Africa, to which I am also indebted for my understanding of what is going on there. The aim of this book, as indicated in its subtitle, is really quite modest. I will consider it a success if it answers the reader's question: "But what do *they* think?"

The Rockford Institute   RICHARD JOHN NEUHAUS
Center on Religion and Society
New York City

ACKNOWLEDGMENTS

I am grateful to Beyers Naudé and the Christian Institute, now outlawed, for first introducing me to some of the issues and actors in South Africa's agony. To the South Africa Foundation which helped me, as it has helped so many people of every political persuasion, on the logistics of my most recent trip. To those in South Africa and here who read the manuscript in whole or in part and offered many valuable suggestions. To Teresa Mancuso for the index and secretarial help always graciously given.

I am also grateful to the Council on Religion and International Affairs, and its president, Robert Myers. The Council, an Andrew Carnegie foundation in New York, commissioned the project of which this book is the product.

I am greatly indebted to William Eerdmans, publisher, and Jon Pott, editor, for their supportive interest in this project, and for their own considerable insights into the worlds of South Africa. Also to my friend and colleague of many years, Peter Berger of Boston University, for keeping me engaged in research on "South Africa Beyond Apartheid" (SABA), a continuing commission of South African and North American scholars examining the possible futures of South Africa.

Finally, and most particularly, I am grateful to the hundreds of South Africans who generously shared with me their time and ideas. Only some of them appear by name in these pages, but all of them have contributed to this enterprise. I hope I have not misrepresented any persons or ideas. I know I have betrayed no confidences. I also know people have a way of saying more than they might have intended to say.

DISPENSATIONS

CHAPTER ONE

AFRIKANER IDENTITY AND DESTINY

THE new dispensation began on November 2, 1983. On that day the white voters of South Africa approved a form of "power sharing" with South Africans who are not white, at least by South Africa's reckoning of whiteness. Some whites railed against the new dispensation because, they claimed, it meant the end of apartheid. Other whites, those in the government, were immensely pleased by the vote. They acknowledged, sotto voce, that it did indeed mean the beginning of the end of the apartheid system that has been the object of moral indignation throughout the world. Then there were the whites of a more liberal disposition. They too were deeply unhappy about the new dispensation. Not because they had any use for apartheid; on the contrary, they detested it and believed that the new scheme is nothing more than a disguise for perpetuating it. As for the Indians and the coloureds (people of mixed race) who are to be included in the new political order, they would be asked for their opinion later. And as for the great majority of South Africans who, as it happens, are black, well, they were not asked because they are not to be included. In their view, and in the view of most non-South Africans watching these strange goings on, apartheid by any other name is still apartheid.

Dispensation is an odd term for a political arrangement, but then South Africa is a very odd country. In other countries it is called a regime or an order or a plan or a program. In

South Africa it is called a dispensation. Fundamentalist Christians in America are usually "dispensationalists" of one sort or another. In that context dispensationalism means a system of interpreting history in terms of a series of divine reorderings of human affairs. The sense is not foreign to what is meant by dispensation in South Africa. You can also dispense something in the sense of serving or dealing it out. Whites in South Africa clearly feel themselves to be in a position to dispense political and other favors to the less favored. And you can dispense with something in the sense of doing away with it. Whites in South Africa feel they are dispensing with those aspects of apartheid that have earned them such opprobrium abroad and generated such discontent at home. But mainly dispensation in the language of South Africa means what the fundamentalists mean by it: an arrangement of affairs in obedience to providence or nature, or both. As we shall see, in the minds of many white South Africans, providence and nature are closely, sometimes inseparably, connected.

The basic reality of South Africa is that there are relatively few white people and an awful lot of nonwhite people. The white people are well-off and in charge of things, while the nonwhite people are, generally speaking, poor and powerless. Note, however, that this statement of "the basic reality" is vigorously disputed from several sides. Some say the basic reality is that South Africa is a geographical region containing many nations and the basic mistake is to think of it as one nation. Others contend that the basic reality is not, at least not essentially, a conflict between black and white, but is a class conflict produced by capitalist oppression. Still others, agreeing that economics is at the heart of the matter, argue that the basic reality is a social and political system that is ludicrously out of synch with the economic facts of life. Then there are those who insist that the basic reality is the defense of Christian civilization against the barbarian hordes of communist aggression. Nor is this an exhaustive list of the ways in which "the basic reality" is stated. How you define the basic reality of South Africa has everything to do with what you think can be done or should be done in South Africa. We will try to listen sympathetically to the diverse ways in which people explain the basic reality, even when the explanations seem highly implausible. But the reader will not go far wrong by beginning with the working hypothesis that "the basic reality" is the first of those mentioned above.

MANFRED is a tobacco farmer near the small town of Rustenburg, about two hours' drive west of Pretoria.[1] In his mid-forties, he is the fourth generation to work this farm and he hopes his children will work it after he is gone.

It is after church on a Sunday in June and, following a solid meat-and-potatoes dinner, we leave the family and grandparents and take a walk around the property. A few hundred yards from the homestead are the bunched huts of the workers. There are about eighty workers, and they are socializing on this day of rest, the adults talking and drinking by their doorways, children playing games, adults and children walking to visit relatives who work on other farms. It is a peaceful scene which, for the American observer, inevitably evokes images of our antebellum South.

Manfred is the kindly master. The accuracy of both words, kindly and master, seems beyond doubt. Of course these workers are not slaves, not in any conventional sense of the term. Within the restrictions of the South African law and economy they are free to pick up and seek work elsewhere—but those restrictions are severe. And, unlike slaves, these workers are paid. Manfred has ten tractors (a tractor is called a "trekker"), and a driver makes 120 rand a month. (In recent years a rand has been worth ninety cents U.S., but during the turmoil of the summer of 1985 it fell as low as thirty-five cents.) In addition, the worker gets housing, medical care, and certain food benefits. A tractor driver, Manfred

3

says, works most of the day and is the elite of the farm workers. The other workers, those who pick the tobacco, for example, get housing, food, and medical plus 18 to 20 rand per month in cash. "They can make more if they work overtime," Manfred says, "but they don't care much for that."

In the summer heat (during our winter months in the northern hemisphere) the workers go into the fields at seven in the morning; in winter they start at seven thirty. At nine they have a half hour tea break and, later, a half hour for lunch, and they quit at one in the afternoon. "That's the way they've been doing it all these years and that's the way they like it," Manfred observes. "Some people say they're lazy, but I say it's just a different way of life and they have a right to it. We've long since learned to adjust to their pattern." At one o'clock they go back to their houses, take a nap, or sit around and talk and drink beer. "It really is their choice," he says, "they don't think more money is worth the trouble of overtime."

Manfred believes most of the workers are satisfied. "But they want more for their children. Some of them make real sacrifices to see their children get an education. I encourage that, but I know too that some of their expectations for their children are unrealistic. Some of them think that education is almost magical in what it can do for the children." I keep probing, trying to find out his inner feelings toward these black workers. He expresses himself tentatively in different ways and then stops, looks at me very seriously, and sums it up this way: "I can't honestly say that I know them, and it would be too lofty to say that I love them, but I know I need them and I know they need me." It is a statement that keeps coming back to me as I talk to South Africans of every color, status, and persuasion. If there can still be any honor in noblesse oblige, the statement is not devoid of that honor. But chiefly I am struck by the nuances, the ambivalence, the moral uneasiness in that statement. I have no doubt that Manfred means what he says. That so many people mean what they say is a large part of the hope, and a large part of the problem, of South Africa.

In one important respect Manfred is not typical of whites in South Africa. He is neither Afrikaner nor English. He is German, descended from German missionaries who came out in the early nineteenth century to bring "The Word" to the Tswana people. The service that morning, in a handsome new building built from a design sent over from America, was all in German, and Manfred's missionary ancestors lie buried in the adjoining graveyard. After the service I talk briefly with a young German missionary who has come in from his station for the day. Except for the modern building, the cars, and the clothes, it seems that this Sunday in June could be Rustenburg in 1883. It seems, but it is not, as the people here well know.

A few years ago the farm was not all tobacco. There were cattle, and there were rustling and killing by "terrorists" from the mining areas, and now there are no more cattle. "We have learned to adjust," says Manfred. He knows the speculations, the fears for South Africa's future. Does he really think his children will be running the farm after he is gone? "Only God knows that. I hope so, I hope so very much. But I tell them that if they're good Christians and if they learn a skill, there will always be work to do somewhere. The world is very big." After the riotous rebellions in Soweto in 1976 and 1977, his brother called it quits and moved to West Germany. "Now my brother is worried about the Russians and wonders if he made a mistake. Ah well, I tell him, none of us has a safe place. You stay where you are and I will stay where I am and we will trust for the best." But what would Manfred do if it really looked like South Africa was on the edge of blowing up? After a pause, he answers with a story. "Somebody once asked Martin Luther what he would do if he knew that the world was going to end the next day. Luther said he would say his prayers as usual, drink his beer to the glory of God, and plant an apple tree. I'm planting my apple tree here in South Africa."

Manfred knows that South Africa just might blow up. Along with almost everybody else, he thinks that whether it does or not depends upon those in power. Those in power are the English and the Afrikaners, but mainly the Afrikaners. Manfred is active in National Party affairs at the local level and is a close friend of the member of parliament. "I am a liberal in fact. I could support the PFP or even Dr. Buthelezi, but that just wouldn't make any sense here." (The PFP is the Progressive Federal Party and Gatsha Buthelezi is chief of the Zulus—on both, much more later.) "Anyone who says he's a liberal around here is immediately making himself irrelevant. The NP is the only politics here and it's on the right course." The right course, according to Manfred, is the course charted by Prime Minister P. W. Botha; it is the new dispensation. "Nobody knows what it's going to mean in the long run. The prime minister has said that. But it's moving in the right direction and almost everybody here agrees with that. We made our feelings clear when the others started the Conservative Party." The reference is to the right-wing party that was formed in 1982 when Afrikaner nationalists split over the new dispensation.

Being neither English nor Afrikaner, Manfred has a somewhat different view of both. "I know that some people in the West think that the Afrikaner is like the German. They even compare them to the Nazis. I've known them all my life and my family has lived with them for more than a hundred years, and they're not like us at all. Germans will follow a führer to the last man and the last drop of blood. The English pretend to be so different, but they can be fanatics too. 'God Save the Queen!' and then they go marching off to the bitter end. The Afrikaner is really the practical one. He's a pragmatist, he makes adjustments." Then he pauses and says in a more skeptical tone, "We have to believe that, you see, because the future is in the hands of the Afrikaner." Manfred is prepared to plant an apple tree on the eve of the apocalypse. Manfred claims to believe that the Afrikaner is at heart reasonable and moderate. Manfred is not typical of thinking in South Africa today.

Will the real Afrikaner please stand up? Some critics question whether there is a "real" Afrikaner, or a "real" Englishman, or a "real" American. They are right to question, no doubt, for the idea of "national character" has been much abused. Stereotypes can be misleading, and yet, contrary to common usage, a stereotype is not necessarily false. It is an imprint left by a reality; a social stereotype is the result when a certain reality leaves the same or a similar imprint upon enough minds. It seems indisputable that "cultural patterns," qualities of intellect, character, and behavior occur more frequently and are more highly valued among one group of people than among another. That at least is the assumption behind our inquiry into the character of the Afrikaner. To quote Coleridge:

> But that there is an invisible spirit that breathes through a whole people, and is participated in by all, though not by all alike; a spirit which gives a color and character both to their virtues and vices, so that the same action, such I mean as are expressed by the same words, are yet not the same in a Spaniard as they would be in a Frenchman, I hold for an undeniable truth, without the admission of which all history would be a riddle. I hold likewise that the difference of nations, their relative grandeur and meanness, all, in short, which they are or do, ... all in which they persevere, as a nation, through successions of changing individuals, are the result of this spirit.[2]

Talk about national character is especially problematic in South Africa. It can play into the hands of those Afrikaners who argue that South Africa is a region of many nations and who draw from that the logic of apartheid, namely that separate development is required for the preservation and growth of distinct nationalities. So keenly, and so understandably, is that way of thinking resented that there are many who would obliterate the very concept of national character. Sectors of the "black consciousness" movement would exclude the question of nationalities altogether and cast the South African dilemma solely in terms of black and white. Marxists, of course, employ a "class analysis" in which both race and nationality are subordinated, if not excluded. And yet there is nobody in South Africa who seriously disputes the existence of Afrikanerdom. And, as our conversations will reveal, almost everybody has an opinion about the character of the Afrikaner. (The opinion, almost without exception, is on what "he" is like, not on what "she" is like, which itself says something about South Africa both within and outside Afrikanerdom.)

Among the first things to be said about the Afrikaner, maybe the first thing, is that he is an African. He says it of himself and others say it of him. African is not, of course, to be confused with "bantu," "kaffir," or "native." They too are Africans, but the Afrikaner is The White African. Mfanafuthi Makatini, the representative of the African National Congress at the United Nations, talking over lunch in New York City: "It is very sad that we are fighting each other, for you must understand that we belong together, we are both Africans. The Afrikaner is not black like I am but he is as much an African. I watch them when they come to New York and you can see they feel the way we do, they are not at home here, they know they belong in Africa. It's not that way with the English, they fit right in here. I watch them, I tell you. You can pick up the English and put them anywhere and they think they own the world."

According to some authorities, the trekboers, the frontier farmers, were the first people in Africa to call themselves "Africans."[3] Afrikaners deeply resent being confused with the white colonialists of the nineteenth century. The widely respected Rockefeller commission report on South Africa, *Time Running Out*, puts it this way:

> If it is a myth that the whites who settled South Africa moved into land that lay empty and idle, so too is it a myth that the South African whites of today are colonialists on the order of those who snatched up large chunks of the globe in the nineteenth century. Their roots run deep. South Africa *is* their land. But it is also the land of many others, some of whom were there long before the whites arrived—and with all of whom they are now inextricably intertwined.[4]

A South African government commission, charged with the responsibility of drawing up constitutional proposals for the "new dispensation," spells it out, as one might expect, more sharply:

> Thus a leading American scholar of the process of decolonisation and independence (Rupert Emerson) has written: "The Afrikaners have produced the most intense and coherent nationalism on the continent," with, he might have added, a new language and distinctive culture; and the British Prime Minister Sir Harold Macmillan referred to the historical significance of Afrikaner nationalism in his "winds of change" speech in Cape Town in February 1960, when he said: "Indeed, in the history of our time, yours will be recorded as the first of the African nationalisms." This is a factor which is often overlooked in external assessments of the South African situation.[5]

The defensive tone in that official statement is something one runs into in talking with most Afrikaners. They feel misunderstood and put upon by the rest of the world, as though they were intruders in the black man's world, and ruthless intruders at that. Gerrit Olivier is a youngish professor of political science at the University of Pretoria. He looks like a comer, and he is. Far removed from the boertrekker in education and manner, he regularly explains the boer-trekker's dilemma in international forums (in those declining few where South Africans are still admitted) and to strangers in his strange land. And so he explains to me: "Yes, we insist we are Africans, but I'm not sure that we accept the full implications of that. We have to learn to understand ourselves as members of the Third World—this is a Third World country. And we're a minority in a Third World country, and, like it or not, the power is concentrated in our hands. Quite frankly, too many whites like it too much. But most of us recognize that the idea of white control over others doesn't accord with the morals of our society. That is the cause of our bad conscience, and we are terribly torn over what to do about it."

Strangers are permitted to ask impertinent questions, so I ask why they don't relieve their bad conscience by letting go of some of the power. "Yes, of course," he says, "power sharing; that is what is going to happen, it's what is happening now. But it has to be done in an orderly fashion. I see you smile, but the fact is that order is essential to justice, there can be no justice without order. You Americans with your Madison and Jefferson, they could assume commonality in the society, a context in which minority rights could be protected. In the U.S., democratic theory was about how to limit government in order to protect the rights of individuals and minorities. That's not our situation. Our problem in Africa—and I don't mean just in South Africa—is how to *create* government upon democratic premises. We look at our fellow Africans on this continent and they're not getting on very well with this. The plight of minorities is horrible and individual rights hardly exist." Then a theme we will encounter in other conversations: "I'm not embarrassed to say that we in South Africa have a mission within the Third World. I mean all of us, black and white, we have a chance to prove that 'African' is not synonymous with chaos and brutal injustice. But the Afrikaner cannot escape his special responsibility. It's fine to say 'share power,' but that doesn't solve

10

our problem. In Holland or Belgium or France parties can change rapidly, into power and out of power, but here that would mean violent confusion, and the dialogue we're involved in requires stability."

It sounds like a conventional argument for gradualism, and Olivier knows it. "Look, what can I tell you? In the final analysis, ultimately, but this is a long time off, the goal is to be the kind of society that America is, even a kind of melting pot. But this isn't America and it isn't Europe. This is going to have to be an African solution. The Afrikaner has no choice but to keep an eye on Europe and America, but now more than ever he has to be an African and look to Africa, and the rest of you must try to understand that."

Afrikanerdom as the first African nationalism. Afrikanerdom as an achievement of the "nation building" that other African leaders talk about but have seldom advanced. To the outsider it cannot help but seem implausible. It is an attractive theory in Gerrit Olivier's spacious wood-paneled office at the university, but one wonders about its attraction or believability in Soweto. Such speculation, however, distracts us from the business at hand, which is to explore the self-understanding of the Afrikaner. Of course his self-understanding may be an instance of "false consciousness." But, whether false or true, whether the Afrikaner is viewed as the friend to be helped or the enemy to be known, how he thinks about himself is a potent factor in this dispensation and in dispensations yet to come. Afrikaners—at least most Afrikaners, it would seem—think of themselves as the most advanced of the tribes of Africa.

To speak of Afrikaners as a tribe touches upon a sore point in their painfully ambivalent understanding of themselves. "Tribal," after all, denotes something primitive, undeveloped, and clearly premodern. The more sophisticated English South Africans speak with thinly veiled contempt of the tribal mentality of the Afrikaner. That is resented by Afrikaners, and many of them go to great lengths to demonstrate that they are every bit as worldly and modern as the English.

The ambivalence is not only in relating to their English cocitizens. It is also a problem in relating to the West. On the one hand, the Afrikaner claims that he is fully part of Western civilization; indeed he is the defender of Western Christian civilization on an otherwise barbaric continent. He believes the West, especially the United States, should appreciate more fully that South Africa is an ally in the common cause. On the other hand, when the West applies its own moral and political ideals in criticizing South African, the Afrikaner rushes to reassert his special identity and special situation as an African.

When Afrikaners describe themselves as The White Tribe of Africa, they do so in part, one suspects, for the shock value of the thing. There is an evident delight in being countercultural in the sense of challenging the global culture of modernity about which many Afrikaners are deeply suspicious. It is also a defensive measure, letting the rest of us know that our standards cannot be applied to the "unique" African circumstances of Afrikanerdom. More important perhaps than those considerations, however, talk about The White Tribe of Africa is intended to strengthen self-identity within Afrikanerdom. Where the rest of us speak of "solidarity," the Afrikaner speaks of the tribe and the *volk*.

Like most national anthems, the national anthem of South Africa is effusive. Written in 1918 long after the supposed defeat of the Boers by the English, it is clearly a Boer hymn. The English translation is something of an afterthought. To the outsider, the effusion spills over into idolatry. "Ringing out from our blue heavens . . . Calls the spirit of our Country, of the land that gave us birth. / At thy call we shall not falter, firm and steadfast we shall stand, / At thy will to live or perish, O South Africa, dear land." And so forth for three verses. Apparently there was some theological uneasiness about addressing the country as though it were the deity, so a fourth verse was added which makes explicit reference to God. The fourth verse is seldom sung.

Much has been written about "civil religion" in South Africa.[6] But that term, as used in American discussions, is too weak to describe the Afrikaner's sense of the entanglement of nationhood and divine purpose. "Civil religion" usually refers to a patina of piety or to the diffused values operative in a society. There is nothing thin or watered-down about the Afrikaner's traditional sense of peoplehood. What may strike us as idolatrous in the anthem reflects the Afrikaner's vibrant sense of God acting in history. The song refers to "our plains where creaking waggons cut their trails into the earth," and so it is the remembrance of God's great deeds cut into the consciousness of his Afrikaner people.

Much has been made of the similarities between Afrikanerdom and the ideology of nazism with its emphasis upon blood, soil, and the *Volk*.[7] That connection is highlighted in the propaganda of those who would portray the Afrikaner as a jackbooted fascist keeping those of impure race under the whip. In fact there was a flirtation with nazism in the thirties and early forties. A few National Party leaders, such as B. J. Vorster, who would later become prime minister, were jailed during World War II for their pro-German leanings. And there were small organized groups, such as the Ossewa-Brandwag, which espoused a "New Order" along National Socialist lines. More impartial historians emphasize, however, that these people had very little contact with or knowledge of National Socialism in Germany. Their pro-German sympathies during the war are better understood as the flip side of their anti-English passions. More important, however, the National Party itself—including most of the leaders who would become the architects of apartheid—clearly distanced itself from those who were sympathetic to the Nazi ideology. Afrikanerdom was not prepared to ground its ideas about race and peoplehood in pagan romanticism about blood and soil. For the Afrikaner, nothing short of the will of God would do.

Afrikanerdom, it is generally agreed, rests on three pillars: the Afrikaner churches, the National Party, and the Afrikaans language. Thoughtful Afrikaners today worry about whether divisions in the churches, joined to the apparently inexorable tide of secularization, may not be weakening the first pillar. The second pillar, in the view of many, may be threatened by the current split in the National Party. As we shall see, it is not the first time there has been a split in the National Party, but it may be the most severe. The third pillar, the Afrikaans language, therefore assumes increasing importance. Professor J. W. Horton, a senior historian at the University of Natal and an archetypical English don, draws ponderously on his pipe while explaining why this emphasis on language is nothing new. "You must understand that the great struggle, the chief concern, of the Afrikaner is that he not be anglicized. This goes back to Hertzog in 1911 and long before that. People forget it now, but the great issue then was not black-white relations but language policy. That is why the Afrikaner has always had such a difficult time making up his mind about the coloured people. The coloured speak Afrikaans. In addition, most of them are Dutch Reformed." When the Afrikaners really came to political power, Horton notes, the chief sign of their success was not that whites were now the rulers. That had always been the case. The symbol of triumph was language. "After the Nationalists came in, there was very little English spoken in the government bureaucracy. Of course, as an English speaker, I have to admit that before 1939 there was almost no Afrikaans spoken."

"Vir kerk, volk en taal"—for church, nation, and language—is the motto of the Afrikaans Christian League of Women. It is one of many volunteer groups that have appeared in order to preserve the tribe's sense of peoplehood as its members have moved into the culturally corrosive worlds of the city and the modern economy. As growing theological

sophistication blurs the image of *kerk* and political contentions buffet the understanding of *volk,* solidarity is secured
in *taal.* It should not be thought, then, that Afrikaans is a
residual phenomenon, something to be shed along with the
former Afrikaner rusticity. Afrikaans is the dominant language in every sector of South African life, except at the
higher levels of business where English speakers are still pretty
much in control. But that too is changing. Most educated
South Africans one meets, both black and white, claim to
have a reasonable facility in both languages. Afrikaner control
in education, however, is leading some English-speaking South
Africans to fret about whether English might not be on the
way to becoming a residual language. Even in business circles
one observes that, when Afrikaner and Anglo talk between
themselves, Afrikaans is frequently the language used. The
Afrikaner insists, and the Anglo has reason not to resist. At
a "Coloured university," before a crowd of several hundred
blacks, a "black consciousness" speaker rhetorically assaults
Afrikanerdom—in Afrikaans. The blacks of South Africa do
not have a common language of their own.

When the Afrikaner speaks to the linguistically deprived, such as myself, he speaks of course in English. The
accent of ordinary South African English is an intriguing mix
of Afrikaans, Scottish, and Cockney sounds. The Scottish
comes through in magnificently rolled *r*'s. But there are important gradations. Some who are self-consciously Anglo edge
off into something like an Oxbridge accent, whereas the more
conservative (*verkrampte*) the Afrikaner, the more is the accent Afrikaans, sounding very Dutch or German. More liberal
(*verligte*) Afrikaners tend to "ordinary" South African English
or even begin to sound quite Anglo. Here too one encounters
curious twists, however. I recall a conversation with one Afrikaner of very enlightened views. He had studied in England
and, aside from his name, might have been taken for an Anglo. As his criticism of Afrikanerdom became more emphatic,
his accent became more guttural. Soon he was sounding like

15

one who had just recently come into town from the farm. I suspect that he wanted to make clear to me—or to reassure himself—that, despite his views, he was no traitor to the tribe.

As important as language may be, however, it seems that most Afrikaners do not think of it as the center of cultural identity. That center is rather located in the events of history. The most explicit, impassioned and ritualized expression of that center is the annual Day of the Covenant, December 16. "For the Afrikaner, Covenant Day is Christmas, Easter, and your Fourth of July rolled all into one," one alienated Afrikaner journalist told me. True Afrikaners, I am assured, are never, never frivolous when talking about the Day of the Covenant. The observance marks the victory of the Boers over the Zulus at Blood River in 1838. Blood River has the force of an incantation in Afrikanerdom. It is a story that has been told and retold innumerable times and the details of it cannot distract us here. (Later we will have occasion to hear Gatsha Buthelezi, now chief of the Zulus, reflect on Blood River. Not surprisingly, his understanding of its significance is quite different from the symbolism celebrated on the Afrikaner's Day of the Covenant.)[8]

Suffice it that in 1838 five hundred Boers, trekking north into Zululand, found themselves surrounded by fifteen thousand Zulu warriors. Some of the men thought they should retreat, but the women were adamant that they had been called to give battle in the name of the Lord. On December 7, a Sunday, the whole company gathered and swore an oath that, if God gave them the victory, they would forever after celebrate the day as a sign of their covenant with him. Sarel Cilliers read the words of the Lord to Moses, "Write this as a memorial in a book and recite it in the ears of Joshua, that I will utterly blot out the remembrance of Amalek from under heaven." On December 16, the Zulu impis (groups of warriors) attacked and at eight o'clock that evening they fell back, leaving three thousand dead on the field and the river flowing red with blood. The Boers had but three wounded and they had, they believed, received God's vindication of the covenant they had made with him.

Near the town of Vryheid in Natal one leaves the highway and drives down a small dirt road into a huge natural amphitheater. Here the thousands of Zulus died and here today thousands of Afrikaners come to observe the Day of the Covenant. There is a monument consisting of sixty-four full-size cast-iron covered wagons. They are positioned as Andries Pretorius's laager was on that day, and now they have turned to the color of dried blood. It takes little imagination to sense the power of this myth of peoplehood divinely established.

The modern mind pretends impatience with such myths. We cultivate a rigorous skepticism toward claims of absolute meaning associated with historical events. Yet today's Afrikaner believer insists that his myth is no less plausible than, for example, the liberal's myth of a moral necessity within history inexorably moving toward a universal community that will have no place for tribe and peoplehood. The meaning of Blood River, he contends, is at least as believable as the myth of Christian Marxists who have read "the signs of the times" and declare that the Afrikaner must get out of the way of the coming revolution which will usher in a race-free and class-free society. The conflict in South Africa is not between myth and rationality (which, it is suspected, may be only another kind of myth). It is a conflict between competing mythologies. Historical myths are contingent. That is, they can be falsified or vindicated by future events. The vow of December 7 was, in Afrikaner eyes, vindicated by the victory of December 16. If or when the crunch comes in the years ahead and South Africa must really stand alone, then, many Afrikaners assert with feeling, they will once again stake their all on the covenant. This is what is meant by "returning to the laager," a metaphor frequently heard in discussions about the possible futures of South Africa.

Blood River was not the only time that God is believed

to have spoken a word of confirmation from his side, so to speak, of the covenant. Some of his words were mightily ambiguous—take, for example, what happened in the Boer War. In 1899 the position of the Afrikaners and their two republics was ludicrously weak. That 70,000 irregulars should go up against the greatest power in the world seemed like madness. The republics were backward, entirely without friends, and completely surrounded. The British had manpower beyond numbering, the latest weaponry and ammunition, and an agreement with the neighboring Portuguese colony that no arms would be permitted to reach the Boers. Yet the war lasted for three years and was only brought to an end after the British had fielded 450,000 trained troops and engaged in systematic atrocities that have become an important part of the Afrikaner myth. Morally, the Afrikaners believed they had won, and enlightened opinion in the rest of the world, including England, tended to agree. If militarily and politically they lost, it was not that God had repudiated the covenant; he was only testing his covenant people. Testings are but for a season, as the scriptures say. The Afrikaner does not fail to point out that the British "victory" was short-lived.

Piet Cillier is an avuncular soul, now semiretired in the department of journalism at the University of Stellenbosch. He was for many years editor of *Die Burger,* one of the major Afrikaans newspapers on the side of the National Party. "We are still living in the aftermath of the Boer War," he says. "It is as important to us as the Civil War is to you Americans. The Boer War marked the beginning of the end of imperialism. You wouldn't know it from the way people in other countries talk these days, but then they believed we were the 'freedom fighters' taking on the forces of oppression. They were right then." The British concentration camps, he says, "shook the conscience of the West."

"But when it comes to history, people have short memories. The whole of Afrikaner thinking, from the very beginning, is that one people should not dominate another people permanently. We are depicted as the great villains of apartheid, but the fact is that we only wanted to give other people the freedom that we had fought to have ourselves. The only practical way to do that was through territorial separation. At least that is the way we thought out the proposition in the 1950s." He allows that the Afrikaner may have been wrong thirty years ago, that now his close friend P. W. Botha is right in wanting to include the Indians, coloureds, and blacks ("He can't say so publicly, but privately he knows the blacks must be included"), but his main point is that there is continuity through all this. "It simply is not true and it is not fair to say that the Afrikaner freedom fighter of eighty years ago has abandoned his principles. We're just having a devil of a time trying to figure out how to extend that freedom to others."

The mix of piety and truculence, of benign intention and willingness to "do whatever is necessary" to ensure survival, is striking in the Afrikaner character. The late Herman Charles Bosman is revered in Afrikanerdom for his tales about the olden days. In *Mafeking Road* the narrator tells how he and his brother set out to fight the British in the Boer War. "We were accompanied by Nongaas [a native], whom we took along with us to look after the horses and light the fires. My father stayed at home. He said that he was too old to go on commando, unless it was to fight the red-coats, if there were still any left. But he gave us some good advice. 'Don't forget to read your Bible, my sons,' he called out as we rode away. 'Pray the Lord to help you, and when you shoot always aim for the stomach.' These remarks were typical of my father's deeply religious nature and he also knew that it was easier to hit a man in the stomach than in the head: and it is just as good, because no man can live long after his intestines have been shot away."[9]

"Praise the Lord and pass the ammunition" was not written by an Afrikaner, but it might well have been. Under Vorster's rule the second most powerful man in South Africa was thought to be General Hendrik van den Bergh, head of the Bureau of State Security (BOSS). If Cillier is avuncular, the general is positively grandfatherly. In truth, his grandchildren were playing about the room as he talked, and talked. One could forget at moments that, in the view of apartheid's most militant opponents, this is the man most responsible for the systematic brutalities of the South African system. He is old now, but erect and physically towering, altogether a commanding figure. He makes no secret of his disdain for "the politicians" who have taken over since Vorster. And he makes no secret of his belief that he knows and understands the Afrikaner. For the general, the religio-political tribal myths are reinforced by naked necessity. He says he is working on a book to be titled *No Boats in the Harbor*. The point is that there is no place for the Afrikaner to go; he will stay and fight.

"There are only two countries in the world of which this is true," the general says. "The other is Israel. The Israelis have burned the boats they had. They could have gone anywhere, but they burned their boats to show that they were determined to stay there. For us it is different. We have no place to go, there is no country in the world that would take us. Make no mistake, nobody loves us Afrikaners, not in the world and not here, certainly not the English-speaking South Africans." For the Afrikaner, he says, the simplicity of the situation is stark. "Either we retain our seat at the table or else we take the crumbs from the floor. We will keep our seat, and we know which seat is *ours*." That does not mean that blacks will go without food. "They will have their own seats, but they will be at separate tables." "Politically, the Afrikaner will be alone at the table, but it will be a large and abundant dining room with plenty of room for other tables." What about P. W. Botha and the proposed new dispensation? "This government is heading for the crumbs on the floor."

"If they want to get us to give up control, they'll have to exterminate us. That's the only way." Afrikaners should, like the Israelis, see that "the United Nations and those other so-called voices of international conscience are mere bloody nonsense." He has thought long thoughts on the possible violence ahead. "The Afrikaners are a stubborn crowd. They know they've made mistakes but they also know that in the whole world their situation is unique. If there is bloodshed, and it could come to that, between black and white, then I can tell you that blacks will die in the millions. Don't think that I have spent all these years in charge of the security of this country and haven't thought these things through. We have thought about it. I can't tell you the details but, make no mistake about it, if the Afrikaner is cornered you will see that the Afrikaner is a fighter." He is standing as he says this and stretches to his full height of well over six feet, slamming a fist into open palm. "Make no mistake about it!"

When I ask the general to look back over his sixty-nine years and say something about the experiences that have most shaped his thinking on these questions, the theme of freedom fighting emerges again, joined to his idea of justice. You must, he says, understand the Anglo-Boer War of 1899–1902 to understand the Afrikaner. "I remember being in Montreal a long time ago and I saw a monument dedicated to those Canadians who 'defended the Empire' in the Boer War. That impressed me deeply. They weren't defending the Empire, they were expanding the Empire." Afrikaners are not interested in empire, in South Africa or anywhere else. "I recall hearing as a boy about Paul Kruger [1825–1904, president of the Republic of Transvaal] and how he said that he was born under the British flag and did not want to die under that flag. That's the whole point—we believe that nobody should have to live or die under somebody else's flag. Every people should have its state, like you have states in America, and then we can come together in some kind of confederation. Then we can say to the black states, 'The day you are viable economically, you can come in too.' But the tables will be separate, and whites would live in a 100 percent white state."

The general says he is not political and belongs to no

party. But his vision is the vision associated with some of the right-wing groups which have broken from the National Party. "This is not a question of right wing or left wing," he protests, "it's a matter of basic justice. The Afrikaner cares about justice and I'm an Afrikaner. Why can you people sympathize with the Jews but not with us?" ("You people" in this connection would seem to mean the whole world, which I at the moment have the doubtful privilege of representing.) "Do the Jews let in all the Arabs? If 'power-sharing' is morally necessary, why is it not necessary in Israel? There are no Arabs sharing power in the Israeli government." In South Africa too he thinks the requirements of survival should be weighed in the moral balance. "Wherever you look in history, where there are different people and minority groups, it's numbers that will decide. You know that in not so many years there will be thirty million blacks. They breed overnight. And then there will be, at most, six million whites. Whatever chance we have now may be gone by then."

In setting forth his version of a new dispensation the general says he is not unmindful of the plight of blacks. "I know that the lot of many blacks will be unfortunate, especially if there is no employment in their own states. And it will be twice as bad if they are not permitted to work in the white states. If that happens, the white man's progress will come to a quick end too." "We whites are the elder brothers; we have to look after them and advance their development."

I am told that General van den Bergh is a fossil, a has-been to whom no mind should be paid. But we will discover many who think as he does. Those who support P. W. Botha's new order, those who are usually younger and more technocratic in mindset, say that the van den Berghs represent an intolerable status quo. They, on the other hand, endorse "a status quo with modifications" leading to fundamental change in the structure of South Africa. They may be wrong, however. The van den Berghs and others whom we will meet are not in favor of the status quo. They want an apartheid radically restructured in order to conform to an Afrikaner morality and sense of justice. "No man should have to live under another man's flag." That same sense of morality, however—combined, not so incidentally, with a lively sense of self-interest—compels them to the conclusion that the black man must be permitted to work in the white state that they would bring into being. The problematic result is that the population of the white state ends up being a majority of black people working for a minority of white people. It is the long way to get back to where South Africa is now.

Taking the long way is not foreign to the Afrikaner. He is an inveterate trekker. Hennig Coetsee, an anthropologist, tells me about a colleague who claimed that he would go on trek, meaning to leave the country, if the referendum turned out the wrong way.

"This too is part of the trek tradition," Coetsee says. Afrikaners have trekked to Kenya, to Argentina, to Brazil. All the time trekking to maintain their religious and ethnic identity, but, of course, by trekking away from South Africa, they lose precisely what they wanted to maintain." Most Afrikaners think it little short of treason even to talk about leaving if and when the crunch comes. In that eventuality, the journey is not out of the country but back to Blood River.

The speech of the Afrikaner is permeated with talk about the trek, talk that is similar to scriptural references to pilgrimage. Educated Afrikaners, without any apparent self-consciousness, speak of setting out on a "new trek," of a spirit of "in-spanning" or "leaving the laager." Like stations of the cross, monuments mark the way of the Great Trek of the last century. One writer notes that the religious intensity surrounding the myth of the Trek threatens to obscure the historical reality. "But the Trek was a real event, nevertheless, often commonplace in its difficulties and burdensome in its dullness but, ultimately, heroic because it was so stupidly daring."[10]

Stupidly daring. I suspect the phrase would not offend

many Afrikaners. Embarked upon a trek inward, the Afrikaner explores memories and loyalties past, looking for a place
to stand in the face of a threatening future. And he discovers
that what some call stupid daring others have called brave
defiance of the allegedly inevitable. And yet others have called
it faith. To be sure, this may be rationalization, a religious
and moral gloss on otherwise naked self-interest, an exercise
in false consciousness blinding the Afrikaner to his own base
purposes. It may be all that, and it may at the same time be
what the Afrikaner claims it is, part of the Afrikaner nature;
it may be what Coleridge called "that invisible spirit that
breathes through a whole people, and is participated in by all,
though not by all alike; a spirit which gives a color and character both to their virtues and vices."

CHAPTER TWO

GOD'S MANDATE TO
THE AFRIKANER

I n 1948 the Afrikaner was surprised by political victory.
Now, almost forty years later, many Afrikaners allow that
the electoral triumph of the National Party in 1948 was something of a fluke. For many others, however, any such admission is tainted by irreverence. For them it was no accident.
They believe as Daniel Malan believed then that a higher
purpose was engaged. Malan, a minister of the Dutch Reformed church and the politician who led the Nationalists to
victory, declared: "The history of the Afrikaner reveals a determination and definiteness of purpose which makes one
feel that Afrikanerdom is not the work of man but a creation
of God. We have a divine right to be Afrikaners. Our history
is the highest work of the centuries."[1]

Malan was a true believer. He believed in a way that,
one suspects, many Afrikaners wish they could believe again.
Malan addressing a crowd at Blood River: "Here you stand on
holy ground. Here was made the great decision about the
future of South Africa, about Christian civilization in our
land, and about the continued existence and responsible power
of the white race. . . . You stand here upon the boundary of
two centuries. Behind you, you rest your eyes upon the year
1838, as upon a high, outstanding mountain top, dominating
everything in the blue distance. Before you, upon the yet un-
trodden path of South Africa, lies the year 2038, equally far
off and hazy. . . . The trekkers heard the voice of South Africa.

They received their task from God's hand. They gave their answer. They made their sacrifices. There is still a white race. There is a new People. There is a unique language. There is an imperishable drive to freedom. There is an *irrefutable* ethnic destiny."[2]

The Afrikaner's identification with Israel is today usually expressed in terms geopolitical and strategic. But the identification rests upon a deeper stratum. For the trekkers, the story of the Old Testament was their story. The identification was deeper than perceived analogies between their experience and the tribulations of Israel of old. They *were* Israel of old in a later dispensation. So literally did they believe that they were a chosen people fulfilling biblical destiny that when some stone cairns, perhaps marking the graves of long dead Koikoi chiefs, were found along the Fish River in the 1770s, the trekkers thought them to be monuments left behind by the Israelites and so named the place Israelites Kloof.[3] Afrikaner history has been rudely pushed from the pages of the Old Testament into the modern world. They may sincerely view themselves as defenders of the West, but their West is not ours. Of course they know about the history of the eighteenth and nineteenth centuries, about the Enlightenment, the Declaration of Independence, the development of concepts of human rights and equality. They know about it, but they did not experience it, it is not part of *their* story.

For many Afrikaners modernity—what we are taught to think of as progress—is a fall from grace. It is hard to believe that you are defending Western civilization and, at the same time, to believe that Western civilization, with the exception of South Africa, has collapsed under the dogmas of godless humanism. Other Afrikaners take a more approving view of modernity. Or, if they do not actually approve, they have concluded they have no choice but to face up to it. For them too it is hard. How do you assimilate two centuries or more of Western history in a hurry? The probable answer is that you don't. At most you can tack it on, accommodating to ideas previously declared to be heretical. The problem is that it looks like accommodationism, and is therefore suspect in the eyes of those who once truly believed and who want to believe again.

A sociologist in her thirties says this is not her problem. "I am a scientist. As a scientist, I think the myths of Afrikanerdom are absolute rot. As a modern women, the values of those who criticize South Africa are my values. They just don't understand the difficulties of trying to straighten out the mess we're in here." But what if the critics refuse to understand and Afrikanerdom is finally left alone. There is a pause and the tone of certainty is gone. "I really don't know. I know I would not leave. Everybody has to have a people and these are my people. You don't have to accept all the religion that goes with it to believe a people might have some sort of worthy purpose in history. What is so wrong with that? You Americans think you have some kind of purpose in the world, don't you?"

This is, at the very least, a sharply tempered sense of Afrikaner destiny. Johan Heyns believes that sense is in need of even further tempering. Heyns, a ruddy-faced, robust man in his late fifties, is professor of theology at the University of Pretoria. In the view of some, he has leaned too far to the *verligte* side of things and has been suspiciously cordial to some of the more outspoken dissidents within the Dutch Reformed church. Yet in 1983 he was elected to the high position of moderator in the Transvaal, an election that was thought to signal a hopeful shift in church thinking. Heyns is very much a disciple of the late Karl Barth. That means, among other things, that he believes there is a powerful discontinuity between human strivings and divine purpose, between what we think God is doing and the absolute truth of the word of God. In Heyns's view, a declaration such as that of Daniel Malan at Blood River is little short of idolatrous.

"In the theological world, and more generally, South Africa is judged negatively because we have invited a negative judgment. We reap what we sow. Over the years we have endured as a theological community, but the theology was self-serving. Until the last decade we tried to theologically legitimate what is manifestly illegitimate. Now we're paying the price." There is a second reason why South Africa is judged so harshly in the religious world, according to Heyns. "We cannot get a hearing because of the world-wide movement toward 'political theology.' " He mentions Johann Metz and Jürgen Moltmann, prominent European theologians who have written about God's work in history through political means. "There is irony here," says Heyns. "In important ways, they're doing what Afrikanerdom did for so long, trying to put a divine stamp on human politics. Of course they're much more sophisticated intellectually, but at heart it's the same effort. The big difference is that their politics are different."

But surely, I interject, he does not want to deny that God might be up to something in history and that, just possibly, we might be able to perceive his purposes, at least in small part. This leads to a discussion of Wolfhart Pannenberg, a German and one of the most distinguished theologians in the world today. "I understand," says Heyns, "what Pannenberg means by revelation as history. It may be very important, and it may be fine for you in Europe and America. But it's dangerous in our context. It lends itself too easily to the Afrikaner perversion of seeing his history as the revelation of God's intent. We can't afford to even entertain viewpoints like that."

Heyns reflects a feeling common among *verligte* Afrikaners. The feeling is that the liberation from the historical fundamentalism of Afrikanerdom is still very recent and very tenuous. In other societies intellectuals may be moving on to something called postmodernity, but the Afrikaner has more than enough to do in trying to come to terms with modernity. One thing at a time, he seems to be saying, especially when that one thing is not yet surely grasped. Heyns and others believe that secularization has to do its necessary work in

South Africa. In other words, political and social reality was altogether too "religionized" in the past. The religious interpretation of reality needs to be countered and checked by other interpretations.

It would be a mistake, Heyns insists, to think this means downplaying religious or theological seriousness. He explains: "You ask about the moral legitimacy of our present government. In the past you would have received a very definite theological answer. Mine is also a theological answer, but it is a very different answer. It has nothing to do with the government being the embodiment of the *volk* or with all those parallels with Old Testament Israel. I quote Romans 13 too. ["Let every person be subject to the governing authorities"—a passage sometimes invoked in Christian history to encourage politicial passivity.] But Romans 13 says absolutely nothing about the rightness or wrongness of this particular government. It doesn't mean that the rule of the National Party is ordained by God. Romans 13 is talking about the nature of governmental power itself in a fallen creation, regardless of how that government is constituted."

As for this government, Heyns leaves no doubt that he thinks it is constituted illegitimately. "If you ask me as an ethicist, someone applying a universal rule of justice, then there is no doubt that the present government is illegitimate. I have no difficulty in saying that as an ethicist, it is an illegitimate government. But it is the government that is a consequence of a particular history.

"Is it a tragic history? Of course tragedy is involved in all of history, but I would not say that our history as a whole is a tragedy. No, I would have no right to say that. I don't know that, I have no basis in the word of God for saying it. If I said that, I would be guilty of the same presumption practiced by those who say our history is the revelation of God's purposes. All I can say is that it's our history, it's not the history of our choosing but we have to do our best with it. You must understand that the Afrikaner is just learning to be theologically modest about himself." It is obvious that for this Barthian such modesty is not a slighting of the theological but is made imperative precisely by the theological approach he espouses. As we shall see, some of Heyns's students, such as the coloured chaplain and political activist Allan Boesak, are not so reluctant to declare what God is doing in South African history.

Beyers Naudé, a former Dutch Reformed dominee who was "banned" by the government for seven years for his activities against apartheid, had told me that "most of our dominees do not have a theological thought in their heads. They get their theology from the Afrikaans newspapers." I report this to Johan Heyns and he does not disagree, at least not very much. "Our church leaders are mainly managers of the religious establishment. That may be deplorable but it is not very surprising, is it? I imagine it's true in other places too." There is the particular problem in South Africa, he says, that church leaders know that the theology they once learned is now viewed as discredited by professional theologians. The result is a tendency among church leaders to leave theology alone, combined with a deep-seated suspicion of theologians and intellectuals in general. "It is a perennial question among Afrikaners whether the theologians can be trusted. Obviously, the theologians have a more critical approach in their study of Scripture but also, and this may be more important, they question the traditional interpretation of Afrikaner history." The latter cuts very close to the bone indeed.

D IRK Fourie is not a professional theologian. He is pastor of a large and affluent Dutch Reformed congregation in a suburb of Johannesburg. Fourie is a big man in his early fifties, effusing the self-confidence one finds in those who know how to get around in "the real world." I immediately think I have met him many times before in the obviously successful head pastors of the important Protestant churches of middle America. He graciously comes to my hotel on a Saturday morning. This too he accepts as part of his ministry, to straighten out Americans and others who have got South Africa all wrong.

Fourie describes himself as a moderate on the spectrum of Afrikaner opinion. He speaks of the "extremists" of the left wing and of the right. Others, however, say he is a leading and exceedingly ambitious spokesman for right-wing Afrikanerdom. For the more militant opponents of apartheid, it is well to remember, distinctions between right and left, *verligte* and *verkrampte,* are ludicrous. In their view, anyone remotely sympathetic to the present order, even if their intentions are reformist, is a racist and reactionary. Talk about left and right in Afrikanerdom is in their view to deal merely with degrees of fascism. In any event, my visitor this morning is wearing his moderate hat. He says he understands the misunderstandings that Americans and liberals in general have about South Africa. He recognizes that we are a bit slow in picking up on the "complexities" of the situation, and he is prepared to be patient.

"You must see, man, that. . . ." I am "man" throughout a lengthy rehearsal of standard arguments. We Afrikaners know "our blacks" better than anyone else. The American approach to race is irrelevant. ("How would whites in America feel if they were thirty million in a country with one hundred seventy million blacks?") South Africa is not one nation but a place of many mininations. We have seen what black rule has meant on the rest of the continent and we have a responsibility to make sure it does not happen here. And, of course, there is much about the communist onslaught. Quite unselfconsciously he says that the question is how the several nations, including the Afrikaners, can find *lebensraum* for development. *Lebensraum,* Hitler's term for the elbow room needed by the *Volk,* is used several times, and then Fourie concludes his survey of the basic situation: "Neuhaus. That's German. I know you're an American, man, but as a German you should be able to understand. The Afrikaner is from the Netherlands and we're like the Germans. We believe in individualism and democracy and freedom." It is an intriguing reading of modern history.

It is not easy to listen to Fourie, but it is necessary. His voice, I have no doubt, is much more representative of Afrikanerdom than are the voices we in the West find easier to listen to. There is, for instance, the representative mix of bellicosity and self-pity. "It is nothing new that people do not like Afrikaners. That goes back to the nineteenth century. The English did all the writing about us. They made us look like stubborn and ignorant and brutal people, and that is believed all over the world. It is not surprising that South Africa's case is not listened to. We are still in the United Nations organization, but when a South African speaks everybody walks out. It is the same with the churches. People like Allan Boesak go around saying we have to be isolated even more, and he will probably succeed. Now the Dutch Reformed church in Holland has said, 'Oh, you wicked people with your apartheid, you are not truly the church.' So they break off good relations too." He adds with a sardonic smile, "It is good to know that there are so many righteous Christians all over the world. I tell you, man, I guess we Afrikaners are the only ones left who are sinners in need of forgiveness."

The sardonic tone aside, there is an element of seriousness now as Fourie gets beyond the rehearsal of standard arguments. It is again the question of destiny. "What is finally going to happen is finally not in our hands. That is true, and we know it. It is up to the Lord. He has led us to this line of action and it has had good results for his kingdom. We have shared the gospel, the whole gospel, with the blacks. Maybe that doesn't matter in some churches today, but we still think sharing the gospel is the main business of the church. Maybe the Lord has no more use for us, but I don't believe that. You can be sure of one thing, man, we're not going to raise the white flag. If the Lord wants us to stand alone, we will stand alone."

The troubling question is raised whether perhaps the Lord has changed his mind about Afrikanerdom. "Let me speak to you as a Christian," says Fourie. "For three hundred years our Lord has said, 'In South Africa, the whites, that is the Afrikaners, are to be a nationalist group, they are to go forward, they will have big problems but they are to get to the top.' Is the Lord now saying to the Afrikaner that South Africa is to be a black country? If that is the Lord's will, then it will happen. There is nothing we can do about it. As it says in Proverbs, 'There is a time to plant and there is a time to uproot,' and if the Lord who planted the Afrikaner in Africa says it is now time for the white man to be uprooted, then that is the way it will be." The note of apparent resignation is quickly modified, however. "But as long as we have the leadership we have the responsibility. As long as we do Christian justice for all the population groups, why should the Lord not want us to continue? Let me ask you, man, what if we surrendered? Do we have a right to surrender? I would have to answer to my children. And I know that I will one day stand before the Lord and he might say, 'Why did you surrender? Why did you give up the leadership that I gave you?' I know we are all sinners but on this question I want to stand before the Lord with clean hands. I do not want the Lord to say to me, 'Why did you not listen when I was speaking to you?' "

The argument of the Fouries is riddled with contradictions, and the logical gaps are glaring. There is no reasonable doubt about the sincerity, however; there is a dimension of ultimate anguish. In many discussions of South Africa that anguish is reduced to something else, something more amenable to the putative sciences by which we think we understand social change. One recalls Unamuno: "These terrible sociologists, who are the astrologers and alchemists of our twentieth century." In this alchemy moral claims are no more than moral pretensions, and our obsession for unmasking becomes the new mask blinding us to reality. Power seeking, tribal hubris, and economic self-interest—those dynamics we can handle, and no doubt all those dynamics are engaged. Also engaged, however, is the moral earnestness of people who believe they are answerable to a transcendent judgment. This does not make their argument more persuasive. Sincerity, far from being the solution, may be a large part of the problem. But to belittle it in the name of modern skepticism is, I am persuaded, a sure way to miss out on what is happening in South Africa today and what may happen tomorrow.

T HE spiritualities of South Africa, and of the Afrikaner in particular, has long intrigued Franklin Sonn. Sonn is a "coloured leader of distinction" by almost anyone's reckoning. He heads up the Technikon near Cape Town, a large and modern training school for young coloureds. In America we might call it a technical school, but Franklin Sonn insists it is more than that, being concerned also for cultural and moral questions that we associate with the humanities. Sonn himself is a man broad in build and broad in interests. He exudes self-confidence and is exceedingly affable. Exceedingly. Middle-brown in complexion, he is sharply dressed and obviously attentive to what some sociologists call the presentation of self. It is hard not to like him, and hard not to believe that his intention is to represent to younger nonwhite South Africans the achievement to which they too can aspire. Despite the system. He emphasizes that: *despite* the system.

"There is an African saying, 'When the elephants fight the grass gets trampled.' Our students here are the grass. Some of them might want to do a little trampling of their own, so they join up with the elephants. But the elephants are true believers. It is a destructive game that is going on between the leadership of the various groups in South Africa. Do not misunderstand, we're concerned about belief and we encourage interest in politics. But belief must be informed, and you have to be trained so that when you get into politics you have more to contribute than more noise and more trampling."

Sonn has been criticized as an "Uncle Tom" (the term is widely used in South Africa). He has a long record of outspoken criticism against apartheid, however. He is aware of the criticism and visibly miffed by it. "Now for many years, time after time, I am reelected to head the union of thousands of black teachers. I know who some of those critics are, I can tell you; they play the game of more-radical-than-thou. They have to make noise to drown out any comment that they lack either achievement or real constituencies."

The acerbic note is not typical of Sonn. The usual communication is one of understanding and urgency, trying to see things from different viewpoints, trying especially to understand the biggest elephant, the Afrikaner. "You start with a person's belief system," he says, "and from that comes his philosophy, and then his values, and then his course of action." The order may seem a little too neat, but that is Franklin Sonn's understanding of moral integrity. "The Afrikaner has moral integrity. I don't mean all of them, of course, but most do. And I don't mean that moral integrity means they're right. They're dead wrong about justice in South Africa. But you have to know the way they act." He has met with the prime minister on occasions and has a qualified respect for him. "P. W. Botha is straight. There are no kinks in the man. He goes from his belief system through to his policies, and he is consistent."

Sonn, who says his model is Martin Luther King, Jr., but who also does not mind being compared to Booker T. Washington ("Booker T. Washington is looking better all the time in America, isn't he?"), is critical of the English and black churches. He is critical because "they say one thing one day and another the next." "They demand that the government do this or that and then, if the government does it, the churches come out and say the change is 'only cosmetic.' " But, most of all, he is critical of the opposition churches because, he says, they refuse to recognize that the Afrikaner too is acting out of moral and religious conviction, however perverse.

"When you refuse to recognize any moral integrity in the opponent, then you are calling for a crusade, for a holy war, and that is always a very unholy business."

It is frequently said that the coloureds of South Africa are or can be in a mediating role between white and black. This is thought to be more the case with the Cape coloureds, those in the south of the country near Cape Town. The coloureds to the north and east, up in Natal, are generally more English in language and manner. Many Cape coloureds are members of the Dutch Reformed Sending Kerk (Mission church) and most speak Afrikaans. (It is pointed out that young coloureds often speak Afrikaans to their parents and English among themselves.) P. W. Botha has often spoken publicly and, many think, movingly about the special relationship between whites and coloureds. He need not mention that the special relationship is a very literal relationship of being blood cousins, distant and not so distant. Franklin Sonn says this special relationship need not humiliate coloureds in relation to whites nor elevate them in relation to blacks. "I understand and I sympathize with those who say we must all call ourselves black. I have no problem with that, so long as we don't try to deceive ourselves about our history and the facts of South Africa. If all of us who are not white are black, then we have to see that there are different ways of being black, and being coloured is one way of being black. It is a way in which maybe we can understand the Afrikaner in a different way."

Such understanding is important, says Sonn, because "we have only three ways we can go." "We can go the way of cataclysmic revolution, or of a different and reforming government, or of working with the reforms of this government. I think that only if we work the third way will the second way become to some degree more likely, and the first way, which would be disastrous for everybody, can be avoided." It is a dangerous deception, Sonn claims, to describe South Africa only in political and economic terms. "You cannot understand the Afrikaner or any African if you leave out the spirit. I am afraid that is what some of our churchmen opposing the government are doing. I do not understand them. They think they have to play to the Marxists of the ANC [African National Congress]. How is it possible for Christians to believe in the spiritual presence of Christ—even though we cannot see him, we know he is with us and strengthening us—and at the same time to agree with those people who say there is no reality other than what you can physically feel and touch. I am not a professional theologian, but I don't understand it. I am afraid that churchmen who play the game of revolutionary materialists are being used temporarily, and then, when they are no longer useful, they will be thrown aside."

But is it realistic to talk about loving your oppressor? "What is realism?" Sonn quickly returns. "It is realistic to recognize that things are not so simple as oppressor versus oppressed. It is realistic to recognize that the powerful are not completely in control of their situation. They are human beings too, with sin, and limits and not always knowing what is right. . . . You cannot overlook the quality of persons. I have learned to place a great deal of faith in people who I know twice a day have their quiet periods of thought, their quiet period with God, who read their Bible and pray earnestly about what they are doing. I have no doubt that P. W. Botha is such a man." But what difference does it make if your oppressors are pious? "It makes a very big difference! It is a help to know that the Afrikaner knows the meaning of righteousness. It makes it possible to challenge him on the level of his sense of decency and moral and religious feelings. When you quote the Bible and he knows you are not using the Bible just to make a political point, then you have his attention. Believe me, I have seen it happen, often."

Franklin Sonn does not want to demonize the opposition. "Many blacks do that here, and many Afrikaners demonize the blacks. Americans and Europeans demonize the Afrikaner. A few years ago I visited Yale in your country and the students made it very clear to me that I should speak telling them how terribly oppressed I am. They did not want to hear about South Africa, they wanted me to posture for them. I confess that I resented it. They wanted me to perform for them. They thought they knew what an 'authentic black' from South Africa should say, and I failed to fit the role they had assigned to me. I am sorry I disappointed them, but I think it was important that they learn something about the realities of South Africa." It is not, Sonn emphasizes, a matter of portraying the "realities" more favorably; it is a matter of portraying them more accurately. "There is enough bad news to tell about South Africa without having to invent anything."

The bad news and the good news are sometimes hard to separate. "If the Afrikaner thinks of himself as a very moral man, is that bad or good? It is probably both. It means he can do evil with his whole heart, but it also means he is vulnerable to being questioned on a moral level. This is what is happening now and this is a big difference. Before the Afrikaner was engaged in wrongdoing unashamedly, but now he is ashamed about the wrong. That is why this is such a critical moment in our country." Sonn says he is not so naive as to think that a change of heart or of moral judgment is the only thing that can bring about change. "Oh yes, I know about the other forces, the economic and political and military. Yes, I've been listening for years to the secular English analysts you mention. They have it all programmed how economic patterns will force change. They put up their charts and their graphs and explain why certain things are inevitable, and then the next day somebody else has a different set of graphs and charts. I am more inclined to trust the person who takes into account the moral and religious convictions of others." Sonn says that one of the endemic weaknesses of the white "liberal" opposition to the government—the Progressive Federal Party, for instance—is that it appears to be so secular. "The black African and the Afrikaner are alike in being spiritual creatures. They will not really trust anyone who does not speak to the soul."

Franklin Sonn acts on his belief that there is in fact a bond of shared belief with the Afrikaner. He tells about a recent conference he addressed in Cape Town. It was an Afrikaner medical convention, and "I told those doctors that the structure of South African life is not only unjust, it is sinful. I spared them none of the criticisms but I put them in a Christian context they could recognize. I tell you, after that some of them came up to me almost in tears. It was as though they were asking, 'What must we do to be saved?' " Alas, not all Afrikaners are ready for the mourners' bench.

A MONG the smugly saved, or so it seems, is Carel Boshoff. Professor C. W. H. Boshoff is the son-in-law of Hendrik Verwoerd, premier ideologist of apartheid and prime minister from 1958 until his assassination in 1966. He was at the time of our meeting also chairman of the Broederbond. Some months later he would be removed from that position when he publicly joined right-wing forces in fighting P. W. Botha's proposed new dispensation. The Broederbond is the powerful and allegedly secret fellowship that is the glue of Afrikanerdom. No outsider is supposed to know who belongs and, of course, cannot know who is the chairman. The Broederbond is journalistically portrayed as a combination of the Ku Klux Klan, the Masonic order, and the gestapo. More sober observers note that the Broederbond has changed dramatically in recent years. Some say it has become a more progressive and open association, others that it is a shadow of its former reactionary self. In any event, Professor Boshoff does not deny what others assure me is the case, that he is the chairman of the Broederbond. To be sure, neither does he affirm it. But he does not deny it, for he cannot tell a lie.

I take him to be in his mid-sixties. The estate, some distance from Pretoria, is expansive and surrounded by high walls which block out the view of lesser homes in the surrounding housing developments. The thought strikes me that it would be a likely site for a last stand. Professor Boshoff raises horses and he goes on about the importance of purity in breeding. He also has a huge bull mastiff dog and he calls it Leo. "Since I call a dog Leo, the children ask if I had a lion would I call it Hund," he says with a chuckle. "Maybe I would." He fixes me with a knowing look. "You can call animals whatever you want, but you have to call people what they are." I am not sure what the knowing look means, but it is filed for reference.

Inside the imposing house, the parlor is surprisingly dark. The small windows, heavy curtains, the many pieces of stuffed furniture covered by a material between corduroy and velvet—the parlor is like so many in South Africa, stolid. Very like Professor Boshoff himself. The requisite introductory remarks are blessedly brief. These, typically, consist of the condescending observation that visitors to South Africa cannot possibly understand the situation, that South Africans are viciously misunderstood, but that it really doesn't matter that much because we will take care of our business in our own way, thank-you. After assuring you that they really do not care what you think of them, Afrikaners go to great lengths to change your mind, or to change what they assume your mind to be.

Yes, there is no doubt that the Afrikaner has a powerful sense of moral accountability, Boshoff agrees. "That does not mean that others have a right to call us to account. We are accountable to God. We do not accept what some of the churches say, that apartheid is a sin. What do you mean by apartheid? If apartheid means isolating people and not serving them across color barriers, then I agree it is a sin. But that is not what is meant here. Apartheid really means pluralism; the goal is the realization of their own life for the several nations. If it is simply a structure for estrangement, it is sin. But in fact it is a structure for mutual development. No matter how much the Zulus develop, for example, they are still part of the Zulu nation. That is the way they want it, and that is the way we want to help them to develop. Nowhere in the scriptures does it say a state must be multicolored. We are working for a commonwealth of different nations, not for a unitary state."

This is of course the orthodoxy of those who oppose Botha's new dispensation which would include nonwhites, if only symbolically, in a unitary state. The orthodoxy is not seriously challenged on moral grounds, according to Boshoff. "You expect us to take the South African Council of Churches seriously? They are essentially an arm of the World Council of Churches." And, it is implied, we all know about the World Council of Churches. I ask, perhaps too innocently, why the Dutch Reformed churches do not make their case in the ecumenical arena by, for instance, joining the English and black groups in the South African Council (SACC). "I think you know the answer to that. They do not want us. And why should they when they have already decided we are no Christians? We can make no contribution there under those conditions. Our big need is more unity within the Dutch Reformed family." He is referring to the three white bodies within the Dutch Reformed church (about which more later) and, more important, to the split within Afrikaner religion over the new dispensation—a split, not so incidentally, for which many Afrikaners blame the Boshoffs of South Africa.

Boshoff is attempting to delegitimate the delegitimaters. Those who challenge the moral legitimacy of Afrikanerdom will in turn have their legitimacy challenged. This, in his view, is easy to do with the English whites and the Marxists of the ANC. The one group is secularist and the other materialist and both are therefore without moral standing. The churches of the opposition pose a dicier problem. Boshoff proceeds to argue that the real church, the church that is doing the work of religion rather than of politics, is the Dutch Reformed church. "The English churches talk so high about their concern for the black man. But what church do the black and coloured people belong to? The Dutch Reformed church. We are the ones who brought them the gospel and have worked with them all these years. . . . Our enemies in the World Council of Churches talk about how evil imperialism is and how we should respect indigenous cultures. We agree with them. That is why we have different churches for different nations, but all within the Dutch Reformed family where we can work with one another while still respecting our differences." (Here is a curious but common twist that at first surprises an American in Afrikanerdom. The language and the logic which we connect with "black separatism" and "black power" in America is echoed here by the apologists for apartheid. In truth, it may not be an echo since some of them have been using it for decades. It is a curiosity that has not gone unnoticed among black South Africans and is part of the dispute between "black consciousness" proponents— who are sometimes accused of promoting racial separatism— and the supporters of ANC who favor a "class analysis" of the South African dilemma.)

Granted for the moment that the bulk of the evangelism and pastoral care among nonwhites has been done by the Dutch Reformed, and granted there have been "heroic" missionary efforts in places as far away as Nigeria and Kenya. Granted all that, how can the Dutch Reformed accuse the English churches of being mainly political when the Dutch Reformed church itself has been the chief popular prop for apartheid? "No, that is not true," says Boshoff. "Maybe it used to be that way but it is not now," protests this supposed defender of the way things used to be. "Maybe even until recently some of our dominees would start with Genesis 11 and then go through the Bible demonstrating that apartheid is God's will. But then there were people who not so long ago went through the Bible proving that slavery was in God's design for the world. There were people like that in your country too. I don't know about your country, but our people do not use the Bible that way these days." Does that mean the Afrikaner is adjusting to reality, that he is becoming more pragmatic? In response the stolid almost gives way to the indignant. "I don't know what is this 'reality' you talk about."

(Remember Franklin Sonn's similar statement. The nature of reality is a lively topic in South African discussions.) "It is not a matter of adjusting, and it is certainly not a matter of pragmatism. Pragmatism is not an Afrikaans word. The Afrikaner is not pragmatic. We live by principle based on scriptural truth."

So it is back to principles. Is the South African government morally legitimate if one accepts the principle that legitimate government rules by the consent of the governed? "We do not accept the principle," says the chairman of what some claim is "the real government" of South Africa. That said, he goes on to contend that the Afrikaner governs with more consent than was the case earlier. "When the English ruled, government was entirely a white affair. Only when the Afrikaners had a place in government did we have things like the Land Act of 1936 which made clear that South Africa was not just for whites." In the apartheid house of mirrors, be it noted, legal restrictions about where blacks can live and work are seen as advances for blacks because they at least gave formal recognition to the existence of blacks in South Africa. The English, it is thus revealed, were more oppressive because, in their muddling way, they just took white rule for granted. The whole structure of apartheid is witness to the Afrikaner's disinclination to take much for granted.

My idea of governmental legitimacy, Boshoff instructs me, is a modern conceit. He cites Romans 13 ("Let every person be subject . . ."). "A government, whether it acknowledges it or not, is the servant of God. It is not based upon consent or some kind of social contract. Is an American who does not consent to your government free to break all the laws of that government? Of course not. No, the people must decide. Paul Kruger said, 'Vox populi, vox Dei' and that is still the Afrikaner democratic principle." Really? But four-fifths or more of the people in South Africa are denied a voice in this government. At this objection he laughs uncomfortably and opines that maybe the question of governmental legitimacy can only be pushed so far. "The fact is that since

1948 this government has maintained itself and it will maintain itself, even if it does not have the consent of some of the people." And then a metaphor frequently encountered in discussions with South Africans: "The fact is that you cannot unscramble eggs, especially when they have been scrambled for two or three decades." The metaphor is more often employed by opponents of apartheid who argue that the political order must be as unitary as is the thoroughly scrambled economic, social, and spiritual life of South Africa.

We will encounter more confident and consistent apologists for apartheid than Carel Boshoff. In truth, he was something of a disappointment. The chairman of the Broederbond, one felt, should have been more formidable. None of Verwoerd's charisma came with the dowry, it seems. Some may see in this an instance of Hannah Arendt's "banality of evil." Perhaps it is no more than another example of the Peter Principle, of talent rising to the level of its incompetence. In any event, the arguments of the Boshoffs are a very long way from Daniel Malan's exultant belief in the Afrikaner's divine election to rule and care for the lesser breeds of humankind. Maybe that is the argument they would like to make but haven't the nerve for it. And Carel Boshoff, at least, seemed unable to make an argument on grounds more mundane. Although we tried from several angles, he never could be quite persuasive even to himself (or so it seemed) on why race as a component of nationalism is different from racism.

As I was leaving, he showed me one of the horses he breeds. It is small, almost a pony it seems to me, and he says the breed was brought over by the original Huguenots in the middle of the seventeenth century. Then one of the native tribes got hold of it and mixed it up with other breeds. "It has taken many years and much work to get the foreign strains out and get back to the pure breed. That is the important thing now, you understand, maintaining the purity of the breed." This was accompanied by another—and long—knowing look. I think I understood.

CHAPTER THREE
PRETORIA'S HIDDEN AGENDA

I N the bitter 1983 campaign for the new dispensation the prime minister repeatedly declared, "There is no hidden agenda." When the returns were in and 66 percent of the voters had approved his constitutional reforms, P. W. Botha said it again. Many people do not believe him when he says there is no hidden agenda, and they find comfort in that. Talk about a hidden agenda refers, of course, to the suspicion that the new dispensation is just the beginning, that in time blacks too will be counted as citizens in the political order. For some that is a suspicion, for many others it is a hope.

The right-wingers who broke away from the National Party claim that the 700,000 who voted No in the referendum are on their side. But that is not very plausible. The "liberal" Progressive Federal Party (PFP) also called for a No vote, and it must be assumed that at least some of its members responded to their leaders' call. On the referendum there was this curious alliance between far right and what passes for liberalism in white South Africa. The Conservative Party (CP) did not believe Botha when he said there was no hidden agenda. The PFP, on the other hand, claimed to believe Botha and therefore argued that the new dispensation meant that the exclusion of blacks would now be irreversibly entrenched in the constitution of the land.

One and a quarter million whites followed Botha's bidding and voted Yes for the new dispensation. It should not be thought, however, that this means 1.4 million believed Botha when he said there is no hidden agenda. To be sure, many who voted Yes undoubtedly did so because they took Botha at his word. But many others—especially those who ordinarily vote with the PFP—voted for Botha precisely because they did not believe him. In sum, Botha's victory represents the impressive political achievement of speaking to the majority in tones adamantly conservative while, at the same time, winking at the minority of voters whose support he needed to embark upon more radical change. This, at least, is the interpretation of those who, unlike Franklin Sonn, are not so persuaded that P. W. Botha is straight as an arrow.

"Successful politics in South Africa is the politics of stealth." The speaker is a youngish man, an English speaker, as they say there. I will call him Harold. He is a cross between an academic and a foundation officer, and he is as contemptuous of the traditional Afrikaner as he is respectful of P. W. Botha. Botha's government, in his view, represents a break from Afrikanerdom, but the break must be disguised with great subtlety. Botha and his colleagues are the new technocrats who have moved beyond Afrikaner myths. "They understand economics and the ways that politics must be accommodated to economic logic. They know that apartheid makes no economic sense. And if the economy goes down they know that, despite all the rubbish about returning to the laager, they will have no political support among Afrikaners or anyone else." The economic argument against apartheid is widespread among English speakers. Among business leaders, both English and Afrikaner, it is almost universally embraced.

The politics of stealth takes time, Harold emphasizes. "I remember," he says with a smile, "a U.S. ambassador who came over in the early sixties. He said that after his state department briefing in Washington he had the distinct impression that his mission in South Africa was to preside over U.S. interests during a period of transition from white to black rule." The naivete about South Africa exhibited by

Americans amuses the *verligte* as much as it infuriates the *verkrampte*. *Time Running Out* is the title of one important American study of South Africa. "The choice of a title was completely predictable," says Harold. "For thirty or fifty years now people have been saying about South Africa that the clock is set at five minutes to midnight. When there is a blow-up like 1976, they say it is two minutes to midnight, and when there is a long period of quiet, they set the clock back, but never farther back than five." Like so many others, Harold urges that we understand South Africa "in historical perspective."

Not that he is lacking a sense of urgency. In the context of white South African opinion, Harold is recklessly urgent for change. And he expresses excitement about what is happening now: "Botha's readiness to split the National Party is the most important event in Afrikanerdom since the Nats came to power." In order to understand the constraints of the politics of stealth, a brief excursus on 1948 is required. The government of Jan Christiaan Smuts was up for reelection. Smuts was for many a revered figure, a military leader of distinction and the kind of politician who people call a statesman. (I remember as a child seeing his picture on the cover of *Life* magazine and assuming Smuts was in a world class only slightly below Roosevelt, Churchill, and Stalin.) It is commonly thought now that he was too much a statesman for his own political good. There is some irony in the fact that Smuts had a strong hand in writing the charter of the United Nations. In the frequent judgment of that organization now, South Africa is the prime violator of the principles its leader helped author.

At home Smuts's opponent was Daniel Francois Malan, whose impassioned rhetoric we have already sampled. Malan had long been viewed as a troublesome maverick, a fanatical populist and racist, a figure not unlike that of George C. Wallace in the American sixties. Events took a more ominous turn, however, when Malan and his followers got control of the 1938 centennial celebration of the Great Trek. They whipped Afrikaner loyalties and anxieties to a fevered pitch among the *volk*, with whom Smuts seemed to be losing touch. The enemies of the *voortrekkers* were portrayed as being all of a piece: black savage devils, imperialist English South Africans, and Afrikaner Judases who betrayed their people for the coin of international prestige and "respectability," as the English speakers measured out respectability.

Thus the lines were drawn at the eve of World War II, and the war etched them more deeply. We have earlier noted that some Afrikaner leaders were pro-German (or anti-English, as they would have it), but the leadership of the "purified" National Party generally avoided that trap. The leadership did not hesitate, however, to rail against Smuts for having joined South Africa to the "English" cause. Since South African soil was not threatened, they declared, it would have been more seemly in a sovereign nation to remain neutral. That Smuts approved of "Afrikaner boys fighting England's wars" simply revealed that the great man was himself more English than a true son of Afrikanerdom. After the war, the situation deteriorated. As one English-speaking historian told me, "Veterans flocked into the towns bare-footed and empty-bellied and convinced that somebody had played a cruel trick on them. That somebody looked very much like General Smuts."

By 1948 there was the additional tension over unruly blacks. It did not seem that the Smuts government was on top of the situation. The massively threatening black population was getting out of control, or so Malan and his colleagues claimed. Thousands of blacks had been simply disregarding the laws, leaving their assigned areas for squatter camps adjoining the cities. There had even been strikes by black workers. But what could you expect when Smuts himself had publicly expressed qualms about racial segregation and some of his closest aides had indicated that eventually the color bar would have to go? The perceived aloofness of

Smuts the international statesman, postwar dislocations, economic recession, and, above all, racial fear made 1948 an auspicious year for those who would assault the establishment in the name of apartheid.

It should not be thought that apartheid was all fear and resentment. There was, as we have seen, a sense of moral purpose, however self-deceptive. And there were intellectuals who had taken a long hard look at South Africa's options and had concluded that apartheid—or "separate development," as they now prefer—was the only way to go. Professor G. A. Cronje was one of the early ideologists, and he wrote in 1945:

> The racial policy which we as Afrikaners should promote must be directed to the preservation of racial and cultural variety. This is because it is according to the Will of God, and also because with the knowledge at our disposal it can be justified on practical grounds. ... The more consistently the policy of apartheid could be applied, the greater would be the security for the purity of our blood and the surer our unadulterated European racial survival. ... Total racial separation ... is the most consistent application of the Afrikaner idea of racial apartheid.[1]

In 1948 the time had come for a more "total" approach. The Smuts government, resting upon an English-Afrikaner coalition of political, economic, religious, and cultural leadership, certainly did not realize its time was over. The election results took everyone by surprise, including, almost certainly, Malan and his colleagues. From the establishment's viewpoint it was one of those things that simply is not done. In fact the Malanites had not won a majority of the vote. But, together with the erstwhile Afrikaner Party, they were able to put together a working majority in parliament. Apartheid—until recently a radical solution articulated by a few discontented intellectuals and vulgarized by demagogues at the margins of South African life—had come to power.

Apartheid, then, has not been forever. Thirty-eight years,

viewed "in historical perspective," is not such a terribly long time. Admittedly, the victims of a system of injustice have some difficulties in attaining historical perspective, but we are not at the moment talking with the victims. We are talking with Harold, and Harold and those like him tend to view apartheid as something of an aberration in South African history. In 1948 the Nationalists were the barbarians that C. V. Cavafy says the modern world is waiting for. It was hoped that "they would be some kind of solution." Or such was the hope of some English speakers at the time. "But they have turned out to be no solution, no solution at all," says Harold. "Their solution is the problem." That apartheid was not going to work the way its proponents had promised soon became apparent.

In principle apartheid was installed in 1948. In practice it took a decade or more just to devise the regulations and attempt to implement them. By the sixties it was obvious that the implementation was not going according to plan. A rash of additional regulations dealing with segregation and security had more the appearance of shoring up a failing order than of pioneering the future. By the mid-seventies, apartheid's friends and foes agreed that there was a crisis. By 1977 the new prime minister, P. W. Botha, was talking about the need for a new dispensation. "At the end of the day," says Harold, "people will look back on the attempt to establish total apartheid as a fit of craziness."

Total apartheid includes "petty apartheid" and "grand apartheid." Petty apartheid refers to the day by day interactions between the races. It is similar to the Jim Crow system established in the American South after the Civil War—separate drinking fountains, restrooms, park benches, and the like. In the early seventies South African facilites were littered with "white" and "nonwhite" signs. At least in the cities most of those are gone now. (In the countryside they were not needed to keep people in their place.) The government has frequently declared that the day of petty apartheid is past. The suggestion is not that it was an evil to be repented of, merely an impracticality to be dispensed with. Petty apartheid was, after all, so petty.

Grand apartheid is something else altogether. It is with respect to grand apartheid that people speculate—some in fear and some in hope—about the hidden agenda.

The politics of stealth is not easy. You want to reveal your hand to some people, letting them know that more is afoot than you can publicly say. But it is hard to do that without running the risk that they will tell others who must under no circumstances be told. The resulting uneasiness is especially evident in conversations with government officials. A rather heavy-handed instance is the conversation with an assistant consul in New York about my getting a visa. An initial contact by telephone suggested there would be no difficulty on the visa, and I filled out the papers. Some weeks later there is no visa and the date of departure is fast approaching. Upon inquiring I am informed that the visa will not be ready in time, and may not be possible at all. Assuming they have checked into my suspiciously leftist history, I muster expressions of outrage and get an appointment.

The assistant consul is a blond and burly embodiment of Afrikanerdom and he sits quite intimidatingly behind his desk. "Let me be candid with you," he says. He explains, with candor, that the South African government is experiencing difficulties. Because of the booming economy civil servants are leaving to take higher-paying jobs and the paperwork on visas is all backed up. I express some surprise, noting that it was my impression that South Africa was a country of great efficiency. "May I be candid with you?" he inquires. I assure him he may. Well, I am a Lutheran pastor and, "It has not escaped our notice that for a long time the Lutheran church has been taking an excessive and unconstructive interest in our affairs." I thought that most elegantly expressed. After I explained that I was not going on official business for the Lutheran church, and that I intended to report quite objec-

tively, and that even Lutherans might not be invincibly ignorant about South Africa, he said, "May I be frank with
you?" Making a mental note that we had progressed from
candor to frankness, I encouraged him to bare his soul, as it
were. "You must understand," he said, "that our relationship
with the American administration is at this point extremely
delicate. I believe it is extremely unlikely that you would
write anything favorable about us, but, even if you did, we
would not welcome it. At this delicate point, the less attention paid to us the better."

A middle-level civil servant may not know whether, in
fact, there is a hidden agenda. If there is such a thing, he
almost certainly does not know from whom it is to be hidden
or to whom a peek might be permitted. The question of my
visa was referred to "higher authority." And a week or two
later, for reasons unexplained, it came through. Such ambivalence and uncertainty, as well as inconsistency, is common
in conversations with government officials, as it is also in
their actions. One week they seize the passport of Bishop
Desmond Tutu, the best known and one of the most outspoken opponents of the regime. A little later they allow him to
leave for the assembly of the World Council of Churches,
where he excoriates the government and all its works and all
its ways as the virtual reincarnation of Hitler's Third Reich.
Yet a little later they refuse visas to two relatively apolitical
bishops (almost nobody can be entirely apolitical about South
Africa) from Europe who intended nothing more than a pastoral visitation with the brethren in South Africa.

"The politics of stealth is the politics of confusion,"
explains Harold. "They can't let one another in on the secret."
Harold has read Max Weber and the sociological literature on
the nature of bureaucracies. "All that is true here," he said,
"but with some odd twists. The Afrikaners are fierce bureau-
crats, but their bureaucracy is not really a modern thing. It
has more to do with ethnicity, with the *volk*. They take a
modern instrument like bureaucracy and use it to fend off

modernity. The apartheid system is the biggest bureaucratic monstrosity you can imagine. You have no idea how many inspectors and regulators it takes to make sure that people don't relate to one another in forbidden ways or say things they aren't supposed to say." Then Harold lets me in on the secret which is, he believes, the key to understanding the Afrikaner: "The Afrikaner is a socialist at heart and when he gets power he's a socialist in practice." This turns out not to be such a big secret. It is repeated to me by dozens of English speakers and by *verligte* Afrikaners, especially by those in the world of business.

The alleged socialism is of a curious sort. Socialist "solidarity" is in this case with the *volk*. Instead of a socialism perceived as the vanguard of the future, this socialism is the besieged protector of a sacred past. It is like other socialisms in that its government seems unable to keep its hands off things, to let them be. Afrikaners are, as the saying goes, forever fixing things that aren't broken. Things end up getting broken. One may question whether socialism is the right word for the Afrikaner mindset. Certainly it is not Marxist socialism. Yet it shares with Marxism a collectivist approach to the ordering of society. In talking with one *verkrampte* ideologue, he even let slip the trendy term "wholistic" in describing the Afrikaner way of putting society together.

Those who write about modernity, democracy, and market economies have urged that the characteristic mark of democratic capitalism is that it recognizes distinct spheres of social activity. Economics is one sphere, politics another, and culture—including religion and values—yet another. That approach is anathema to Marxists who propose a political economy that "gets it all together." And that approach is anathema to the traditional Afrikaner for whom economic life must be subordinated to the ordering institutions of party, church, and language. In his eyes, modernity and liberalism promise nothing but rampant individualism and the fragmentation of order and meaning.

An additional and complicating factor in South Africa is that the presuppositions of democratic capitalism are also alien to black tribal traditions. Students of Third World development have frequently noted the ways in which traditional social patterns resist 'the development of modern economic and political institutions, as witness the enormous problems leaders throughout Africa have had in "nation building." The animus that many black South Africans express toward capitalism is in large part an animus toward what is seen as the fragmenting individualism of modernity. Their enthusiasm for "African socialism"—traditional community, with a patina of Marxist rhetoric—finds its counterpart in the Afrikaner's devotion to the *volk*. Remember the conversation in New York with Mfanafuthi Makatini of the African National Congress. The revulsion against the anonymity and fragmentation of New York City, he noted, underscores the shared "Africanness" of the Afrikaner and his black opposition. It is a case of tribalisms in conflict.

The politics of stealth that Harold speaks of is distinctly modern and deeply offensive to the Afrikaner. When I mentioned the idea to conservative Afrikaners, most of them were visibly indignant. "That is absurd," Dominee Dirk Fourie declared. "That is not possible in our way of thinking. It would be immoral." In the modern politics of hidden agendas, the left hand must not know what the right hand is doing. But for the architects of apartheid the whole point of power was to join hands in establishing a cooperative order that would, at last, make sense. First it must make moral sense, then political sense, and somehow the economic sphere would take care of itself. To the "modernizers" among the white rulers of South Africa, apartheid did not make sense as a concept and turned out to be disastrous in practice during its short-lived reign.

"You can't just tell people that their dream was an illusion," explains Harold. "The Afrikaner has a steep emotional investment in it. That would be too wrenching, and it would be political suicide for any Nat leader." According to Harold and many other English-speaking whites, neither could Botha challenge the government bureaucracy head on. The bureaucracy, which mushroomed after 1948, is filled with Afrikaner true believers. It was and is, in the minds of many, palpable evidence that the Afrikaner is determined to take total control of the society. "People talk about the Dutch Reformed church and the Broederbond, and they are very important, there is no doubt of that," observes one English political scientist. "But they overlook the government bureaucracy. If apartheid still has a church of the truly faithful, that's where you will find it." Among the modernizers the opinion is commonly expressed that the bureaucracy, especially that part of it charged with implementing the apartheid system, is the main check on Botha's power, and upon the candor with which the government can state its purposes. That is why a strong executive presidency is so crucial in the current constitutional reform, it is said. Only a powerful president who is freed from the constraints of parliament and the party politics that is entrenched in the bureaucracy can move South Africa forward. This is sometimes called the "Gaullist model of leadership," and it is implicit in the new dispensation that was approved November 2, 1983.

"The politics of stealth is the politics that recognizes the limits of politics," says Harold. His connections are mainly with business leadership, so it is perhaps not surprising that he thinks economics is the "lead factor" in changing South Africa. In this view, common among business leaders, the hidden agenda is exposed by economic realities, of which intelligent politics is a reflection. Most people allow that Botha and those around him are intelligent. "The blocking power of the bureaucracy is limited," according to Harold. "The conservatives are caught in a Catch-22 situation. They don't know much about exercising power, but the one thing they know for certain is that their government needs a strong defense. A big defense costs big money, and they know they're not going to get money from outside South Africa. So they need taxes, and for taxes they need the production of wealth. They may mutter against capitalism, but they also know for certain that wealth comes from a market economy. Here comes the Catch-22: You can't have a free market without free labor and the great bulk of the labor in South Africa is black."

That is the reality of the hidden agenda that dare not speak its name in the political arena. According to this analysis, the present and growing "adjustments" in the apartheid system have very little to do with a change of heart or ideology. They have everything to do with economics. "We can't have a growing economy with millions of people perpetually rioting in the streets," observes an economist at the University of Cape Town. It is economic self-interest, not moral pressure or persuasion, that has brought into being black trade unions and will bring into being some kind of "political accommodation" for urban blacks who are an essential part of the economic mainstream. This view of affairs is not untouched by cynicism and contains an element of economic determinism similar to the Marxist ideology it so adamantly opposes. Fear—and therefore the need for a massive defense system—combined with greed—the desire of whites to maintain what may be the world's highest living standard—dictate the not-so-hidden agenda.

"Yes, but what that overlooks is that people are not always rational, and politicians can be plain stupid. In fact they often are." The speaker is Peter Sorour, director general of the South Africa Foundation, and I have just asked him about this economically dictated agenda. Like many whites in leadership positions, he is of Afrikaner and English descent and admits his primary loyalty is to his mother's (the English) side. The South Africa Foundation is a nongovernment agency supported by corporations. Depending on whom you talk to, it is a public relations firm for capitalist oppression or an important instrument for progressive change. "The economic logic is clear enough," says Sorour, "but it is not fair to say that the Afrikaner is simply illogical. It is more fair and more accurate to say that the Afrikaner has other things on his mind than economics." I am then served, once again, a brief history of the Great Trek with its emphasis upon divine destiny and its deep-seated resentment against the "outlanders," especially the English, who "invaded" the Afrikaner's land in search of gold and diamonds.

"The traditional Afrikaner was not interested in politics for its own sake. He has no use for power or imperialism. He wants to be left alone. For centuries he was quite willing to be left out of the great matters of world affairs—he wanted to be left out. But in this century he became convinced that the only way he could protect his culture and religion against the English was to seize political power. The important value is the culture; political power became important as a way to protect the culture. Economics was a secondary consideration." Sorour hastens to add that he is not suggesting that the Afrikaner is indifferent to material benefits. "I am simply saying that, if you get these factors in the wrong order—culture, politics, and economics—you are never going to understand the Afrikaner and what he is trying to do here."

There is no doubt that Afrikanerdom is in crisis, says Sorour, "but the solidity of Afrikanerdom began to erode a long time ago." It did not start with the Sharpeville shootings of 1960 nor with the Soweto riots of 1976. "It started with World War II. The most important thing about the war from a South African angle is that it brought the industrial revolution to South Africa. Before the war, South Africa produced only agricultural and mining products. It processed and sold them in exchange for manufactured products from elsewhere, from England in particular. The war changed all that; we had to start manufacturing our own goods. Not only factories for ammunition and war goods but processed foods and other basics. The story is not unique to South Africa. Factories and industrialization means urbanization. When the soldiers came back from Europe—and there were many, many soldiers— they were horrified to discover slums and other things that go with urbanization. It was not the South Africa they had left, it was not the South Africa they were told they were fighting for. This, I am sure, was the beginning of a strong distrust of the people who had been in charge of their country."

Economists talk about the push-pull factor. "At the same time Afrikaner farms had been divided through many generations and that could only go so far. So sons were being pushed off farms that had become too small to be viable, and at the same time they were pulled to the opportunities of the industrialized cities. Some Afrikaners began to go to university and to qualify for the commercial world, and that posed another problem which continues to this day. They were succeeding as the world measures success, but that was just the problem, it was as 'the world' measures success and they had been brought up to be suspicious of the values of 'the world.'

"In 1948 the Afrikaner was in a very antigovernment mood. The same thing happened in England after the war when Churchill was turned out. But here there was also this feeling of an old world, a preindustrial world, being lost. The hope was held out that they could retrieve the old world while still enjoying the benefits of the new world. It is not an uncommon human hope. But here there was also this uneasiness about being 'of the world.' The Nats won because they convinced the Afrikaner that he had to get worldly power in order to protect his other-worldly values."

According to Sorour, apartheid was not at the heart of the Nationalist victory. "Once, much to their surprise, they came into power, they had to solidify, That's where the ideologists of apartheid came into their own. The most shameless and demagogic of the politicians played the *Swartgevaar* [Black Danger] card which had been in their hand all along. It is easy to be moralistic about this, but politicians do it all the time, even in America, or so I am told." That is said with a smile. "Politicians are in the business of staying in business. They need to strengthen and expand their power base. What they will say and do for that purpose does not always make sense in other terms. In fact, just the opposite is true. When politicians are floundering in changes they cannot control, that is when they are most likely to use nonrational or even irrational arguments, such as appealing to the *Swartgevaar*." I fail to ask him whether his observation might be pertinent to the current government's invocation of "total onslaught" by the external enemies of South Africa.

"It is a great mistake to underestimate the nonrational," Sorour notes. "After the war the whole picture in South Africa could have been changed if we had been open to the millions of European immigrants who would have come. There was a debate at the time, but those who favored the immigrants lost. The Nats opposed immigration for two reasons. First, they were afraid that these immigrants who wanted so desperately to come would identify with the English opposition. Clearly, they could not become Afrikaners. You see still today that the Portuguese and the Jews and the Italians and everyone else—in the eyes of the Afrikaner they are all 'the English.' Everybody who is not an Afrikaner is English, and to be an Afrikaner you have to be born an Afrikaner. The second reason the Nats opposed immigration is religious. They were worried that many, maybe most, of the immigrants would be Catholic, and you must never underestimate the degree of anti-Catholicism in the Afrikaner view of the world."

The relevance of "what might have been" is highly debatable. But perhaps the consideration of the ways not chosen helps us to appreciate—against the arguments of determinists of all sorts—the contingent and accidental in historical change. Sorour speculates on what might have been: "If the immigration decision had gone the other way, we would have an entirely different situation. There would have been problems, I'm sure, but they would have been different, and I believe they would have been more manageable. Two or three million immigrants might have come, but think if it was only one million. By normal population growth that one million would be five million now. If you put that together with the coloured population there would be thirteen or fourteen million whites, or at least nonblacks, with common interests. In that case the white and black population would have been nearly equal. Obviously, an accommodation would have been much easier. Then we would have been in a situation a little more like your American situation where integration does not mean overwhelming domination. Please understand, I am not making a moral judgment or trying to excuse what has happened here. I am simply saying there is a connection between demographics and demagoguery. If the population realities had been different, the appeal to the *Swartgevaar* would not have been so potent."

THESE, then, are some of the people who believe that there is a hidden agenda in the new dispensation. They are glad to believe it. Others believe it and are anything but glad. Professor A. D. Pont is a founding member of the HNP. The initials stand for the Herstigte Nasionale Party, which means the Reconstituted National Party. It came about in this way. After the assassination of Prime Minister Verwoerd in 1966, B. J. Vorster took his place. Within the ruling circle were those who thought Vorster no fit successor and soon a serious rift developed between "revisionists" and "traditionalists." Vorster was counted as a dangerous revisionist. (While it is P. W. Botha who says "adapt or die," we are again reminded that there were earlier divisions over alleged departures from Afrikaner orthodoxy.) The big issue then was over Afrikaans-English cooperation. The traditionalists, led by Albert Hertzog, son of the legendary General Hertzog, contended that English-speaking South Africans were altogether too liberal to be trusted with governmental responsibility. One thing leads to another and one issue embroils another. The particular embroilment of 1969 was multiracial sports teams playing in South Africa. Hertzog protested this as apostasy from apartheid, Vorster dismissed him from the cabinet, and the HNP was formed.

People like Professor Pont would seem to have good reason for believing that the new dispensation is just one more point on a continuing slide away from apartheid. Consider again the time scale: in 1938 the ideologists of apartheid unfurl their banner; in 1948 they seize power; in 1958 apartheid is supposed to have been entrenched; in 1968 Afrikaner leadership is divided over what to do about a system that obviously is not working; in 1978 the "counterideologists" under P. W. Botha are calling for a new dispensation to include coloureds and Indians. And in 1988? Professor Pont knows that historical change does not always happen so neatly by decades, but there is an eerie rhythm and a consistent direction. "Botha is the last in a series of little men who succeeded the giants. He even makes Vorster look like a giant. I have no doubt about it, Botha is selling us down the river into a black dominated country."

The HNP has never succeeded in being much more than a protest movement. After the "Muldergate" scandal came to a head in 1978, C. P. Mulder formed the New Conservative Party. (Muldergate, the reader will remember, involved sundry skullduggeries and misuses of vast funds to promote pro-South African sentiment abroad, notably in the U.S.) But both the HNP and the NCP were quickly overshadowed when in 1982 the Conservative Party was formed under the leadership of A. P. Treurnicht, who had been a member of the Botha cabinet. In fact, the NCP, together with a few other right-wing groups, folded itself into the Conservative Party. Such, all too briefly, is the taxonomy of organized political reaction with which Professor Pont unabashedly identifies.

Sharp-boned, rosy complexioned, and quite bald, the professor is a man who relishes an argument. Twenty or so years ago he publicly charged that Beyers Naudé and his ilk were communists. They sued for libel and won, and Pont is still today making payments to them for damages. He treats the matter lightly; it is but another wound honorably borne in the everlasting battle for truth. "We must also speak the truth in criticizing separate development," he says with marvelously rolled r's. I ask for an example, and he cites the fact that black workers must travel for many hours to and from their jobs in town, thus being denied adequate time with their families. "We Afrikaners believe in the family, and this is an injustice we must answer for." My inquiries elicited no other examples of injustices under apartheid.

"The question of whether our rule is morally legitimate depends on whether you begin with the political system or with the nation itself. The English-American idea begins with the political system, everyone must have the vote and then you call that democracy." I ask whether he agrees with an American conservative who described South Africa—very disingenuously, I thought—as "a democracy with a limited franchise." "No, democracy is not the central issue. Democracy or any other system must be in the service of the nation." "It is the nation that received this fatherland and only those who belong to the nation that received the fatherland have the right to vote." But would not that exclude also the English-speaking South Africans? No, because already in the last century Paul Kruger institutionalized the idea that after seven years of residence a non-Afrikaner could become a citizen and member of the nation. I remembered that ten years ago in South Africa Japanese and other nonwhite businessmen visiting the country were permitted to stay in hotels as "honorary whites." In Pont's view, it would seem, everyone who belongs to the political community is an honorary Afrikaner.

"But that's the point," he says, "the political community must reflect the cultural community." I indicate that there are blacks who are culturally far closer to the white rulers of South Africa than are many of the Portuguese and Italian immigrants of recent years. He allows that in a superficial way some blacks may be so culturally advanced, but he is severely skeptical that any black could really close the cultural gap. I name some South African blacks whom I have met, people of highest educational attainment and ability, people who are holding positions of great responsibility in the university and white business enterprises. Pont is impatient with this line of questioning. "All mixing across color lines has been unacceptable in our history. You cannot rewrite that history to suit your fancy. In 1834 one of our forefathers took wives from the native tribes. He was like Solomon, he took the daughters and sisters of kings in order to forge alliances. But there was never the slightest question that these women were therefore Afrikaners. Among us it has always been true and it is still true today, once you go outside the color barrier you can never come back to the nation."

Is this not racism? (He has said that he agrees with the current teaching of the Dutch Reformed church that racism is a sin.) No, it is not racism, it is nationalism. "It happens that race and color are factors that distinguish one nation from another." But, in actual fact, is he not saying that it is *the* factor? Is it not the *only* factor, since Portuguese and Italians who are culturally different and clearly from other nations are admitted to the political community? And, if it is the only factor, is it not racism? Resisting this line of inquiry, Pont allows that he is none too happy about the government's welcoming attitude toward Portuguese, Italians, Latin Americans, and others. "It is going much too far, to include them simply because they are white. When you do that, it does begin to look like racism. I'm against that."

"Protecting our culture and our nation, that is the whole issue. The issue is not race. The issue is not that we are the last bastion of civilization. The sooner we get over those ideas, the better. The issue is whether the Afrikaner nation will have a place under the sun. . . . You ask abstract questions about the meaning of racism and democracy and so on, but we are more pragmatic than that. It is a question of whether the dam is going to break. However different the

Italian and the Portuguese may be, they are not a deluge that is going to swamp us. The blacks are, and they will, unless we keep the dam in place. Botha and the liberals want to poke holes in the dam because they say it will relieve the pressure. You can be sure it will relieve the pressure, and we will be drowned."

The dam is the homelands policy, what used to be called the Bantustans. That is where blacks will, according to their several nations, find their political community. "But this government is not serious about the homelands policy, about separate development and everything else we fought for. 'Adapt or die' really means adapt *and* die. Let me ask you, what do you make of this talk about finding a political accommodation for the urban blacks? You do not need to answer. You make of it the same thing I do and everybody else does. And you can be sure that, despite what they say in public, the black leaders know what it means too. It means they are going to be included in the political community, and sooner rather than later. I believe that God gave us the fatherland and the responsibilities that go with it, but, if this happens, it means the end of the nation."

Does he think there is a moral alternative? "Moral!" he almost spits the word. "When it comes to South Africa everything must be so moral! Look at West Germany and Sweden and France—they have millions of guest workers. Do the Turks and the Italians there have rights as citizens, do they elect the Swedish government? Of course not. But who says that is immoral? It is an arrangement from which both sides derive benefits. That is all we are proposing here for the blacks." In this connection it is necessary to understand that people of Pont's view—indeed almost all white South Africans—contend that they did not take the land from its natives. When the white man moved in, the land was usually unpopulated, sometimes scarcely populated, but always undeveloped. Disinterested historians agree there is considerable merit to the contention. What is not clear is how the events of one hundred or three hundred years ago bear upon today's situation. With respect to the migrations of peoples and development of nations, questions of original possession tend to seem a bit academic. More than one Afrikaner of conservative persuasion asked me whether it would have been more moral if the Afrikaners had followed the American example in dealing with native peoples. I am sure there is a good answer for that.

The hidden agenda seems to be hidden only from the willfully blind. Pont sees it and Sorour sees it, but their response to what they believe they see is diametrically opposed. Chief Gatsha Buthelezi of the Zulus claims not to see it. But it may be he is pressing for a quite different design than Botha's for the political inclusion of black South Africans. The leadership of the Progressive Federal Party claims not to see it. But it may be that its liberal credentials depend upon maintaining a common front with Buthelezi. Many coloured leaders claim not to see it. But it may be that they merely think it will not work and do not want to be caught on the wrong side when the black majority takes over. The African National Congress leaders claim not to see it.

CHAPTER FOUR
ARISTOCRACY AND CASTE

I T has been said that revolutions are declared impossible before they happen and inevitable after they happen. The prospect of violent revolution in which the black majority would take over South Africa is very much on the minds of almost all South Africans. Among white South Africans, few people claim that revolution is impossible. Many say it is so improbable that it is a distraction from any serious discussion of the futures of South Africa. Very few think revolution inevitable—at least not in the next decade, or three, or five.

If there were to be such a revolution, the question asked is what would happen to the nonblacks in South Africa. The 4.5 million whites in South Africa make up a little over 16 percent of the population. (That assumes that we count all the blacks within the traditional borders of South Africa and forget for the moment the semifictional "homelands" in which blacks are supposed to find their citizenship.) Sixty percent or 2.7 million of the whites are Afrikaners and 1.8 million are English speakers. The new dispensation proposed that the "browns" be included, which means 2.7 million coloureds and about 850,000 Indians. If, as the government hoped, these two groups could be persuaded to go along, it means that 8 million people, or about 29 percent of the population, would be on "the wrong side" of a black revolution. Of course such gross statistics can be misleading, for there are sharp differences within these population groups. In addition, blacks in South Africa are not a monolithic group. (*Verkrampte* Af-

67

rikaners are painfully ambivalent on this score: when invoking the *Swartgevaar*, blacks are depicted as a monolithic threat; when justifying apartheid, blacks become separate peoples with a primary loyalty to their several tribal "nations."| Nonetheless, the figures given above constitute the arithmetic of Armageddon in the incessant frettings about South Africa's future.

Come the revolution, most Afrikaners say they know where they will stand. They may not be as bellicose as General van den Bergh, with whom we talked earlier, but they say they will fight and will give better than they get. They are not so sure about the English speakers, however. The English, in the general's phrase, still have boats in the harbor. In the conventional picture of South Africa, the English are cast as the more moderate, sophisticated, secular, and practical sector of the white population, and there is no doubt considerable truth in that. Public figures such as Alan Paton, Helen Suzman, Donald Woods, and Harry Oppenheimer present "the human face" of South Africa to the world. They deplore the vulgarities of the Afrikaner and his barbarous apartheid. This, needless to say, does not go down well with the Afrikaner.

Some writing about South Africa employs the term "Anglokaner," meaning to include all whites. It is an oxymoron that has not caught on with either Afrikaners or English. The differences between these groups are deep and long-standing. No doubt some differences are being overcome as the Afrikaner has become more educated, urbanized, and affluent. But he is still reminded that the English are the natural aristocracy of South Africa. For thirty-eight years, the aristocrats have been outsiders in the political life of South Africa dominated by the National Party. The whole point of the Nationalists was to seize power from the English. At the same time, many Nationalists resent the fact that the English have derived the benefits of the apartheid system without bearing the political and moral odium of it. Even more galling is what is viewed as a pattern of moral posturing by English speakers who condemn the political order on which they depend for the protection of their privileges.

Analysts of the new dispensation of 1983 have made much of the government's effort to "co-opt" coloured and Indian support for white supremacy. That is understandable. But too little attention has been paid the co-optation of the other political outsiders, the English. P. W. Botha needed and he received the support of the traditionally more liberal English speakers who had in the past voted with the Progressive Federal Party. Rejecting the PFP's "purist" argument that the new dispensation means approval of apartheid, these English speakers accepted the government's invitation to buy into "evolutionary rather than revolutionary" change. This portends a significant change.

Ejected from political power in 1948, the aristocracy maintained its preserve in the world of business. The political empire of the Nationalists and the economic empire of the Harry Oppenheimers were, as one observer put it, like neighboring principalities. They could not help but relate to one another, but the style of relating sometimes looked like the conduct of foreign affairs. With the new dispensation it may be that cabinet meeting and corporate board room have been edged close enough for conversation. It may even be that a realignment of political, economic, and social forces will make more recognizable that new man, the Anglokaner. These things may be, but by 1985 business leadership, including Afrikaner leaders, was increasingly outspoken in protesting the government's hesitation and clumsiness in moving toward change. There is nothing new about saying that time is running out, but it is very new that Anton Rupert, the country's foremost Afrikaner business leader, is saying that.

Alexis de Tocqueville's distinction between aristocracy and caste is suggestive in understanding the English in South Africa:

> The French nobility, after having lost its ancient political rights, and ceased more than in any other country of feudal Europe to govern and guide the nation, had,

nevertheless, not only preserved, but considerably enlarged its pecuniary immunities, and the advantages
which the members of this body personally possessed;
while it had become a subordinate class it still remained
a privileged and closed body, less and less an aristocracy,
but more and more a caste.[1]

More broadly applied, Tocqueville's distinction illu-
mines the larger crises of South Africa. That is, a real aristocracy, as distinct from a caste, maintains its authority to
"govern and guide" by virtue of its ability to include and
discriminate on the basis of talent and achievement. A caste,
on the other hand, must classify people according to race,
nation, or ethnicity, in order to protect itself from being judged
by the criteria of accomplishment. White rule is a caste system, as is white-brown rule. After 1948, the English speakers
had become a caste within a caste. There will be no true
aristocracy in South Africa as long as the majority of its people are excluded from full participation. What happened in
1983 is that the English, who once thought of themselves as
the aristocracy, may have gained political leverage in moving
South Africa beyond its captivity to caste.

A measure of political leverage will not be restored to
the English except grudgingly and under the pressure of necessity. Among many Afrikaners there is a deep feeling that
the English do not really belong. Surprisingly, the same sentiment is frequently expressed by coloured and black leaders.
Harold, our very English English speaker, declares, "I identify
with universals. I have no use for nationalistic feelings. I am
at home in the Western cultural tradition, especially when it
comes to civil and political freedoms. I could live as well in
the U.S.A. or Great Britain or Canada. I do not need to stand
under a flag, I do not want to stand under a flag." It is a
worldview alien to the traditions of the Afrikaner, the Cape
coloured and the Zulu alike. "I would miss the veld, and
friends of course, but I cannot say that I have any patriotic
feelings about South Africa as such. I think I am represen-

tative of the people I know and respect." Harold is, in the jargon of the social sciences, deracinated. The Afrikaner fears he is representative of English speakers. The Afrikaner trusts particularities more than universals. General Smuts made the mistake of becoming an "international Afrikaner," which many thought to be a contradiction in terms.

The suspicion is that the English will not stay and fight. David Kramer embodies and plays upon the tensions between English and Afrikaner. He is a singer and comedian, the grandson of a Jewish immigrant, who brings to life Afrikaner characters who even get Afrikaners laughing at themselves. And he also plays to English audiences. The university students laugh when an Afrikaner police sergeant in one of Kramer's songs concedes that he has not had a haircut "for almost two weeks." The English laughter disappears, however, with the concluding verse:

> You and your friends
> In your faded blue jeans,
> You think you know
> What everything means.
> You've got big mouths,
> You've got the degrees.
> But when the stuff starts to fly,
> Then you'll run overseas.

"What do the English believe in? Tell me that." The challenge is from an Afrikaner member of parliament, a man thought of as a moderate. "They believe in money and their comforts, and maybe some of them believe in something like 'Western values,' but they don't believe in anything that is uniquely South Africa. What they believe in they can get elsewhere if they have to. They don't believe that God put them here, right here, for a purpose. To tell the truth, I don't think most of them believe in God."

The greater secularization of the English is frequently remarked. John de Gruchy of the University of Cape Town, and himself English, is a leading student of religion in South

Africa. He notes that one reason why it is hard to challenge the Afrikaner morally on apartheid is that the challenges have historically come from the English churches. "The Afrikaner has a hard time believing that the English are morally serious. I have to admit his disbelief is not without reason. If you ask what the English who came here really believed in, well, they believed in the empire. Of course there were the missionaries too, but that was all tied into an empire that somehow was advancing the progress of history and was always just." According to de Gruchy, this "civil religion" of the empire began to collapse when the empire itself was challenged and the religious component of it was under attack by the secular Enlightenment, Darwinism, and related foes of religious commitment. "So all that remained to the English as a group was a kind of secular individualism," de Gruchy believes. "And this degenerated into cynicism, into apathy toward social and political issues, a laissez-faire approach to life. As far as Calvinists and Nationalists here could see, the whole thing was indistinguishable from the age-old enemy called liberalism." Among Afrikaners liberalism is a very dirty word indeed. As with certain fundamentalists in America, liberalism is equivalent to secular humanism.

"The English churches and English people who want to raise a moral challenge have a very real handicap," says de Gruchy. "It is not just the prejudice of the Afrikaner. Or maybe it's a prejudice reinforced by experience. The English who are morally and religiously serious have not developed a theology or an ethic that is indigenous to our situation. This means that, whether they want to or not, as I'm sure they don't want to, they sound like echoes of foreign ideas. And, in the world as it is, most foreign ideas about South Africa are alien also in the sense of being hostile to South Africa. So the Afrikaner does not take very seriously the charge that he's using religion to justify his own situation when the charge is made by people who, in his mind, are using religion to promote what is finally just a different politics. Morally speaking, the Afrikaner feels he has the stronger hand because he at least believes in his religion."

At Potchefstroom, an Afrikaans university, I was struck that the school's statement of purpose was filled with high devotion to Christian ideals and the training of God-fearing young people for the responsibilities of leadership. A professor to whom I pointed this out immediately produced, for contrast, the statement of the University of Witwatersrand. Wits, as it is called, is an English school and thought to be a hotbed of liberalism. The Wits statement is called the "dedication" of the university and it has been ritually renewed each year since 1959: "We affirm in the name of the University of the Witwatersrand that it is our duty to uphold the principle that a university is a place where men and women without regard to race and color are welcome to join in the acquisition and advancement of knowledge and to continue faithfully to defend this ideal against all who have sought by legislative enactment to curtail the autonomy of the university. Now therefore, we dedicate ourselves to the maintenance of this ideal and to the restoration of the autonomy of our university."

"There you have it," said the professor at Potchefstroom (called Potch). What did I have? "You have the problem with the English. I do not disagree, you understand, with the idea of academic freedom. I support it with all my heart. But you have to be committed to more than freedom. Autonomy is not enough. Freedom is a fine ideal but freedom by itself is just a vacuum." It is a familiar argument. In the rest of the world it is usually an argument against liberal democracy that is heard on the left. But it is not only on the left that worries are expressed about the limits of freedom, about what happens when freedom is divorced from a cultural matrix of shared values. In South Africa the English are widely perceived as a people without normative values, certainly without values that are grounded in any transcendent beliefs. The analogy should not be pushed too far, but Afrikaners talking about the deracinated English are reminiscent of earlier Eu-

ropean anti-Semites who deplored the "cosmopolitan root-
lessness" of the Jews. As we shall see, the leaders of the very
substantial Jewish community in South Africa are keenly
aware of the danger of being classed with the English as a
people who really "do not belong" in South Africa.

In another sense, of course, the English elite does have
an historically rooted sense of belonging in South Africa. Unfortunately, the symbols of English belongingness almost
inevitably rub the Afrikaner the wrong way. They are reminders of the days when the Afrikaner was seen as little
more than the dirt under the English boot. The country Afrikaner was, in the language of Kipling's day, "lower than the
kaffirs." It was not only the English who looked down on the
Afrikaner. The Dutch in the Cape Town establishment, those
who were *real* Hollanders, shared the contempt for the Boer
and were embarrassed that he claimed a kinship with them.
"Oh no, it isn't just the English," says a sophisticated Afrikaner academic who is quite self-consciously only one generation from the farm. After taking time out for a discursus
on the relative merits of California and South African wines,
he continues. "This is what really frightens the Afrikaner,
that the English disease is contagious. We talk a lot about
Afrikaner solidarity, but in our past and present, we have seen
the Afrikaner climb the ladder and become more and more
like the English. In higher government and professional circles in Pretoria, the Hollander and Afrikaner, you can't tell
them apart, and you can't tell either from the English. We
only talk more about the English because we don't want the
painful reminder that maybe all of us want to become, in fact
are becoming, more like them. It is easier to talk about 'them'
as though the line between us is still secure."

He quickly adds that, on the political and economic
levels, the line has to be blurred and must finally disappear
if South Africa is to survive in anything like its present form.
"If only we could abstract the cultural from the political and
economic, most Afrikaners would feel more comfortable about

the future. We have no lack of fears. The fear of black dom-ination is the one we talk about the most in public. But there is another nightmare that is just as big; the nightmare that the English are going to win after all. We fought them in a horribly bloody war and in 1948 we thought our success was complete. But now we really need Anglo-Afrikaner unity. And to many Afrikaners that comes down to fending off one nightmare by embracing the other." In deciding between the nightmare of black domination and the nightmare of the En-glish disease, the blood of race is thicker than the blood of nation.

Afrikaner inferiority feelings relative to the English run deep. For example, this statement by Anton Rupert, an Af-rikaner and one of the "princes" of South African business and finance. "Since the early thirties, when one out of every three Afrikaners was indigent, we have fought for and won a place in the economy of the country through study, dili-gence, daring, audacity, and perseverance. We have built brick by brick and proved not only that the Afrikaner in this coun-try can compete on equal terms but also that South Africans can compete anywhere in the world."[2] It seems a strange boast in a country where Afrikaners have been in a majority in a competition limited to whites. Even more touchingly, Rupert announces: "In a relatively short period of just over 300 years, we have made two original and important contri-butions to world culture: our unique Cape Dutch architec-ture and the vigorous Afrikaans language." Cape Dutch architecture is indeed charming but it, along with the Afri-kaans language, is of limited interest outside South Africa.

Many Afrikaners told me about the cultural sterility of black Africans. Why, even the wheel was unknown south of the Sahara until the European came. They do not mention, although they surely know, how thoroughly derivative is the "culture" of South Africa, dependent at almost every point upon the English. In religion Afrikanerdom is distinctive, but in no aspect of religion has it made a contribution recognized as world class, so to speak. Revealingly, one of the arguments used by Afrikaners who support the new constitutional order is that it rids the country of one of the last remnants of English imperialism—the "Westminster system" of parliamentary government. Nat politicians regularly declare that the new dispensation "at last gives us a government that is uniquely South African."

THE English in top business positions profess to be determined modernizers, as a general rule. In their view the history of conflict, contempt, and resentment between English and Afrikaner is so much baggage to be discarded so that South Africa can "get on with it." Yet the distinctively English past is pervasive in South Africa and is unabashedly celebrated by those who continue to declare that there will always be an England. Cape Town is surely one of the most beautiful cities in the world, and one of the loveliest things about Cape Town is the Mount Nelson Hotel. In the quiet lounges of its rambling Victorian dignity, it is quite possible to believe that the Great White Queen still reigns and all is right with an essentially British world. At night the plumbing rumbles and the jackets of the Indian and coloured waiters are somewhat frayed. But come time for tea, when silver-haired men in blazer and regimental tie are joined by their ladies who guiltily select cream-puffed sweets from groaning oak carts, then all talk about South Africa in crisis seems quite droll.

The Mount Nelson sits on an assiduously landscaped hill looking down upon a long boulevard lined by historic government and other buildings, including the parliament. (For reasons that need not delay us here—but not unrelated to Anglo-Afrikaner conflicts—the government of South Africa is divided between Cape Town and Pretoria.) The Mount Nelson does look *down* upon the parliament. Very gently, I broached the question of politics with a gentleman at tea. "Oh yes, well you never know what those chaps are doing down there, do you? . . . I can tell you that in '48 when they took over some of us were quite unsettled at the prospect of their running the country. But, you know, they learned the ropes after a while and are not doing such a bad job of it." The tone suggested that, if Botha and his boys began to mess up, well, we would just have to take over again. The suggestion is ludicrous of course, but, for a brief moment, it seemed almost plausible. One should not think that Afrikaners are not admitted at the Mount Nelson. I am assured they are. It is only that they are hard to tell apart.

At the Durban Club an Afrikaner would have to be very well disguised indeed. I am the guest of a retired and inordinately British gentleman who shows me through the elegant spaces, including oak-paneled rooms named for British prime ministers and sundry heroes. We ascend a sumptuous staircase lined with portraits of the royal family, including one of Edward VIII. "He was quite a naughty fellow, wasn't he?" my host asks, and I acknowledge I had heard it said. At the top of the staircase, the queen's picture. "She has turned out rather well, don't you think? We are all very pleased with her. She's quite a girl." I allowed as how I had not thought of her in quite that way, but reflected to myself that it was nice they were not going to give her her walking papers any time soon.

At lunch in the club's dining room my host remarks that it is a shame that more visitors don't see this side of Africa. "Soweto and Kwazulu and all that, well that's South African too of course, but this is equally South Africa." More than equally, I should think, from his perspective. It is not that he is uninterested in nonwhites. To the contrary, he is eager to instruct me in their ways. "You have to understand this about them . . ." and "You have to understand that about them. . . ." I must understand about these Indian chaps who are waiting on us. "It is quite remarkable, you see, they are very loyal. They put in twenty-five or thirty years service and then they get their gold watches, and they know that they have achieved something." He acknowledges that some of the younger Indians are less obliging. As for the blacks, "You have to understand that they tend to the tips." That means they are particularly careful about their heads and hands and shoes. "They must always be well-shod. They spend an enormous amount of money for shoes, more than you or I would." Later we visit a shop selling Zulu art. "These people are very good with their hands, you know." Nothing was said about their natural rhythm. At lunch I had inquired, delicately I thought, about Jews and the Durban Club. "Jews don't want to come here," my host said a little peevishly. "You have to understand that it is their own choice that they do not come as guests. They are rather touchy, you see, about not being admitted as members." In any event, he assured me, they have their own club and they like it better that way.

It is easier to be a bundle of unselfconscious prejudices in Durban. Easier than in Johannesburg, a vulgar and booming city for which a poet might do what Carl Sandburg did for Chicago. Easier than in Cape Town, a gracious minicity with a bad conscience about what South Africa has become, a city often compared to San Francisco but like Boston in its stateliness. Durban is different. At the center of Durban is the Durban Club, a piece of the empire, even of the Indian raj. I am told there are 440,000 Indians in Durban and about 250,000 whites, mainly English. Just outside, but clearly beyond the pale, is Kwazulu, the homeland of South Africa's largest single "nation." Along the beachfront of the Indian Ocean, high and stark white hotels present a tackier side of Durban. It is a favored holiday spot for those white South Africans who have not taken to the new "sin cities," the imitations of Las Vegas that have cropped up in "independent" homelands which permit entertainments forbidden in South Africa proper.

About the segregated beach of Durban's waterfront strip the story is told of an Asian who inquired whether this is the Indian Ocean. "No," he was told, "the Indian Ocean is five hundred yards farther up the beach." The strip is called the

Golden Mile and is garishly decorated with strings of lights, yellow, red, and white. Along the beach, across from the tourist hotels, the City of Durban has erected Minitown. Miniature trucks crawl along miniature highways, and miniature people watch a football game. The players are all white, as is the crowd, except for a small group of darker hue off to the side. They presumably are Indian or coloured, as are the few people in the miniature church. One suspects that some miniature mind thinks this is what Durban is today, or will be again. "Durban is essentially an English city," a professor at the University of Natal tells me, "and the Indians are more English than we are." He thinks it too bad that visitors to South Africa usually see Johannesburg, Pretoria, and Cape Town before coming to Durban. "If they came here first they would get a quite different impression of our country. We'll be the last to go. That is, if Buthelezi can keep his people under control." Buthelezi's people are, of course, the Zulus.

It is all pitiably distant from the vision of Cecil Rhodes who wrote in 1877: "It often strikes a man to inquire what is the chief good in life. . . . To myself the wish came to make myself useful to my country. . . . I contend that we are the first race in the world, and that the more of the world we inhabit, the better it is for the human race. I contend that every acre added to our territory provides for the birth of more of the English race. The absorption of the greater portion of the world under our rule simply means the end of all wars."[3] In Durban the flag descends slowly, slowly to the strains of "Abide With Me," offered up to whoever is the keeper of lost dreams.

Not all the English of Durban are dreaming backwards. Not most of them, I suspect. A prominent businessman spoke to me in the company of his fellows and no eyebrows were raised when he declared, "I've been to your city and I must say I like New York. You go out on the street and all the different races are there, and there's a kind of excitement in the air. You may have a few rich blacks living on Park Avenue but you avoid problems because the peoples don't mix socially. They have their places where they live and the whites have their places, and so forth. I believe it's realistic to think it will be like that here someday." It is not exactly the liberal vision of what New York ought to be, but it is perhaps an advance on what Durban is.

The English of Durban tend to think of themselves as more racially tolerant than the other whites of South Africa. "It's the chaps in Pretoria who have produced this mess, you understand." The speaker is a director of community services in Durban. "You will hear Afrikaners say that the English started the apartheid system, but that's rubbish. We did not have to have a system, we had *understandings* between the different groups. Then the Afrikaner came to power and he said, 'Now we'll show you how to do this thing right,' and he started passing all these regulations to regulate the obvious. You don't have to have a law that says that white and black should not marry. It is insulting to everybody. We weren't facing an explosion of interracial marriages, not that any of us noticed. But the Afrikaner is afraid of everything." That, he gave me to understand, is the main difference between the English and the Afrikaner. The English are confident, the Afrikaner afraid. "For the Afrikaner the three big concerns are unity, survival, and hegemony. If you threaten unity, you threaten survival, and therefore you threaten dominance."

But, when the English were on top, did they not have the same concerns? Perhaps, but it wasn't so apparent. "The Afrikaner is always in a sweat about it." The aesthetics of perspiration is close to the perceived difference between English and Afrikaner. "It is not considered nice to say it," explained one English matron who is also an antiapartheid militant, "but, yes, it is in large part a matter of style. Even when they come over to our side, there is still something of the boertrekker about them, you understand." She described for me a meeting of the PFP in the elegant Johannesburg suburb of Houghton. Frederik van Zyl Slabbert was there, the leader of the opposition. It was thought that having an Afrikaner at the head of the PFP would broaden its appeal beyond English liberals. "Everyone was very considerate, but I'm afraid it was a disaster. He simply wasn't at home with our people." I had talked with Slabbert and seen him on the platform. He is a thoughtful, articulate, and eminently presentable man. "But I need not tell you," she told me, "there are some things you cannot quite put your finger on." One such thing, it appears, is that Slabbert tried some remarks employing country humor which was not well received in Houghton.

Another remarkable woman we shall call Mrs. Kilburn. She and her husband are antiapartheid activists of long standing. She is involved in an agency designed to help blacks deal with the myriad housing, work, and mobility laws of the regime. The formation of her agency was inspired, she says, by the various consumer action groups, such as Ralph Nader's, in the U.S. She has a great admiration for things American. "The cause here is not that different from the cause in America," she tells me. She is a woman of about fifty, I dare to guess, and chic in dress and manner. But surely, I object, the cause in South Africa is not concerned with issues of feminism and gay liberation, as it is in the States. "Oh, you would be surprised. I am told that gay liberation is very big in South Africa." As for feminism, "It is really not a factor. We have so many more urgent things that we must attend to."

There is a problem now with the servants, she explains. That may sound trivial, but it is very real. Apparently the live-in domestic is becoming a luxury, and many new houses do not have facilities for that. So people come for one or two days a week and the government housing authorities are frowning on that. But if they cannot stay around for short periods in different places nor live in one place for a long time, where are they to go? It will create an explosion in the demand for housing for blacks. I inferred from this, perhaps incorrectly, that there is much to be said for having live-in domestics.

The Kilburn home is, by her own description, "opulent." "It is an embarrassment for me to invite blacks. It is an embarrassment for them and for me." Does she have Afrikaner friends? "Oh yes, but they are all Afrikaners who agree with us." A few days earlier I had asked an English couple at dinner whether they had any Afrikaner friends. The husband, who was giving me a very positive picture of South Africa, immediately said they did indeed, but the wife demurred. "You don't have any Afrikaner friends that you play golf with or would invite home to dinner," she objected. "Oh well," he responded, "if you mean *that* kind of friend, no, then I suppose you're right."

Of Mrs. Kilburn I inquire whether it is not important to the cause to talk with the opposition, even with Afrikaners in government. "Would you propose that the Jews should have talked with the Nazis?" she shoots back. It seems a question worth brief exploration. Does she believe that P. W. Botha is comparable to Hitler? Yes, although they are not alike in all ways. She does not believe, for example, that it is the deliberate intention of the government to kill off millions of blacks. "But that may still be what they will end up doing, whether to avoid revolution or in fighting the revolution." I relate the complaint of a moderate Afrikaner who said he had been spending years, in vain, trying to engage liberal English folk in a new conversation about the future of the country. He deplored what he said was the unnecessary polarization in South Africa. "I'm afraid I find that hard to believe," she responds. "Even if he's telling the truth, I'm not the person he's looking for. I'm sorry, but I still don't think you talk with people who have killed six million Jews."

Mrs. Kilburn is not at all morose. On the contrary, her words and manner suggest a feisty delight in being involved in a great cause. "I know that we're a small minority, I mean people who think like us. But I am very hopeful." I ask about the fears that the executive presidency in the new dispensation could lead to some kind of dictatorship. "Oh, that could happen, but it is not in the Afrikaner genes to be dictators or to live under dictatorial government. So the idea of dictatorship, martial law, and so forth, that's not so alarming." She is not alarmed for her own person or family because, "if you have money you can go where you want." The experience of being a Jew helps, she says. "There may be some people who don't want you but, if you have the means, you can make clear that you don't need them." She herself, she says, can live quite happily elsewhere, in England or the U.S., for example.

The bulk of the money for the agency with which she works comes from the U.S., from foundations such as Ford, Rockefeller, and Carnegie. Being funded from abroad may hurt the agency's credibility in some circles, she says, but there is no choice since there is no money in South Africa for this sort of work. I ask her about the frequent claim by South Africans of all sorts that Americans tend to think they understand the problem in South Africa but in fact do not. "Yes, I've heard that said, but I don't think it's true. The people I know in New York and places like that understand the situation quite well. We are in agreement on what is wrong here and what needs to be done." Does she even at moments think this government possesses what people here refer to as "a will to reform"? "No, not for a moment. The idea that the new constitutional proposals are a step toward negotiation is ridiculous. You cannot negotiate if you exclude the people you have to negotiate with, the blacks. And that's what these proposals do."

But she must surely then have some rather dour thoughts about the future of South Africa. "Yes, but there are signs of hope. The theatre, for example, exciting things are happening in the theatre. All kinds of experimentation is going on, and you can begin to see the shape of this becoming a united and multiracial society." She hopes that her group, as small as it is now, "is representative of what the future of South Africa will be." And if worse comes to worst and she leaves, what would she miss most about South Africa? The answer is immediate: "I would miss the hopefulness, the sense that we are doing something new here, that we might be some kind of encouragement for multiracial harmony also for other parts of the world."

B ASIL Hersov is an English-speaking "modernizer" of a quite different stripe. As a friend of his remarked, "Basil is the epitome of what we mean by the 'New South African.' " That we are speaking of white South Africans is taken for granted. In the opinion of some of the black leaders with whom we will be speaking, Hersov and his ilk are simply the newest and the slickest of apologists for oppression. In the view of other blacks, the Hersovs represent the last slender hope for the possibility of black-white negotiation that might stave off the revolutionary armageddon. For Hersov, the ancient baggage of Afrikaner-English hostility has largely been transcended, at least at the level of the top leadership of which he is part. The New South African is generally described as a technocrat. He is pragmatic, anti-ideological, undramatic, ready to do what must be done within the context of what can be done. From the traditional Afrikaner perspective, this is liberalism. Somewhat to the surprise of the American liberal, South African liberalism is most firmly ensconced in the business leadership and, as we shall have occasion to see, in the top echelons of the military.

Basil Hersov is not Harry Oppenheimer. Nobody else is Harry Oppenheimer. It is explained to me that Hersov represents the transitional generation of business leadership. In Oppenheimer's heyday government and business were separate principalities, the one Afrikaner and the other English. Hersov represents a consolidation of progressive Afrikaner-English leadership. The transition, according to this somewhat hopeful picture, is toward the leadership that will take the final and necessary steps toward the inclusion of all South Africans in a democratic capitalism of shared prosperity and opportunity. Many think that prospect either implausible or undesirable. But Hersov is persuasive, if not always convincing.

Hersov is chairman and managing director of Anglo-Vaal, one of the giants of South African business. Anglo-Vaal is heavily into mining, which still makes up a third of the country's enterprise, and does a business of over two billion rand per year. I notice that offices in South Africa lean to the stodgy—much wood, drapes, and lumpish furniture. This one is no exception. But there is nothing stodgy about Basil Hersov. In his mid-fifties, with a full head of graying hair fashionably but unpretentiously coiffed, a gray silk suit with a bit of red lining displayed, the very articulate Mr. Hersov, third generation South African, crosses his legs and leans back to offer a brief explanation of the whole world. He would, one suspects, be quite at home as a corporate head in London, or representing a British firm in New York.

Yes, what I have been told about a unitary economy requiring a unitary state is correct. "The steps that have been taken are irreversible. This is what frightens many whites, especially Afrikaners. The balls have been set rolling and, once they're rolling, there's no way to stop or control them. I think they're rolling in the right direction." The changes of recent years, he believes, are dramatic. "But I have to add that, if I were black, I have no doubt I would think they were much too slow."

"I am very encouraged by Botha. A wise politician who is primarily concerned about keeping his seat would not have done what Botha has done. He has put his neck on the line, and a man doesn't do that if he's just playing games." Botha, according to Hersov, has broken with the Afrikaner mindset that 1948 meant that the *volk* had come to power and must never relinquish it. "There is a curious analogy between the black and the Afrikaner experience. In the long term, maybe it means that the Afrikaner is in a better position to handle the future than the English would have been." On the one hand, he says, the Afrikaner panics in the face of black determination because he recognizes in the black his own, Afrikaner, history of struggle against oppression. That same recognition, however, can help the Afrikaner to understand and accommodate the black. "In the relationship between Afrikaner and black," says Hersov, "there may be wisdom in the notion that you send a thief to catch a thief."

There is the problem of the Afrikaner's linking of white supremacy with a "covenant" with God. "It is Blood River and all that. I have often had this experience with Afrikaners. You can go so far on the economic logic, and the logic that a secure defense means that everybody has a stake in the country, and so forth, and the Afrikaner will agree. But then you reach a certain point and he says, 'Now you're talking about my faith,' and then you can't go beyond that." He allows that the aristocracy did become something like a caste when it abdicated political control to the Afrikaner. "Harry Oppenheimer and a very few others saw that it was a mistake to stay aloof from politics, but most English speakers were quite willing to leave the forms of political leadership to the Afrikaner and his strange ideas. That goes way back in this century, the United Party with Smuts and all the others, there were always Afrikaners at the head. The English were too relaxed about this because they thought that nothing could really be done without them. But, of course, in 1948 things got out of hand and everything changed."

But now things are changing again. "P. W. Botha is encouraging because he recognizes that there must be a meld between the political and the financial. I could vote for Botha, but I don't think I could vote for his party. There is too much in the party program that is anathema to me, the homelands policy, the ignoring of black aspirations, and so forth." Does Botha really believe in the homelands policy? "No, no, I'm sure of that. I talk with him. I talk with senior cabinet ministers. They know and they say that everything is in a state of transition. The homelands policy was a neat mathematical juggle, an effort to divide the black population. They may not know what should replace it, but they know that the mathematics of the homelands policy makes no sense."

Hersov then strikes a more cautious note. "Their great fear, and I must say it is also our great fear, is not without foundation, however. A sudden transfer to a one man one vote situation would mean that whites would be swamped, and the consequences of that could be very bad for everyone." Then there is the anxiety about whether blacks are ready to govern. "Of course the Afrikaner has an endless number of horror stories about what has happened in Africa when blacks got control. But they regularly overlook some more hopeful situations, such as Zimbabwe and Swaziland and Kenya. In Swaziland there are no great problems. The phones go out every once in a while, but our telephone system isn't perfect either." He adds that Swaziland has the advantage of having only one tribe. "They are all Swazis. Here we have these different tribes, and tribal wars have been the curse of Africa."

Isn't he making the argument favored by the defenders of apartheid when they invoke the need for separate development of the different "nations"? "No, not at all. As I said before, separate development is no longer on, the balls are already rolling and they're irretrievable. But that does not mean we close our eyes to the potential for conflict and bloodshed. As we move toward a unitary society, we have to have structures that will anticipate and avoid that kind of bloodshed. As I understand this government, that is what it's trying to do. No, let me say I am convinced that is what they're trying to do."

"I admit we don't have many hopeful precedents in Africa. Even Kenya now has moved to a one-party state, but when I talk to the leaders there I do not think that is necessarily oppressive. The ideal they have in mind is not unlike the American situation, as I understand it. The loyalty of the leaders is not to a party line or just to one tribe but to represent their constituents. That is what we are working for here, a party or a system of parties where everything is not based on race or tribe or ideology." He smiles and shrugs his shoulders, "I know that may sound idealistic, but that has to be the goal."

Hersov says he wants to believe that neighboring Zimbabwe offers some kind of reason for hope. "I have told the prime minister [Botha] that it is a mistake to paint an absolutely bleak picture of what is happening in the rest of Africa. That only intensifies the idea that South Africa is facing a 'total onslaught,' and that induces the siege mentality of pulling around the wagons, the whole idea of the laager." Hersov himself, however, seems uncertain about whether Zimbabwe is in fact a hopeful exception. "We have a terrible time trying to keep our people there, they all want out. Even people who spoke out for giving [Zimbabwe's prime minister Robert] Mugabe a chance are losing heart. They say that in business and agriculture there is very little future there, almost no incentive to invest."

He speaks with a certain sadness about Zimbabwe and its leader, Robert Mugabe. Some of the most militantly reactionary whites in South Africa are refugees from Rhodesia after it became Zimbabwe. Hersov has no use for their strident "Never Again!" opposition to black rule. Hersov wants to be hopeful that Zimbabwe will be a break from the pattern of brutality and chaos that has generally marked postindependence Africa. Being hopeful is obviously an effort. "My impression is that for most blacks in Zimbabwe, black rule hasn't made that much difference. Perhaps that is always true of the peasants in a revolutionary situation. The color of the boss has changed. Too often it simply comes down to having a different set of bosses, and the new bosses very quickly become like the old bosses. Maybe some of the peasants have more land, maybe not. If so, it is more heavily taxed or is really under the control of the new bosses. In a situation like Zimbabwe, the people who get squeezed are the chaps in the middle, and they are the ones who produce the wealth. In Zimbabwe, for example, you have a raising of wages, a minimum wage, and then they peg the profit that you can make, so your profit margin finally dwindles to nothing. You end up with no investment, no production, no jobs, no food." Feeling he has become too morose, Hersov tosses his head and says, "Well, I hope it will not come to that."

Since our conversation the situation in Zimbabwe has continued to decline. Mugabe has harassed his political opponents such as Joshua Nkomo and Bishop Abel Muzorewa. Against the supporters of his one-time ally Nkomo he has unleashed a North Korean-trained military unit, resulting in massacres that have been protested by the Catholic church and international human rights groups. Muzorewa, who had been prime minister during the transition from white rule in Rhodesia, complained that Mugabe's rule is more oppressive than that of Ian Smith. Ironically, Mugabe has also taken to having military squads break up squatters camps around the capitol city of Harare and forcibly drive people back into the countryside. British writer Paul Johnson has dubbed the forty-five-plus independent African nations as "Caliban's Kingdoms." Uganda, Central African Republic, Biafra, Ruwanda, and on and on—the list is long and depressing. Opponents of black political participation in South Africa are inclined to recite the details of the horror with unseemly relish. The Hersovs are not ignorant of the horror, but neither will they agree with a determinism that says the horror is the only alternative to white rule.

"Look, let's face it," says Hersov, running his hand through his hair, "ours is a ghastly situation. Of course other countries may be worse. There are other places in the world that have racial discrimination, but we are the only ones who write it into law. We invite the condemnation by claiming to have a high regard for law." Nor does he think the Western press should be criticized too harshly for operating by a double standard. "That's their business. It is natural that they concentrate on what is wrong. They have the freedom to say it about South Africa and within South Africa, so they go about their business of saying it." Then comes an appeal, together with the schoolboy metaphor, that becomes familiar. "But we need some encouragement from the West too, especially from the U.S. And we need to encourage the prime minister and others here when they do something right. If you beat a schoolboy all the time for his bad behavior, and then he does something right and you still beat him the same way, what is he to do? He throws up his hands and says, 'Well, what difference does it make? I may as well be bad.' That is the way it was only a few years ago. South Africans were very resentful and very defiant and very dismissive of what others thought. They were convinced that the Western nations would never give them a fair hearing anyway, so world opinion be damned."

I told him about a friend, an American journalist, who visited South Africa for two weeks. Afterwards she said that the usual experience was not hers. The usual experience, she explained, is that people come to South Africa in a simplistic and judgmental frame of mind and then return "overwhelmed by the complexities and pleading for understanding for the white South African's dilemma." "With me," she said, "exactly the opposite happened. I was prepared to learn about the complexities but was overwhelmed by the simplicity of the brutal fact that a white minority is determined to exclude forever a black majority from the rights of citizenship in their own land." Hersov allows that, yes, in some ways it is a simple black-white question. What is not so simple, he says, is what can be done about it. Of one thing he is sure: it is not "forever."

"I know better than to say the world should be patient with us. We should not be patient with ourselves. Building trust between people who have been suspicious and hostile to one another is not a simple thing." He adds that trust cannot rest upon charity or sentiment alone; it has to be structured so that everyone understands clearly that cooperation is in their own interest. Such a structure, in turn, must finally be based not upon group classification but on acknowledged merit and achievement. Although it may not be so simple for the whole country, he believes the experience of Anglo-Vaal and other "progressive" corporations can point the way toward building such trust.

"Seven years ago we had discussions here when we were first becoming serious about nondiscrimination. One of the things we discussed, if you will believe it, is toilets. Some of my executives talked to me at great length about what we would do about separate toilets and whether we should now put up signs saying that from now on these toilets are for everybody. And I said, well, did we ever have signs saying they weren't for everybody? And he said no, it was just understood. And I said, well, the word should be passed so it is just understood that there is no discrimination also at this very basic level." Hersov smiles almost sheepishly at the pettiness of all this, but then says, "These day by day questions can be as important as the great policy decisions when it comes to how people get along together." The question of the company canteen came up. It was said that some whites would object to eating with blacks. "My answer was simple. If they did not want to eat in the company-subsidized canteen they could go out to a restaurant for lunch and pay as much as they would pay for a whole month of lunches in the canteen."

The discussion of toilets and canteens is reminiscent of the lunch-counter phase of the American civil rights movement. But South Africa is also becoming familiar with questions similar to "quotas" and "affirmative action." Shortly before I met Basil Hersov, Anglo-Vaal had appointed a black man as director of personnel, a very senior position. "When we made the appointment I instructed that the publicity going out on this be the same as any other publicity about a promotion. It should not make a big thing about his being the first black man to reach that level in the company. Quite frankly, it's a little early for him. He hasn't had some of the experience in labor negotiations and the such that would ordinarily go with that job, but we're going to help him and I think he's up to it. Some of the white labor leaders in the mines are likely going to say they aren't about to sit down with that bastard, and initially we might have to send someone else to the negotiating table, but N'Tuli [the personnel director] understands that."

Hersov acknowledges that corporations are still feeling their way when it comes to advancing blacks. "For example, we had one black we were cultivating for executive leadership. He had a doctorate in mathematics and other impressive credentials, but he just could not get along with people. When I finally had to tell him that it was not going to work out, he protested and pointed to all the certifications he had on paper. But we had looked into that and we found that also at the university people had moved him along irregardless of merit because nobody wanted to discourage a black man. Nobody wanted to say no." I suggest that in a corporation it might be possible to hold the line on merit, but does he really think that kind of rationality will work in the political arena? "I don't know. I would like to think so, of course. Keep in mind that there are rational black leaders who know that, when they do get political power, they want a South Africa that is productive and prosperous. Whites are not the only ones who have been impressed by the disasters in other countries when merit and economic common sense are ignored."

A unitary society in which all South Africans have a stake, will it come by negotiations or by white design? "By negotiations, clearly," he answers. "It is an illusion to think that whites can impose a design that will last. The President's Council [the body drawing up the proposals for constitutional reform] is already a kind of negotiation. Although he is not physically present, the black man is very much at the table when they deliberate. Everybody knows that. That is finally what the deliberation is about." The physical presence of the black man at the negotiating table will close the gap between illusion and reality, but Hersov knows it will not be closed easily. "I assume there will be more violence. I think most of us are braced for that. The temptation is to forget that violence comes from different motives and takes different forms. For the government, the temptation is to attribute everything to communist influence." He says that nobody should doubt that communist influence is there too, "But the blacks are not a monolithic community with monolithic interests that can be manipulated by any one force."

Does he expect that Western opinion about South Africa will change any time soon? "No, not in the near term. What is needed is a clear statement that we are moving toward a unitary society, backed up by clear evidences of change. Americans and others can speculate about the so-called hidden agenda in the constitutional reforms, and I am convinced there is more afoot than is publicly said now, but why should others give us the benefit of the doubt?" There is a heavy history to be overcome. "For twenty or thirty years Western opinion has been conditioned to think of South Africa as a pariah nation. The media have been understandably influential in this, but we can't expect them to suddenly start reexamining their assumptions. We have to take the initiative, we have to give them good reason to look again and see whether they got it right on what is happening here."

No matter what happens, South Africa is not going to become popular overnight. "But the focus of world attention could be shifted. The emphasis would no longer be on the denial of rights to blacks in South Africa; it would be on the fact that the way to achieve these rights is too slow, it is taking too long. But that would be a very welcome shift." Another shift that is welcomed by almost all white South Africans is the Reagan administration's policy of "constructive engagement." "I know that some people claim that Carter's policy, if you can call it that, put pressure on South Africa for change, but that is a mistake, I believe. Indiscriminate condemnation backfires here, especially in government circles. During the Carter years, many government people here said, 'We're damned if we do and we're damned if we don't, so why should we give a damn what Washington thinks.' " Reagan, in Hersov's rather typical view, has given some encouragement for change. "The feeling is that we have an opportunity now, perhaps just a passing moment of opportunity, to demonstrate that we are serious about constructive change."

Hersov is not sure the government appreciates this as fully as it should. "Some people think that we should be applauded when we let up on some of the rigors of the old apartheid system. I call this change by exception. It applies, for example, to what has happened to so-called petty apartheid, as well as in other areas. The government simply looks the other way when a law is violated and then, after a while, it says, 'Well, that law isn't being enforced anyway so we can drop it from the books.' That may be good but it isn't enough. I understand why politicians prefer change by exception. If they made a straightforward statement, 'We should abolish this law,' it would create an enormous fight."

Despite his sympathy for the political tactic of change by exception, Hersov emphasizes that changes must be made which are not merely momentary exceptions but are "in some sense irreversible." He points to the example of job reservation. This is a system in which, by law, certain jobs are "reserved" for whites. Job reservation laws have been dropped and in practice job reservation is widely ignored. It is still a factor in mining, however, where white unions have historically insisted that the better jobs must be for whites only. "The government would have a fight in changing the law, but it would be worth it. It would be symbolically important, but also a substantive step, demonstrating that we are changing not only by exception but also by legislation and determination."

Finally, we turn to the question of the deracinated English. What is Basil Hersov's stake in South Africa? He makes it clear that he has the means to live anywhere in the world. I had no doubts on that score. "But I do not intend to leave. Wherever I would be, I would be a South African, I wouldn't be at home anywhere else." Hersov stands under a flag. "I know some people may not feel this way, but I get a kick when I see the South African flag flying overseas, when I see South Africans overseas speaking out and especially when they achieve distinction. When I think of South Africa, it is really not with any color at all, black or white. It is almost the idea of South Africa which I am very, very proud of. I am very proud to be a South African." As with so many South Africans, Hersov views his country through the eyes of others. Tocqueville remarked the same thing about early nineteenth-century Americans; their opinion of themselves was defiantly posited against their anxious estimate of what others thought of them. It indicates, no doubt, a feeling of inferiority, but a feeling of inferiority mixed with a confidence in one's unappreciated worth.

"When people in other countries, especially in America, remember South Africans' enormous contribution in the last war and how we participated in the Korean War, even though we had no great interest at stake but only because we believed it was right, when they remember that, I am very proud. And when our contributions in these struggles of the Western world are forgotten by others, then I am disappointed, extremely disappointed." "I will say this," Hersov concludes, "and it's not because of racial pride, because, as I said, I don't think of South Africans in terms of black and white, but I believe that South Africa produces above average people who succeed. And if we have the nerve to move beyond the ghastly mess we've gotten ourselves into here, I think the world will see that too."

And blacks, do they have such warm feelings for South Africa? "Let me confess frankly, I don't know what blacks want or what they think. I know individual black people and it seems we don't disagree on this idea of South Africa, but maybe the blacks I know have a good reason to agree with me. I am realistic about that, but I am not cynical. I don't think a black man who wants to succeed in business is insincere for that reason, any more than a white man who wants to succeed is insincere. But I confess I don't know. I would hope that blacks want something along the same lines of the South Africa I want. I hope there is some meeting point about what the future of our country should be. I can only hope."*

It is a hope commonly expressed among the English of South Africa. Sometimes it is expressed in tones forlorn and sometimes in tones defiant. And sometimes it is expressed in tones so confident as to be smug—"of course this is the way it will be, the logic of the situation makes it inevitable." I have come to place what modest hopes one can have for the future of South Africa in the hopes forlorn and defiant. There is nothing inevitable about a promising future for South Africa. There is reason for encouragement in the rapprochement between some English speakers and some Afrikaners around the realization that apartheid, petty and grand, is a moral and practical disaster. The express determination to find another way, a way that will give everybody a stake in a South Africa that is democratic and productive, is some reason to not give up on South Africa. That is about all that can be said, and it cannot be said with much certainty. The hopeful thing is that ten years ago it could not reasonably be said at all.

The English once thought of themselves as the aristocrats of South Africa. Some of them still do. The best of them

---

*Since our conversation, Basil Hersov has been sharply criticized for his role in the 1985 abortive strike by black mine workers. While much larger enterprises, notably Anglo-American, worked with the miners union, Anglo-Vaal and a few others engaged in what has been described as union busting. In addition, Wells N'Tuli, the personnel director he discussed, is said to have been excluded from significant decision making.

know now, however, that they were only at the top of a caste system, and since 1948 they have not even been that. The Afrikaner thought to become the new aristocrat. That might have been possible a century or a half century ago. But when he triumphed the Afrikaner discovered himself in the latter part of the twentieth century. It is a time in which aristocracy and caste system are understood to be incompatible. The caste systems which thrive in this epoch are usually those that claim to be Marxist in one sense or another. They are caste systems that categorize people by class—proletarian, capitalist, land owner, and so on. The only aristocracies that are possible are the aristocracies of achievement in open societies that describe themselves as liberal and democratic. The Afrikaner took over too late. He thought to displace the English as the aristocracy, but he cannot claim that position, nor can the English reclaim it. The position is no longer available. Since white South Africans do not want and almost certainly could not have the leadership in a caste system of class categories and class conflicts along Marxist lines, their choices are limited to two, or so it would seem. They can resign themselves to being the object of the world's contempt and ridicule as, in a climate of ever deepening fear, they continue to try to maintain by brute force a nineteenth-century caste system. Or the white rulers of South Africa can risk the development of an aristocracy of achievement in a democratic and, yes, liberal society. It is not a choice between risk and safety, it is a choice between risks. Among the rewards of the democratic risk is the prospect of restored moral credibility, and that ought to matter to people who claim that morality matters. In any event, it is uncertain which choice, if any, is represented by the new dispensation that began in 1983. And, according to some, the escalating violence since then has mooted any dispensation set forth by Pretoria.

CHAPTER FIVE

THE BANKRUPTCY OF WHITE REFORM

I first met Beyers Naudé in 1971. It was in Johannesburg and he was director of the Christian Institute of Southern Africa. The Institute was then engaged in a flurry of anti-apartheid activities, yet despite his fevered schedule Naudé took time to explain his views at length. And he put me in touch with a range of South Africans, black and white, whom I probably would not have known except for Naudé's network of shared concern. Now it is more than ten years later and, although we had corresponded, this was our first meeting since he had become a legal outcast in his own country.

In 1975 the government declared the Christian Institute to be an "affected organization." That meant, among other things, that it could not receive monies from abroad. The Institute had been almost totally dependent upon funding from outside South Africa. In 1977 the Institute and Beyers Naudé were banned. In 1982 Naudé's five-year banning was due to expire and it was widely thought that it might not be renewed. It was renewed.

Banning is an institution peculiar to South Africa. In Orwellian fashion, one is publicly declared to be a nonperson, and, for the duration of the ban, that is the last public acknowledgment of one's existence. The banned person cannot attend public meetings, except to go to church, cannot write for publication, cannot be quoted in print by others, and cannot have more than two people at a time in his home. It is a little like "dormitory arrest" or "room arrest" in some preparatory schools. If, for example, you are caught bringing beer on campus, you are confined to the dormitory or your room for a day or two or three. Banning is a much more serious matter, however. Banning is for three or five or eight long years. Banning is not in response to juvenile pranks, but to what the government solemnly declares to be a threat to the security of the state. It is like dormitory arrest, however, in its attempt to infantilize and privatize the lives of its victims. It denies them the prisoner's status of being a serious offender, and it asserts the right of the state-as-parent to discipline its recalcitrant children. Banning does not work very well, however, and at present, with only a handful of banned persons left, it is thought that the regime is no longer keen on the tactic. It brings powerful criticism from abroad, where people have an easier time understanding trials and political imprisonments and straightforward persecution and even execution of alleged enemies of the state. And banning does not work because Beyers Naudé, for one example, continues to be an important public presence in the life of South Africa.

I call on him at his home in a pleasant middle-class suburb of Johannesburg. Through the front garden almost overgrown with the extravagance of South African vegetation, I am welcomed by a smiling Beyers Naudé, casually dressed and eager to resume a conversation interrupted by a decade that has taken him from almost frenetic activism to the appearance of solitude. Now approaching seventy and seeming to have aged no more than five years since last we met, Naudé continues to be altogether impressive; ruggedly built with a square jaw and riveting grey-blue eyes, it is easy to see why many think he is something like a prophet also in physical appearance.

As the conversation resumes in the comfortably bourgeois living room, I notice a change in his manner. The word for it is serenity and I remark on that. "Yes," he says with a smile, "I'm not recommending banning to anyone, but it is true. I've had time for reflection, for reading, for meditation—more than ever before in my life. I stay in touch with what is happening, but I know there is very little I can do to affect the course of affairs. . . . At first that was very hard, being cut off from the work that meant everything, and it is still very hard at times. But if there is a compensation, it gives me a better perspective. It is the kind of thing that often happens with prisoners, I suppose, although I know their situation is usually much harder than mine. By 'perspective' I do not mean that the struggle is less important, but maybe I find it easier to admit that I may be less important to the struggle. I would like to think that I am becoming more of a man of faith."

The peculiar institution of banning is also a puzzling institution to those who fall victim to it. "I think it's part of their idea, always keeping you off balance, never quite sure what you can do and what you can't do. It's not a question of following clearly written rules." He assumes that all his communications are monitored and his visitors closely observed. Yet he is deeply involved, almost every day, in "pastoral counseling." According to one version of banning, he can only see one person at a time, but there has been no interference when he sees two for counseling. The afternoons are mostly given over to talking with visitors and to study. "And of course I cannot give interviews. So if our conversation should in any way be connected with publication, either here or in the U.S., you understand it would be against the law," he says with mock seriousness. I indicate that I understand perfectly.

He observes that banning may really be harder on the spouse, in this case his wife Ilse. (Naudé refers to her always as spouse or partner, never as wife.) The year before, he says, she almost had a breakdown because of the imposed isolation. "Of course she can see who she wants and go where she wants, but if you are married you do not want to go out to a dinner party without your spouse. And we cannot have more than one person here for dinner."

Ilse is at the time of my call visiting with family out of town. Naudé's preoccupation with the everyday reflects the domesticating of a public figure, which was no doubt one of the government's goals in banning him. Yet it is in the domestic or private sphere that Beyers Naudé has made the most important public statement of his years under the ban. One Sunday in 1980 he walked across the street from the white church where he had worshiped to the social hall where services were held in the Sotho language for black domestics. By resigning his membership in the white church in which he had once been a leading clergyman, Naudé declared his belief that the time for white reformers in South Africa was definitively over.

"Now we are in a time of greater polarization, of necessary polarization. Those people in the churches and elsewhere who think there is a will to reform, as they say, in this government have chosen the other side. I have no doubt about it at all. Botha believes firmly in separate development and is determined that there will never, never be a unitary state." In twenty or twenty-five years, he says, the government will be forced to recognize the inevitability of a unitary state, but then affairs will no longer be in their hands. How will the government be forced? "By violence, not by violence alone, but certainly by violence. I am personally opposed to violence, but that will not stop its increase. It is urban violence and it will become more regular and more sophisticated, and we already see that happening."

Naudé thinks naked fear will finally reach a point of turning. "Already whites are uneasy, some of them are terrified now, and it will come to a time when the great majority is terrified, not knowing where the next bomb is coming from. They'll know about the ideological guidance of black consciousness behind the violence and they'll no longer believe the government when it says the bombs are the sporadic work of a few thugs and malcontents. And then the whites will ask themselves, 'Is it worth it?' and that will be the turning point. That's when they will begin to think about negotiating in earnest." He then cites, as many in South Africa do, the line of one of Alan Paton's early heroes to the effect that when the white man finally turns to loving, the black man may have turned to hating. "When the whites are ready for negotiations," says Naudé, "it may be too late for negotiations."

Naudé says he wants to believe that there are alternatives to the apocalypse and the church should point the way. In leaving the largest white Dutch Reformed church (the NGK—*Nederduitse Gereformeerde Kerk*), Naude sees himself pioneering the path others should follow. He quickly ticks off the reasons why it is no longer possible to stay in the white church: "First, the NGK is no longer a church in the biblical meaning of the term. Second, joining the black church is necessary for Christian unity, and, third, we whites have to be prepared to reverse roles." We discuss the reasons in reverse order.

Is it not somewhat masochistic, or even an exercise in "false consciousness", to think that whites and blacks can reverse roles in South Africa? "It could be that, but that is not what I mean. The temptation is for whites to insist that they have the better insights, theologically and sociologically and politically. So we end up being paternalistic toward blacks. We have to give up that feeling of superiority toward blacks, especially at those points where the feeling might be supported by fact in the sense that we have had all the advantages. It means that for the first time whites would have to be honest. That does not mean overlooking black mistakes, that would be dishonest. Honesty means a deliberate self-subordination, our readiness to be reeducated; we have to learn to be learners under black people who from a traditional viewpoint might in fact be making mistakes."

But, if his leaving the NGK advances the "necessary

polarization," how does that contribute to Christian unity? "That's where my first and second points come together. You cannot speak of Christian unity between churches when one of them is not a Christian church." Any serenity of manner does not extend to substance as Naudé insists on this point. "The NGK says the World Council of Churches is being divisive and undermining Christian unity when it supports liberation struggles and the such, but that is a division for a truer unity. You do not continue to dialogue with churches that are not churches. If you acknowledge them as churches, you are not advancing the solution, you're withholding the solution. The solution is to say clearly, 'This is what the gospel says, this is what Christ requires.' " How does he respond to those who claim to detect an element of self-righteousness in such a statement, or to those who think Christ has been remiss in revealing a political solution for South Africa? "These are evasions, I believe. Of course we should not be self-righteous, we are all to blame, we have all sinned, but if they would move on in a new obedience the solution is clear enough."

"The word of judgment must be spoken," Naudé emphasizes, "for the sake of the gospel. If the gospel truth is to have credibility among the blacks it must be dissociated from the abuses, from the way the gospel has been used to legitimate an oppressive social system." I ask him about those who say that the Dutch Reformed church no longer claims that apartheid is theologically mandatory or even justifiable. "Yes, these statements are interesting and maybe they are well intended. But they are not compatible with the actual practice of the Dutch Reformed church. 'By their fruits ye shall know them,' and the fruit is apartheid." He says the role of the Broederbond is critical. "For twenty-three years I was a member of the Broederbond and I know how it works. It is incompatible with Christianity that a person also has this suspect and secret loyalty. How can a black churchman trust the dialogue with Dutch Reformed leaders when it is no secret that the leaders have a secret loyalty and secret intentions?" The answer, according to Naudé is that dialogue is impossible.

He has not, however, given up on individual members of the Dutch Reformed church, even if he has given up on their church. "We should maintain dialogue with the leaders and especially with some of the younger ones. But the subject of the dialogue must be focused; the question is how can they remain members of churches that are not churches. They must be led to ask that question. It is fine that there are dissidents in these churches, but as long as they remain they are perpetuating the falsehood that these truly are churches." In the Lutheran World Federation and other worldwide bodies the proposition has been advanced in recent years that apartheid is a matter of *status confessionis,* a question of faith. "I agree with that," says Naudé. "But it does not simply mean that apartheid is wrong because it separates white from black at the altar. It means, I believe, that a church that goes along with an unjust social system is not a church." He compares some of today's dissidents in the Dutch Reformed church with those Christians in Germany in the 1930s who hesitated to join the "Confessing church" in unqualified resistance to Hitler. Then he qualifies that a little: "I am not saying that my decision must be everyone's decision. I knew that in conscience, before God, I could not remain a member of the NGK. Others have to pray about it and reach their own conclusion. But I confess that I have great difficulty, very great difficulty, in understanding how any other decision is possible. Not if you really care about the gospel in South Africa. I am sorry, but I have very little patience with people who think they can still have it both ways. The time for that is long past."

To many people in South Africa and abroad Beyers Naudé is a prophet. To some in the establishments of Afrikanerdom he is no more than a turncoat; to others he is a weak man who "broke under the weight of the moral ambiguity of Afrikaner responsibility for this country." That is the view of a former colleague who does not want to be quoted publicly on Naudé. In this analysis, Naudé's radical break from Afrikanerdom represents the flip side, as it were, of the Afrikaner personality. Moral earnestness can take many forms. The desire for fraternal solidarity in a righteous cause can mean commitment to the *volk* or to the liberation struggle against Afrikaner oppression.

Isaiah Berlin says that the civilized person in the modern sense of the term recognizes the relative validity of his convictions, but yet stands by them. "To demand more than this is perhaps a deep and incurable metaphysical need; but to allow it to determine one's practice is a symptom of an equally deep, and more dangerous, moral and political immaturity."[1] In a world of relativities, Beyers Naudé "demands more than this." Whether that demand reflects immaturity or moral integrity or some combination of both, there is no doubt that also in this respect Beyers Naudé is very much an Afrikaner. Afrikaners frequently criticize him for abandoning his people. He may be such a scandal for them, however, because he holds up to them the tradition of moral relentlessness which so many of them have abandoned.

Among opponents of apartheid who tell the story of South Africa primarily in moral terms, Beyers Naudé and the Christian Institute are stage center. The active life of the Christian Institute was little more than a decade, but in that time it was a lightning rod for both resistance to the state and the state's reaction to that resistance. The prominence of the Christian Institute was due in largest part to the fact that Beyers Naudé is a man whom Afrikanerdom cannot easily ignore. Some of his supporters, both black and white, believe that his day is still to come, that Beyers Naudé will yet be vindicated as the forerunner of a "New Afrikaner" who will one day turn a tradition of moral earnestness into the paths of justice.

106

Of course that may be a piece of radical romanticism. There is no doubt, however, that Naudé symbolically implicates the Afrikaner tradition; no banning or other declarations of his nonpersonhood can eradicate him from the consciousness of the *volk*. Naudé was born in 1915 and his father, a Dutch Reformed predikant (pastor), named the boy after General Christiaan Beyers under whom he had served in the Boer War. The father was a champion of Afrikaans culture, and Beyers, embracing his father's vocation and imbibing his passions, early demonstrated qualities of leadership that would mark him as a comer in Afrikanerdom. In 1939 he joined the Broederbond, "in order to serve my people better and perhaps qualify for some position of consequence." Positions of consequence came his way—influential parishes, campus chaplaincies, travel abroad, and in 1958 election as Acting Moderator of the NGK in the Transvaal. During these years he was in lively conversation with young predikants in the black and coloured churches of the Dutch Reformed family, and his thinking about South African society "became increasingly troubled."

"I did not feel at all alone at that time," he explains. It was thought that there were as many as four hundred "troubled" clergy in the Dutch Reformed church, those who had been touched by ecumenical contact with other churches and, most particularly, by the thinking of nonwhite Christians in South Africa. But then the crunch came. There was Sharpeville in 1960, when sixty-nine blacks were killed during a protest demonstration. And then there was Cottesloe. The latter was a meeting of South African churches with representatives of the World Council of Churches aimed at addressing questions of racial justice. From Cottesloe came very "progressive" resolutions in which Beyers Naudé played an important part. One by one, the Dutch Reformed churches distanced themselves from the work of Cottesloe, however, finally condemning both the procedure and the proposals. Relations between the Dutch Reformed church and the World

Council were brought to an end, and Naudé and his friends saw their work in ruins. In 1962 Naudé, together with Albert Geyser and the late Fred van Wyk of the South African Institute of Race Relations, started a new journal, *Pro Veritate,* and in 1963 they launched the Christian Institute. The goal was to solidify and expand the four hundred or more dissenting clergy in the Dutch Reformed church. The reactions and anathemas of the churches had done their work, however, and it soon became apparent to Naudé and his partners that they were supported not by four hundred, nor by two hundred, but perhaps by two dozen of their colleagues in ministry. Until it was finally banned in 1977, the Christian Institute was never able to build a constituency of any size within the Dutch Reformed church.

"We made mistakes, I am sure," Naudé says now, "but I have no regrets about the directions we explored. There were three phases in the life of the Christian Institute. The first was to work within the Dutch Reformed church and try to bring about real change there. The second effort was to work with the so-called mission churches, that is the mixed churches and the English churches. And the third phase was to back black initiatives. The third effort is the one that alienated the churches of all kinds." Others suggest that the Christian Institute was an alien enterprise, almost an antibody in South African life, from the very beginning. They say Naudé's three-phase division is altogether too neat, that from the start the Christian Institute was perceived as an instrument of foreigners hostile to everything South African. It was perceived that way, they further contend, because in fact it was that.

In some respects the Christian Institute was a very major presence in South African life. Even by American standards of "cause organizations" the Institute had impressive resources. "Please remember," says Alex Boraine, a PFP member of parliament and former Methodist leader, "that the formal politics of South Africa includes only a little over four million people. That's about half the size of the population of New York City. This is a very small world and in this very small world the Christian Institute looked like a giant organization." It was not, however, an indigenous giant. For example, the Institute's Study Project on Christianity in Apartheid Society (SPROCAS) had from 1969 to 1973 a budget of over two hundred thousand rand. Of that amount, a little over one thousand rand, or less than one half of one percent, came from churches and other sources in South Africa.[2] The bulk of the overseas money came from the Netherlands, with considerable help from institutions in England. From the viewpoint of the Afrikaner establishment, therefore, the Christian Institute was exported by their traditional rivals, the English and the Hollanders who had been historically contemptuous of Afrikaans culture. "The only thing South African about the Christian Institute," Professor A. D. Pont remarks, "was a few alienated dominees who could be bought by foreign money."

Professor Albert Geyser offers a more sympathetic, but not uncritical, analysis. Geyser was a cofounder of the Christian Institute and a minister of one of the smaller of the three white Dutch Reformed churches (the *Nederduitsch Hervormde Kerk*, or NHK). It alone of the Dutch Reformed churches formally restricts membership to whites, and it was the first of the churches to reject the proposals from the Cottesloe meeting which Geyser had cheered. Geyser had also contributed to *Delayed Action*, a book of essays condemning the apartheid system, and no one was surprised when a church commission found him guilty of heresy in 1962. Geyser appealed to the secular courts and finally both the courts and the church restored his good standing, formally. In fact he and his wife were effectively ostracized from Afrikanerdom. While he is a pleasant, almost jocular, personality, he still speaks with some bitterness of these events. There is a note of deep satisfaction, however, in his telling of a related incident in which he successfully sued A. D. Pont for libel. Pont is, Geyser says, still making monthly payments on the fine assessed by the court.

We meet at the reception desk near the student center at Witwatersrand, and again I am struck by the number of nonwhite students at this "white" university—proportionately more than one would find at many American schools. "Yes," I was told, "and some of the white students are none too happy about it." It appears that an ultraright group at liberal and English "Wits" is led by a Jewish student. Again there is this Anglo-Afrikaner ambivalence. "The English," I am told, "like their comforts, and for those who are better off apartheid is extremely comfortable." The axiom frequently heard is that the English talk PFP, vote NRP, and thank God for the NP. (The NRP is the New Republic Party, a left-over from the old United Party of General Smuts. While the Progressive Federal Party opposes apartheid, it is commonly said that the difference between the NRP and the National Party is in the different styles of apartheid they endorse. The NRP has its base in the English population of Durban and the Natal region.)

But I wanted to hear Albert Geyser on the Christian Institute. Of the three founders—Fred van Wyck and Beyers Naudé being the other two—"I suppose I was the most conservative," says Geyser. "I believed in the original purpose of the Christian Institute, which was to confront the Dutch Reformed churches. We tried to do that from the inside and discovered it was impossible, so we needed an independent base. We confronted from the outside, but we also insisted that we were not outsiders. Perhaps we were naive about being able to do that." The chief goal, he says, was to force the churches to face up to the implications of their theological claims, especially the claims about South Africa being a "Christian society." After the publication of *Delayed Action*, and after Cottesloe, the challengers were abandoned by many whom they had counted on for support. "There was cowardice, of course," says Geyser, "but there was also institutional self-interest, and I'm not sure that that's just another form of cowardice." When one of the three Dutch Reformed churches emphatically rejected Cottesloe, the big NGK felt that it had to follow suit, or else there would be a hemorrhaging of membership to the groups that had rallied to the support of apartheid. "I believe that the church recognized the legitimacy of Cottesloe, but the leaders couldn't say so without causing great political troubles in the churches and in the relationship with the government." The idea of some leaders was that they could disown Cottesloe as such while, at the same time, dealing with its legitimate challenges in their own way, in-house, as it were. "But in fact the repudiation of Cottesloe played into the hands of those who wanted to repudiate the challenge as well. So we ended up farther back than where we had started. The questions raised by the dissidents in the Dutch Reformed church today, for example, are no advance on what we wrote in *Delayed Action* more than twenty years ago! That is why we felt we had to start the Christian Institute."

While Geyser strongly affirms his continuing friendship and admiration for Beyers Naudé, he also believes there was needless confrontation. In the early sixties, he says, he talked with W. A. Visser't Hooft, then general secretary of the World Council of Churches, about the need for protest that is aware of South African sensibilities. "Visser't Hooft understood, I believe, but it may be that he was not really in control of everything being done in the name of the World Council. I am not sure that Beyers always understood the dangers of becoming a captive to the World Council orbit." This is said with reluctance and an obvious effort to be kind. "The World Council always said it was being prophetic but it was inadvertently—and I say this very carefully—working with what can only be called communist tenets." I express some surprise at this, since it is a stock argument of those who would, so to speak, like to see Albert Geyser in the stocks. "Yes, yes," he responds, "but even the devil can be right at times."

"I was troubled from the very beginning in talking with people from the World Council and other Europeans and Americans who wanted to see justice done in South Africa. They always assumed that Afrikaners were acting out of sheer cussedness, they refused to see that there is a very real and existential fear here." He adds that, while Naudé has done heroic work and is substantially right in what he wants to happen, Naudé was too ready to go along with this simplistic portrayal of Afrikaner motives. "Those of us who fight apartheid here, for us the situation only got worse. Especially in recent years we have been torpedoed again and again by the scream of condemnation and criticism that comes from groups like the World Council. It is impossible to cooperate with the World Council when its Program to Combat Racism, for example, is manifestly inspired by communist aims to terrorize our country. How else can we try to explain it when they are giving money to groups that do not even try to hide the fact that they are communist?" In fact the Program to Combat Racism (PCR) which was established by the World Council in 1970 was sharply criticized by both the Christian Institute and the South African Council of Churches. Supporters of PCR note that aid was given to guerilla groups for "humanitarian" purposes and that the World Council expressed "solidarity with" rather than "support for" movements dedicated to violent change. Not surprisingly, such efforts at distancing and distinction were lost on the critics of the Christian Institute.[3]

I relate to him Naudé's description of the three-phased history of the Institute—first to address the Dutch Reformed church, then to appeal to the English-speaking churches, and finally the backing of black initiatives, which did the Institute in. "Yes, that is the way the history is frequently given but I think it is altogether too neat. From the beginning the Institute had a problem with credibility, with being seen as an effort motivated by theological concerns. One problem we had was that at the time the Afrikaans churches were way ahead of the English churches at the level of serious theological scholarship. Theological dialogue was very difficult when the English churches always wanted to put the political questions in the forefront, and the suspicion was that they had to do that because they didn't have the theological sophistication of the other side."

Suspicions were compounded by the Institute's associations. "From the very beginning the Christian Institute had in its stated purposes that it was opposed to communism and communist influence, but of course once it came into existence it was surrounded by people who offered help. This was a very severe temptation when we had so little support, but many of these people did not share in any way the Christian understanding of the Institute. They did understand that policies in South Africa were evil, and it was only in opposition to that evil that certain coalitions were formed; it was not a common agreement regarding Christian responsibility." Geyser says that he and Fred van Wyck, after they had invited Naudé to leave his church post and become director of the Institute, very quickly began to worry about "the young firebrands" whom Naudé attracted. "These people said, 'We're not interested in talk. We're interested in action. Don't tell us about theology, about what you're going to say, tell us what you're going to do.' And Beyers, unfortunately, was somewhat susceptible to that kind of influence, and so it happened that a number of people gained positions of considerable influence in the Christian Institute, people who had, for all practical purposes, no church relationship at all and no visible commitment to the Christian gospel.

"Fred and I protested regularly with Beyers, always in a very friendly way, but the infiltration of the Institute by people who wanted to use it as a political instrument finally won out." According to Geyser, Naudé was attracted to the prophetic stance, and being prophetic meant always "going farther," taking the "radicalized" position. This, he says, was mixed with Naudé's naivete about people's motives. "If

113

someone had help to offer, Beyers chose to believe that their reasons for helping must be his reasons." (Geyser does not mention this, but if there was naivete, it perhaps cut both ways. In its last years the Institute was, according to some accounts, also infiltrated by government agents.) "I have spoken out publicly against the banning of Beyers and I continue to do that, but I must honestly say that I can understand why, step by step, the Institute lost its credibility and looked to many like an alien and subversive institution." In this analysis, then, there was no three-phased development. Challenging dialogue with the Dutch Reformed church was precluded almost from the beginning, and the Institute followed an erratic course of giving itself to whatever radicalism was in vogue at the moment and could gain financial backing from the enemies of apartheid abroad.

Geyser's criticisms are couched in terms most friendly to Naudé. That may be because he believes, down deep, that all three of the Institute's founders were naive about what is possible in South Africa. While personally cheerful, Geyser's prognosis for South Africa is dour. He has no confidence at all in Botha and the so-called hidden agenda for the inclusion of blacks. He understands the "moral logic" of those whites who argue for a smaller "white homeland," but says it is absolute nonsense, as the present idea of homelands is absolute nonsense. Never, he believes, could South Africa defend itself along the crazy borders created by independent black homelands. What, then, is likely to happen? "In four years from now or forty years from now there will be the next world war, and that will bring black majority rule to South Africa. I have no doubt that in a major war Africa will be so strategically important to the U.S. and others that they will have to accommodate African desires, and near the top of those desires will be black majority rule here in South Africa. From the viewpoint of the West, the Afrikaner is expendable."

And what should be done between now and then? "We have to be concerned to plant genuine Christianity throughout this society and that means, most particularly, improving the lot of blacks. I support the PFP and Helen Suzman, not because the program is perfect or is likely to come to power, but because it represents the evangelical calling of the white man in South Africa." No, he is not optimistic. "The world war will come and then matters will be out of our hands, but until then we can work, as I say, and then there is a chance that when blacks come to power they will be more sympathetic to the things that we regard as worth maintaining in this society."

Geyser represents, it would seem, a frankly reformist approach. It is not based on the assumption that the reforms will in fact succeed. The emphasis, rather, is on what might be called the demonstration effect of efforts at reform. The demonstration is to prepare for the inevitable, black majority rule. It is to persuade the rulers-to-be that not everything associated with white South Africa was evil. Among people of this viewpoint, the term "standards" is used a good deal. They insist that they are not in principle opposed to black rule, "if only standards are maintained." Standards refer to law and order, economic pragmatism, decency—in short, all those things which in their view have not been maintained under black rule in most of the rest of the continent. Albert Geyser does not put it this way, but I suspect that his deepest disillusionment with the Christian Institute is that he believes it finally turned against what he calls "the things that we regard as worth maintaining in this society." He is, in sum, a white liberal and, if the Christian Institute had a dogma, it was that the time for the white liberal is irretrievably finished.

REFORMIST efforts of all varieties are aimed at "accommodating" the blacks of South Africa. From the white liberal perspective, the question is how to buffer the impact of black rule, how to preserve as much as possible the values of Western civilization when the inevitable happens. The

115

Christian Institute's sharp break from the reformist mindset was evidenced in the slogan of SPROCAS, "The Future Is Black." There is obviously a play on words here. At one level the somewhat apocalyptic message is that the revolutionary future is very bleak for those who will be caught on the wrong side of the liberationist struggle. In that sense, "The Future Is Black" is a taunting of the whole fear-ridden white establishment of South Africa. At another level, a hope is posited, a way of salvation is offered. The way of salvation is the way of white self-subordination. "We insisted," says Naudé, "that not only in the Institute but in the society itself the time had come for whites to become the students under the leadership of blacks. This is the way of humility, the way of the cross, and it offers the only hope of resurrection."

Having despaired of the white churches, Afrikaner and English, the Christian Institute in the early seventies tried to organize the numerous "independent churches" of South Africa. The independent churches, such as the several "Zionist" groups, are very indigenous, very black, and, for the most part, very apolitical. They are sometimes referred to dismissively as "sects," but some scholars believe the independent churches claim the allegiance of half the blacks in South Africa. Many blacks who belong to the "brand name" churches—whether Dutch Reformed, Roman Catholic, Lutheran, or Methodist—also take part in these independent movements, finding in them elements of ecstatic worship and spiritual healing which are missing in the more respectable groups. The Christian Institute was searching for a proletarian base, as it were, from which to advance radical change.

Naudé does not argue with the consensus that the effort to organize the independent churches was something of a flop. First, the independent churches are almost fanatically independent. The labyrinthine network of groups is made up of spiritual fiefdoms in which competing leaders jealously guard their own turf. Second, the beliefs and piety of the independent churches are profoundly other-worldly. In Marxist terms, they are the "sigh of the oppressed" or the opium of the masses. Professor Gerhardis Oosthuizen, a student of South African religions, remarks: "There was nothing more fanciful than the idea that the independent churches could serve as a base for radical white organizing. These groups are based on supernatural beliefs that are designed to provide a black refuge from the white world in all its forms."

The third problem the Christian Institute encountered is not untouched by irony. While the whites said they were subordinating themselves, they were still the ones providing the money. The few blacks who were prepared to cooperate by assuming the putative role of superiority over whites deeply resented the fact that whites still wanted them to account for the expenditure of funds. In 1971, when the program was still new, I spent several hours with one of the black organizers of independent churches, a very engaging young man. "They [the Christian Institute] receive the money from overseas and they can do anything with it they want. Then they give it to us and we can do anything with it we want. This is Christian trust," he explained with a sense of wonder at having discovered something almost too good to be true. It turned out not to be true, and by the mid-seventies the effort to make the independent churches a base for radical change was in a shambles and was finally abandoned altogether.

The Institute also had a Black Community Programme and a White Community Programme (BCP and WCP). The black program stayed alive by gravitating around the various black protest movements which are a staple in the South African situation. WCP, however, foundered in its search for whites who wanted to be liberated by surrendering their privileges in "creative response to black initiatives." The white constituency for black theologies of revolution turned out to be disappointingly small. According to Peter Walshe, an American who has written a sympathetic history of the Christian Institute, WCP "faced an intractable sociology."

117

The WCP was planned as a broad range of catalytic efforts which would activate a critical social consciousness. This consciousness, it was rather desperately assumed, must be lying dormant among at least a small minority of whites in the multi-racial churches, opposition political parties, the business community, white trade unions and youth organisations. At first the "target group" was to be the "liberal affluent establishment . . . with their hypocrisy and built-in racism/exploitation which they inflict daily through their institutions." . . . In trying to generate activities, the WCP would "not draw back from tactics of polarization where these seem to be creative and necessary."[4]

Desperate assumptions abounded. As the Christian Institute became more radicalized it became more marginal, and as it became more marginal it became more radicalized. The story is painfully familiar to those who lived through the sundry radicalisms of the sixties in America and Western Europe. A difference is that in South Africa it was happening a bit belatedly. Another difference is that it involved only a minuscule handful of whites, but they were whites who wanted to be on the right side of a revolution of the oppressed, which—at least numerically—seemed more plausible there than in, for example, the U.S. Yet another difference is that, for a time, their activities were handsomely funded from sources in Amsterdam, Geneva, and New York who had experienced serious setbacks in "making the revolution" at home and hoped that "the movement" could be sustained by their radical partisans in South Africa.

The Christian Institute allied itself with those who were seeking a "new revolutionary praxis" in the black consciousness movement led by Steve Biko, who later died while in police custody. Peter Randall of the Institute cooperated with Biko in publishing a series of tracts, the most famous of which was *Cry Rage*, banned in 1973. Walshe describes it admiringly as "a collection of invective, anguished poetry and indomitable hope."[5] As Mrs. Kilburn, with whom we spoke earlier, turned to the theater as a depository of hope in a time of desperation, so also the Christian Institute programs were allied with theatrical expressions of protest. In 1973, *Black Images* inveighed against "Uncle Toms" who thought there could be gradualist and reformist change. In the finale there was powerful staccato music, heavy drumming, flashing strobe lights, and angry voices of the stage crowd as the play moved into the praise of revolutionary black leaders and ended with the challenge: "Everyone says Yes to FREEDOM. Everyone says Yes to BLACKNESS. But how many are prepared to die?"

The stage was declared to be a "liberating weapon." In 1974 some of the leaders of radical theater were arrested and charged with conspiracy to "stage, present, produce and/or participate in inflammatory, provocative, anti-white, racialistic, subversive and/or revolutionary plays or dramas." While the arrests were understandably condemned as oppressive by some white liberals, it must be admitted that the charge was a fairly accurate description of what the revolutionary theater claimed it was doing.

It should not be thought, however, that black radicalism was limited to what Americans have come to call "reverse racism." There is a positive dimension, represented, for example, by Lutheran Bishop Manas Buthelezi who worked with the Christian Institute and was later to become a leader of the South African Council of Churches. Bishop Buthelezi attempted a positive reinterpretation of the radical posture, depicting the black man as the saviour of the white. Had it ever occured to the black man, he asked, that if

> white people are lost . . . he may be held responsible? God will ask: "Black man, where were you when the white man abandoned my Gospel and went to destruction?" When the black man answers, "I was only a *kaffir*, how could I dare to preach to my *baas* [master]?" God will say: "Was Christ's resurrection not sufficient to liberate you, black man, from that kind of spiritual

and psychological death? Go to eternal damnation, black man, for you did not muster courage to save your white brother."

In the mid-seventies, though, it was no longer clear what that gospel entailed. Increasingly murky was the connection between Christianity and violence. At that time Canon Burgess Carr, the Anglican leader of the All Africa Council of Churches was calling for a divorce between the gospel and the "sentimentality" of nonviolence. Liberation movements should be unequivocally supported, he said, because they represented only "selective violence" while white oppression was "collective violence." Nonviolence was "an untenable alternative for African Christians." The liberation struggles "helped the Church to rediscover a new and radical appreciation of the Cross. In accepting the violence of the Cross, God, in Jesus Christ, sanctified violence into a redemptive instrument for bringing into being fuller human life." For many Christians this was an intriguing twist on the traditional assumption that the political and religious leaders who conspired in killing Jesus had done something wrong.

In 1971 Beyers Naudé indicated that he had been persuaded to the World Council of Churches view that South Africa was headed for "civil war." Speaking to white students at Natal University, he declared, "I personally do not believe that we are going to avoid a confrontation of violence of some kind. But I do believe that the whites are still in the position of power to diminish the harmful and unpredictable results of such a conflict. There is still time—but time is running out." In our conversation more than ten years later he speaks of the violence that will of necessity precede genuine negotiation between black and white. "I do not endorse violence," he says, "I never have. . . . I confess I become very impatient with people who get so exercised about the violence of radical change but are not disturbed about the violence of the status quo." In this way of thinking, promoted by various liberation theologies, revolutionary violence is more accurately termed counterviolence against the "systemic injustice" of the social order.

The analysis of "systemic injustice" also led the Christian Institute to a reappraisal of capitalism as the root evil of oppression. In its later stages, according to admirer Peter Walshe, the Institute was able to "free itself from the stultifying grip of capitalist culture" and to join "the worldwide thrust toward more egalitarian social structures, the establishment of which could renew the basis of legitimate government." Walshe and others sympathetic to the Institute point out that this does not mean the Institute favored communism. The commitment was not to communism but to "democratic socialism." The difficulty is sometimes acknowledged that those who shared the commitment in southern Africa were engaged in armed movements backed by forces that did not hesitate to call themselves communist. The difficulty in making these distinctions no doubt played a part in the South African regime's unfavorable attentions to the Christian Institute.

By 1975, Naudé had moved toward a more "advanced analysis." Speaking again at the University of Natal, he asserted: "The majority of our African, Coloured and Indian community will never voluntarily accept the present economic system of distribution of wealth and land which the capitalist system, buttressed by a myriad of apartheid laws and regulations, has imposed on them." This touches on a critical item in any evaluation of South Africa. Business leaders in the several communities, plus many academics, oppose apartheid because, among other reasons, its "laws and regulations" interfere with the operation of a free market. In their view, capitalism with its free (and therefore nonracialist) flow of labor and opportunity is the radical alternative to the apartheid system. Their view is not shared by the groups to which Beyers Naudé made the Christian Institute "creatively subordinate." According to Naudé, the alternative to apartheid-cum-capitalism is "African socialism along the lines promoted by Julius Nyerere of Tanzania." Already in 1975 Naudé was urging a reassessment of "the role of capitalism on the one hand and historic communism on the other hand, especially to ascertain to what degree the emerging form of African socialism could provide a more adequate and just answer to the problem of affluence and poverty which both the first and third world is currently facing."

Naudé's vague tone of questing uncertainty is shared by many who are "on the left" in South Africa, especially by those whose primary audience is the left in Europe and America. Nadine Gordimer, for example, the gifted and popular South African novelist writes about her ambivalences in the "interregnum" between apartheid and black majority rule. She hears radicals speak about the glories of communism and she knows that what they say is not true but she does not speak out. "I am silent because, in the debates of the interregnum, any criticism of the communist system is understood as a defense of the capitalist system which has brought forth the pact of capitalism and racism that is apartheid, with its treason trials to match Stalin's trials, its detentions of dissidents to match Soviet detentions, its banishment and brutal uprooting of communities and individual lives to match, if not surpass, the gulag." She believes that "the choice for blacks cannot be distanced into any kind of objectivity: they believe in the existence of the lash they feel. Nothing could be *less than better* than what they have known as the 'peace and security' of capitalism." The oppressive regimes that have to date called themselves socialist are, she insists, "perversions of socialism." A socialism with a human face, a democratic socialism, is still the goal. "There is no forgetting how we could live if only we could find the way. We must continue to be tormented by the ideal."[6]

The refusal to settle for nothing less than the ideal, even if it means defeating the better in the name of the best, became a characteristic of the Christian Institute. Combined with that is the belief that nothing could be worse than the present misery. I ask Beyers Naudé how he responds to critics who accuse him of a naive utopianism that confuses earthly possibilities with the promise of the kingdom of God. "If there is confusion," he says, "God must be responsible for it. The incarnation means that all his powers and all his promises are involved in our human struggle for justice. The Bible teaches nothing about a kingdom of God that is not part of that struggle." Then I ask about the second proposition, that a revolutionary future could not be worse than the present. Is it not evident from historical experience that miserable and oppressive situations can become many times more miserable and oppressive? "Perhaps that is true. Perhaps the generals are right and millions of blacks will be killed and the result will be an even more oppressive black rule. But I do not think so. The Afrikaner will negotiate before it comes to that. But those who ask these questions do not understand the basic point that the Christian Institute was trying to communicate. These questions are not ours to answer, maybe they are not even ours to discuss. That is what self-subordination means. These questions are for the black man to answer now and the whites must learn to accept the answer that the blacks give."

After the riotous insurrection of Soweto in 1976, the Institute pulled out all stops. It defied the government at almost every possible point, calling for economic sanctions against South Africa, urging general strikes, more stridently assailing capitalism and the bourgeois democracy represented by the legal system. In the words of Peter Walshe: "These commitments were already quite enough to invite destruction. Nevertheless the Institute pushed forward in its confrontation with the state, well past the point of no return."[7] The Institute declared its support for the outlawed revolutionary organizations, the African National Congress and the Pan Africanist Congress, in the name of "the biblical values of justice, freedom and human responsibilities." Sensing its end to be near, the Institute urged whoever was still following to be of good cheer. "We shall overcome, we shall overcome in Him who said 'Do not be afraid: I have overcome the world.' "

The last issue of the Institute's journal, *Pro Veritate,*

railed against the "weak folly of those who think in terms of trying to reform the Government. A false Gospel, an evil binding ideology, cannot be reformed." It must be demolished and replaced by a "total and fundamental change." The handwriting was on the wall declaring "that this ungodly and revolting society will be destroyed." Looking back five years later, I ask what he might have done differently. Naudé smiles wanly; it is obviously not a new question for him. "Oh, personal things of course. I'm certain I sinned against charity at times in personal relations. . . . But not the Institute itself. Except perhaps we should have learned earlier that the most important thing is to back black initiatives. We wasted time thinking there might be this so-called will to reform among whites. There wasn't and there isn't now. If I may offer some advice, don't believe it when you talk with whites, and when you talk to blacks keep in mind that they're ten times more radical than anything they will dare to say to a white man."

We had talked a long time. Tea was finished, and through the sun-dappled garden someone was arriving for pastoral counseling with Beyers Naudé. To many he is South Africa's premier white hero, to others he is a turncoat, to yet others he is a poor soul who lost himself in a maze of prophetic rhetoric and vague good intentions. It has been observed that there is a significant difference between being, in Paul's words, a fool for Christ and being just a plain fool. Judgments of Beyers Naudé are sharply divided, and the final judgment is reserved to a court higher than ours. But no fair-minded person should doubt that, whatever Beyers Naudé has been and is now, he intends that it be for Christ.

EPILOGUE

Not long after our conversation, Beyers Naudé's banning was lifted by the government. Like the banning itself, the action is unexplained and perhaps inexplicable. Certainly it was not because Naudé had become a more compliant citizen of South

Africa. In short order, after Desmond Tutu had received the Nobel Peace Prize and had been elected the Anglican bishop of Johannesburg, Naudé replaced him as general secretary of the South African Council of Churches. He promptly began to gather together some of the old hands from earlier days. "It's the Christian Institute all over again," said one admiring observer, "only this time the churches are with him." Naudé figured prominently in the highly politicized funerals for victims of the turbulence of 1985. He is perhaps the only white man in South Africa whom revolution-minded blacks carry in procession on their shoulders.

In August 1985, Albert Geyser died at age 67. A few days before he died he had written an open letter to P. W. Botha, pleading with him to confess his own guilt and that of the National Party in perpetuating apartheid. He warned Botha that all efforts at reform would fail so long as the Broederbond was allowed to "undermine and circumvent the democratic processes." Although they had long since cast him out, Geyser apparently had not abandoned hope that those in power could still be brought to share his understanding of "the things that we regard as worth maintaining in this society." He made no apologies for being a reformist to the end.

Toward the very end of 1985 Beyers Naudé and I had a leisurely two-hour conversation when he was passing through New York. The year of reintensified activity seemed to have taken its toll. He seemed older and more tired, but as firm as ever in setting forth his convictions. We talked, as you might imagine, about the ways in which the "troubles" of the past year had, and had not, changed the basic terms of conflict in South Africa. I was especially impressed by his parting comment; perhaps it was more in the nature of a confession: "I suppose one thing has changed for me. I find myself worrying more and more about who will be around as a force for reconciliation when the really hard times come. I have always believed, you know, that that is the absolutely essential role of the churches, and I still believe that. When it's all over somebody will have to reconcile people and heal the wounds, and there's nobody to do that except the churches. But now I'm not at all sure that we will be ready for it when the time comes and everything is swallowed up in violence."

CHAPTER SIX

DESMOND TUTU
AND INSTITUTIONS OF PROTEST

O UTSIDE South Africa Desmond Tutu is undoubtedly
the best-known black in South Africa. Within South
Africa his prominence is rivaled only by that of Gatsha Buthelezi, chief of the Zulus, and Nelson Mandela, the long imprisoned symbolic leader of the African National Congress.
Tutu's stature is different from theirs, in some ways more
fragile, in some ways perhaps stronger. Buthelezi is the apparently unchallengable leader of the largest single population
group in South Africa. As long as he lives, he will be a major
actor in any comprehensive settlement of the country's affairs. His prominence is firmly grounded in an unavoidable
natural base, so to speak. Mandela is a much more ambiguous
figure. His leadership role is not only symbolic, it is almost
mystical. In talking with three black youth in Soweto who
insisted that Mandela is "our leader," I asked them what they
know about the man and his views. As is usually the case,
they cited moving passages from Mandela speeches of more
than twenty years ago. Yes, but how do you know what Mandela thinks today? "He believes what we believe. We know
that, we can trust him. Tutu and Buthelezi are always saying
different things," the young man named Nelson explained.
Mandela in jail is a figure of compelling force; Buthelezi and
Tutu are actors—pronouncing, condemning, advocating, reacting, feinting, and appealing—within the exigencies of
sometimes dramatic change.

Unlike Buthelezi, Tutu does not have a strong natural base. In 1984 he received the Nobel Peace Prize, and this was undoubtedly a factor in the sudden intensification of international interest in South Africa. At the time, Tutu had been teaching at General Theological Seminary in New York City and touring the United States on behalf of the antiapartheid cause. Later, after returning to South Africa, he was elected Anglican bishop of Johannesburg. During the violence of 1985 he earned the grudging respect even of his severe critics for standing up to young blacks who—acting as judge, jury, and executioner—were brutally killing other blacks whom they had pronounced guilty of "collaboration" with Pretoria. In at least one instance, Tutu physically interposed himself between an enraged mob and its intended victim. On another occasion he publicly announced that he would leave the country and never return unless the killings ended. The killings continued, and Tutu stayed, but observers were forced to take a new measure of a man whom many had previously dismissed as no more than another noisy cleric.

Bishop Tutu had made his mark as a general secretary of the South African Council of Churches. The council includes fifteen Protestant churches with a membership that is about 80 percent black. It does not include the Roman Catholic church, although Catholic leadership cooperates with some of its efforts, nor does it include the bulk of the fast-growing independent churches. And of course it does not include the big Dutch Reformed churches, although the "daughter" coloured and black churches (now increasingly being called "sister" churches) are moving into the SACC orbit. While the constituency of the SACC, then, is impressive on paper, it is far from clear whether, or in what ways, it represents its membership. If financial support is an indicator, well over 90 percent of its funding comes from overseas. This is in part because most of the members of its member churches are very poor. At the same time, they contribute substantially to their own churches. It is in larger part because Tutu and the SACC represent what he frequently refers to as "the international community" in South Africa. This is both strength and weakness.

In a country obsessed by international opinion, Bishop Tutu has a certain leverage. But his opponents also use this against him, claiming he is nothing but a tool of the revolutionisms associated with, for example, the World Council of Churches. In fact Tutu is a moderate in the most literal sense, moderating between the most militant external and internal opponents of the white regime and the reformist elements within the country's leadership. The moderator's lot is not always a happy one. As was the case with the Christian Institute, overwhelming dependence upon outside forces for support creates the temptation to play the tune of those who pay the piper. Also the friends of Tutu say that he has sometimes succumbed to the temptation. It is understandable that he takes help where he can get it. The tenuous support of the member churches, combined with government harassment, combined with internal fiscal scandals, made the SACC a fragile base for the leadership of Desmond Tutu. Tutu's prominence today would seem to depend upon international publicity, a force of personality, a depth of piety, and a political dexterity that is remarkable in a man who insists that he is not a politician. That insistence may be part of his political savvy.

This conversation with Desmond Tutu took place in his Johannesburg office. It is in a building that houses a number of church and other antiapartheid organizations, including the Women's Defense of the Constitution League, popularly (or unpopularly) known as the Black Sash because its members wear a black sash in silent protest demonstrations. It is immediately apparent why Tutu is often described as "impish." He is a small man given to being simultaneously urgent and humorous, prophetic and self-deprecating. He says right off in a most friendly manner, "So I hear you are collaborating with the enemy this time." This, he explains, because I called him from the offices of the South Africa Foundation. The Foundation, he says, "is viewed as a public relations office for the government" and is therefore "not on our side." There is no hostility in the remark, only the implication that one cannot be too careful about the company one keeps.

Today the bishop is not in ecclesial garb but wears a brown suit, striped shirt, and a big wooden cross with a silver figure of Christ. During the course of our conversation and the serving of tea (which seems inescapable in South Africa), Tutu takes time out for a phone call from a colleague. In expansive manner he leans back in his large swivel chair, looking and sounding quite like a politician or preacher in black Brooklyn, U.S.A. "OK . . . You can tell him for me. . . . Right on. . . . Keep the faith, brother." I look about the office filled with certificates, citations, and pictures of friends and their children, both black and white. There is a photo of Tutu and his wife shaking hands with Pope John Paul II in St. Peter's Square, and a framed plaque from St. Philip's Church in Harlem. Other testaments lie on the shelves; there seems not to be room for all the honors bestowed. (In 1982 Columbia University awarded Tutu an honorary doctorate but his passport was momentarily impounded, so the president of Columbia and others flew to South Africa to give the degree in a public ceremony at Witwatersrand University. Thus the award got much more attention in South Africa and the U.S. than it otherwise would have received. A few weeks later Tutu had his passport back and went off to visit friends in the U.S. Such are the willy nilly, keep-them-off-balance, and usually inept ways in which the government deals with its opponents.)

The phone call attended to, Tutu returns to serious and uninterrupted conversation. Yes, he says, there are signs of change in the Dutch Reformed church but it may be too late. They may not be saying it officially any more, but most Afrikaners do believe there is a biblical justification for apartheid. Tutu agrees with Allan Boesak, who at the Ottawa, Canada, meeting of the World Alliance of Reformed Churches in 1982 had apartheid condemned as a heresy. "We have to say that apartheid is anathema, a clear contradiction of Christian faith. If the Afrikaner agrees with us on that, fine, then we have something to talk about. Once he is no longer talking about apartheid, then he can talk about certain cultural differentiations. I may even be sympathetic to that. It is true that not all South Africans are alike culturally; we have to take that into consideration. But we cannot consider it if there is still a racialist element in the question," says Tutu. (Tutu's father is Xhosa and his mother Tswana.)

But moving the Afrikaner beyond "primitive apartheid thinking" is not enough. "They may no longer be talking about race," Tutu explains, "but then it merely becomes more apparent that they are talking about power. The idolatry of race is replaced by the idolatry of power. They are guilty of the idolatry of power, political power has become God for them." Tutu is not cheered by the so-called technocrats who want a nonracialist meritocracy. "This is the beginning of a different strategy and the government may agree to it. They do away with discrimination based on race alone and in that way they co-opt some blacks who gain substantial material privileges. The idea is that these privileged blacks will serve as a kind of buffer, a solid middle-class between the whites and the blacks who are left out." To the extent this happens, and Tutu says it is already happening at a very rapid pace, "the race question, the old question of apartheid, will become a class struggle. Yes, I think that is what we are seeing now."

The idolatry of power is disguised in democratic dress. "Nobody should think that we have democratic institutions here. We have an oligarchy, a very smart oligarchy. It uses democratic forms to ingratiate itself with the West, to pretend it is part of the West." Would the South Africa for which Tutu hopes be democratic? "Of course. But that does not mean we simply imitate the West. We have to develop authentically

African forms of democracy," he cautions. Whatever else that means, it does not mean agreement with those who say that a democratic and open society must be accompanied by an open or free market economy. "Blacks believe in community," Tutu says. "But now we are beginning to lose that and that is one reason I loathe capitalism. It is against community, it is all competition and selfishness. You see blacks today who actually boast of their ulcers because that is a symbol of their success. As you know, I have seen this in America too, so I'm not just talking theoretically. Are people happy under capitalism? No, from everything I have seen capitalism gives unbridled license to human cupidity, to the law of the jungle. Capitalism and the free enterprise system—it is unfreedom, it is morally repulsive," and with that the bishop wrinkles his nose and puts up his hands in defense against the threatening inroads of the West.

Those who may find Tutu's views repulsive, however, should hesitate before dismissing him as just another "Third World ideologue." It is true that he rails against transnational corporations, deplores the disproportionate consumption of global wealth by the few, condemns the ecologically disastrous rapacity of the First World, and calls for redistribution through a new international economic order. Nonetheless, he has also spoken out against the antidemocratic and brutal rule in many independent African countries. Prompted by the barbarities of the Idi Amin regime in Uganda, Tutu declared in 1977: "In the newly independent Third World countries, we have often seen serious inroads into civil liberties and human rights. The position of the people has often been worse under their own rulers than it ever was under their colonial masters. There is often no freedom of speech, or press freedom. Criticism of the abuse of power by largely totalitarian military dictatorships is frowned on. Political dissent is not allowed, on the pretence that developing countries cannot afford the luxury of having a democratic system, or that one-party states are not necessarily dictatorships."[1]

I ask him whether, for example, the one-party state of Julius Nyerere in Tanzania is "necessarily a dictatorship." He is visibly taken aback. While most students of development have in recent years abandoned a long-standing romance with Nyerere's version of "African socialism," he is still a sacred figure for many. Tutu allows that, while Nyerere is a very great man, he does not represent the kind of democratic rule which Tutu favors. I mention that in his indictment of the antidemocratic nature of the South African government, he cited "the hypocrisy of claiming to be committed to a free enterprise system while, at the same time, restricting the mobility of labor and refusing to let people achieve at the level of their abilities regardless of race." Is he not calling on the South African to practice the free enterprise that he says he loathes? He chuckles, saying it is a point well taken. "Maybe I am saying that, maybe not. I know that they need to be challenged for not practicing what *they* say *they* believe. But I don't claim to be an economist, and I am not a politician, despite what some people say, I am a churchman, and my concern is for the integrity of the church of Jesus Christ. I have to be careful not to pretend that I have the solutions, but I have to be even more careful not to be too cautious in crying out against the evils of the present situation."

Even those who would like to deny it find it hard to deny that Desmond Tutu is a deeply spiritual person. Some of his critics on the left think he takes the Christian ethic of loving your enemies altogether too literally. "The trouble with Desmond," I was told by a friend of his who is a supporter (some say a leader) of the African National Congress, "is that he really thinks the whites can be converted." I mention to him Tutu's statement that the Afrikaner is guilty of idolizing power. "He's correct, he's correct about that. But then why doesn't Desmond understand that the only thing that the Afrikaner understands is revolutionary power?"

In truth, Bishop Tutu flirts with that understanding of things. But the flirtations are checked by the experience of

133

another power. "I make no apology for the fact that I try to be a man of prayer," he says. "I know that some people think piety and politics are opposed, that piety is an escape from the hard world of politics and suffering and so forth. I don't believe that." He suggests that the secularized activism of some Western Christians is a peculiarly Western disease. "We Africans are spiritual beings. I can speak for myself, I *know* the transcendent power of God, the power that is more important than the mundane. I don't mean to say that the mundane is less important, the two are held together for me in my experience of Christ. I can tell you that I could not justify the things I'm trying to do on a purely humanistic kind of reasoning. I wouldn't try to do that. As a Christian, I don't have to try to do that. These are Christ's brothers and sisters, God's children, and I am called to serve them and God will bless this work in his way and in his time. It's as simple as that."

It may be as simple and as complex as that to a man who is through and through an Anglo-Catholic. Daily mass, a daily regimen of prayer, regular quiet days and retreats— these are the things that Desmond Tutu says matter most. It is a way of life he learned from the fathers of the Community of the Resurrection, and most particularly from Trevor Huddleston. In 1945, at age fourteen, Tutu came down with tuberculosis and was visited regularly by Huddleston, then priest of a black suburb of Johannesburg and one of the best-known clerical opponents of the apartheid system. Tutu looks back to that meeting as a decisive point which, despite some years of resistance on his part, led him to ordination in 1961, six years of priestly service in England, and then, in 1975, to the position of dean of Johannesburg. One of his first decisions as dean was not to live in the very pleasant deanery in a "whites only" section of Johannesburg. The fact that he, together with his wife Leah and their children (one of whom is named Trevor, after Huddleston), lives in an upper class house in the black township of Soweto is often noted by his detrac-

tors, both black and white. But Tutu believes that the decision "to live among my own people" was and is an important
symbolic statement.

The making of symbolic statements about what ought
to be done in a world requiring concrete choices is perhaps
a vocational hazard of clergy in politics. Like clergy, politicians make extravagant statements but, at least in democratic
systems, are held somewhat accountable for what they say.
Not so with clergy, who can always retreat into the explanation that they were only speaking symbolically or, as it is
said, "prophetically." As an American friend and clerical activist is fond of putting it, "It's my job to call for justice to
roll down like mighty waters; it's someone else's job to work
out the irrigation system." It seems that in certain moods
Desmond Tutu is inclined to agree also with Barry Goldwater
that "extremism in the defense of liberty is no vice and moderation in the pursuit of justice is no virtue." An example
may be his strident strictures on capitalism, inconsistently
combined with his advocacy of a free labor market and the
advancement of democratic values. There are other examples.

"Those who approve of apartheid or even tolerate
apartheid are saying Jesus be cursed." Does the Dutch Reformed church approve or tolerate apartheid? "Yes." Can a
church that says Jesus be cursed be a true Christian church?
"That is not for me to judge. God will judge. We have to try
to deal with them as Christian brothers." Tutu says he agrees
with the World Council of Churches slogan that "the world
sets the agenda for the church." At the same time he insists
that the church must not be conformed to the world. "If our
faith is truly transcendent, then Christian teaching must be
a radical corrective of what the world falsely thinks is important." Such apparent inconsistencies are not surprising.
They touch on questions that confuse most religious folk.
And Bishop Tutu is not a theological scholar with the leisure
to hone his expressions to verbal exactitude. Apart from his

centered reality in prayer and altar, he is a controversialist who is riding a tiger.

In his public role he speaks to diverse audiences and, as with some politicians, his fiddling with the fine tuning of his message is sometimes too obvious. Addressing church groups overseas, he routinely compares South Africa with Hitler's Third Reich and leaves little doubt that if things go on as they are, substantive change will come about at the cost of revolutionary bloodshed. Speaking in South Africa, he is more restrained. Perhaps because at home it is illegal to advocate violence. More likely, I choose to believe, because Desmond Tutu is deeply committed to nonviolence. A speech in 1978 to a church conference in Pretoria represents, it would seem, what Tutu most wants to communicate:

> In South Africa . . . the Church of God must sustain the hope of a people who have been tempted to grow despondent, because the powers of this world seem to be rampant. It does not appear that significant political change can happen without much bloodshed and violence, and it seems that God does not care, or is impotent. The Church of God must say that despite all appearances to the contrary, this is God's world. He cares and he cares enormously, his is ultimately a moral universe that we inhabit, and that right and wrong matter, and that the resurrection of Jesus Christ proclaims that right will prevail. . . . He is a God of the poor, of the hungry, of the naked, with whom the Church identifies and has solidarity. The Church in South Africa must be the prophetic Church, which cries out "Thus saith the Lord," speaking up against injustice and violence, against oppression and exploitation, against all that dehumanises God's children and makes them less than what God intended them to be.[2]

Let justice roll down like mighty waters. The rhetoric is amenable to many specific applications, and one suspects that Tutu intends it that way. "Remember what happened to

Muzorewa," Tutu advises me. I am told by others that he frequently brings up Muzorewa as an example he does not wish to emulate. It will be recalled that in Rhodesia Bishop Abel Muzorewa tried to strike a compromise in a power-sharing arrangement with the former white rulers. Zimbabwe/Rhodesia was short lived. As Rhodesia became Zimbabwe, Muzorewa was unceremoniously swept aside by Robert Mugabe. Muzorewa was not radical enough, he was not attuned to the rapidity of change that few foresaw in Rhodesia and that relatively few foresee now in South Africa, but which many believe is certain to come.

To some, Tutu is carefully positioning himself to play a leadership role in whatever circumstance unfolds. To others, it is not so much positioning as it is posturing. They point, for example, to his part in the divestment campaign. The divestment campaign, which aims to get foreign companies to withdraw from South Africa and thus bring antiapartheid pressure to bear upon the government, looks very different from the inside of South Africa than from the outside. The campaign has made headway in the United States with some churches and universities pressuring companies to divest from South Africa. If that does not succeed, the churches and schools have in many cases divested their own portfolios, so to speak, refusing to have anything to do with companies operating in South Africa. By 1985 a growing number of state and local governments in the United States were also in-volved in the divestment campaign, although this was being challenged in the courts. It is against the law in South Africa to advocate divestment and, while on a trip in Scandinavia in the mid-seventies, Tutu appeared to do just that. This was supposedly part of the government's reason for the erratic granting and withholding of Tutu's passport.

In the U.S., proponents of divestment generally recog-nize that divestment is not going to do much economic dam-age to South Africa. It is nonetheless seen as a useful instrument of "consciousness raising" and as yet another way to express the outrage of "the international community" against the apartheid system. Within South Africa, few people disagree with the conclusion of the Rockefeller Foundation report, *Time Running Out*, that divestment is a nonstarter. Standard arguments against divestment include the belief that Japanese and other foreign companies would gladly fill any economic space created by American withdrawal, that such withdrawal would chiefly hurt black workers who are benefited by economic growth and the more progressive policies of American companies on nondiscrimination, and that withdrawal would undercut the tenuous development of black labor unions in recent years.

One coloured leader with a reputation of being radical put it this way: "Don't quote me, but the entire divestment idea is turning out to be an embarrassment. It was not really our idea here in South Africa at the beginning, you know. Our friends in England and America thought it was something they could do because these were their companies and maybe they didn't like corporations very much in any event. . . . But now we're stuck with this and we can't say it's not a good idea because our friends have made such a huge investment in it, and they really are our friends. So when we're overseas we can't come out and say we're against divestment but, on the other hand, because of the law we can't say that we're for it. So, as I have said privately to some people here, maybe it's a bad law that is doing some good—at least it prevents us from having to be dishonest with our friends overseas."

Without revealing who told me this, I ask Tutu about the logic of it. He disagrees most emphatically. "It is a question of solidarity with the forces of justice all over the world," he declares. But what if in fact divestment does not work, or, if it did work, what if it might do more harm than good? "That is not the question. Who knows what works? What I know is that we cannot choose where we will stand in solidarity and where we will not. I know all the arguments about how divestment will hurt black workers, but I am not persuaded." And if the arguments turn out to be true? "Nobody said the struggle would be without costs. Those who bear the cost of oppression must naturally bear some of the cost of their own liberation."

In 1983 the SACC called for "internal divestment." That is, member churches were asked to refrain from doing business with or investing in companies that defend apartheid. It could not help but appear to be a pathetic gesture. At the time the SACC, always internally weak, was staggering under the blows of government investigation and revelations of fiscal scandal. Lutheran bishop Manas Buthelezi, president of the SACC, allowed that divestment might not be a good thing in itself but "the options to follow other paths are eliminated daily." Bishop Tutu allowed that the program would bring no business to its knees but it nonetheless "has symbolic value and offers the churches an opportunity to convey a message."[3] In the view of his critics, and some of his friends, Tutu's approach to the divestment issue is an instance in which positioning slides into posturing.

While he sometimes speaks about violence, revolution, and economic assault, Bishop Tutu the moderator also positions himself in relation to other possibilities. When we move away from discussing "the struggle" in global terms and ask what, concretely, the government must do, Tutu has a standard list of four items. With slight modifications, these items have appeared regularly in his public statements of recent years. In an unprecedented meeting between the government and religious leaders, Bishop Tutu once put them also to P. W. Botha. Here is how he sets them out:

"What would be required for me to believe that this government is serious about change? I can answer in four words: citizenship, pass laws, removals, education. The first thing is for the government to commit themselves in principle to a common citizenship in an undivided South Africa. That means abandoning the homelands idea altogether, putting it in the dustbin where it belongs. Maybe they can't do it right away, but at some point they have to say this in so many words. Then the pass laws have to go. There is nothing so hateful and demeaning to the majority of people in this country. Of course that will have to be a phased process. I hate the term 'influx control,' I absolutely hate it. But, at the same time, nobody wants to see chaos in this country. There must be some kind of control of population, but it must not be racist, it must not be demeaning to one group.

"The third demand is an end to all population removals, all this absolute nonsense and horrible evil of uprooting people and sending them to places that have never been home to them and can never be home. . . . Millions of people have been coerced into these Bantustans—they don't call them Bantustans but that is what they are—and live in tents without adequate water or food and no chance to make a living. It is a horror, an abomination, and it must stop. They can stop that immediately. They don't need to proclaim a unitary state immediately, they don't even need to say they're abandoning the homelands idea, they can just stop it.

"And the fourth thing is a uniform education system. They can say right now that all the universities are open, regardless of race. If they still have black universities, they should be able to appoint blacks who have credibility in the black community, on the basis of their real leadership, not because they pose no threat to the government's power. If the government were to do these four things, it would not be enough, but they would get us started. Then, as I told the Prime Minister, I would be the first to tell black people: please give the government a chance, they are trying to bring about real change."

THERE would seem to be several Desmond Tutus, and perhaps there must be if he is to continue to be a major actor in South Africa and in the world's perception of South Africa. When playing to Western audiences and to what he believes are the more radicalized black youth in South Africa, he is not out of step: the homelands policy is today's Auschwitz, racial conflagration in South Africa might well trigger the Third World War, Christians must get on the right side of the global revolution, the question is not whether there will be violent revolution but how violent it will be, responsibility for the amount of bloodshed required is entirely up to whites, cooperation with communists who pose only a hypothetical threat is better than collaboration with the present oppressors of the poor, and so on.

Bishop Tutu is not above employing naked threats. When in 1982 the constitutional proposals came out, offering a modicum of participation to coloureds and Indians, Tutu addressed those communities in a speech in Durban: "The blacks will never forget when they are free in a genuinely democratic and nonracial South Africa which is coming, whatever anybody else may try to do or tell you, that when that happens they will remember that Indians and coloureds deserted us and delayed our liberation, with all that would have meant in the high cost of human suffering caused by apartheid. Make no mistake about it: if you go over to the other side, then the day of reckoning will come. Let coloured and Indians make no mistake about it!"

There is a Tutu issuing revolutionary jeremiads against all who would be co-opted into liberal bourgeois opposition to the liberation struggle. And there is a Tutu who has this to say to black journalists in South Africa about their responsibility to the black community:

> I remember vividly how I was inspired as a youngster by reading the black American journal *Ebony*. It warmed the cockles of my heart as I contemplated the odds against achieving anything worthwhile, reading about those brothers and sisters in the U.S. who had made it, also against daunting odds. I didn't know anything about baseball then, but I thrilled at Jackie Robinson's achievement of breaking into the major league, by playing for

what were then called the Brooklyn Dodgers. How many of us grew inches because of films such as "Stormy Weather"? I don't think it was particularly memorable, but it had an all black cast, and wasn't that something in those far off days?

You have a tremendous role to play in lauding black achievement, and telling our people that we *can* make it against all kinds of odds, and that the sky is the limit.[4]

Tutu lauds black self-advancement and, at the same time, condemns "cosmetic" improvements that only delay the day of reckoning. He cannot be Mandela and he does not want to end up being Muzorewa. I ask him about this. More specifically, I ask if it is a good thing that there are now blacks moving into middle and top management in some major corporations, even a growing corps of black millionaires who live, as Tutu lives, in the upper class homes of Soweto's select subdivisions. "Yes, this is a dilemma, I don't deny it. We want our people to get ahead but not so far ahead that they forget the people they have left behind." As for his own home and the car he drives, he says, "Do you think black people would be better off if I lived in a little box and rode the public coach into my office? I don't think so. A leader has a responsibility to look like a leader. Does this mean we have compromised with the system? I don't think so. My commitment to the struggle is evident in my work, and I believe this is true of many other blacks who want to use their success for the liberation of their brothers and sisters who are not so successful." Hard ideologues dismiss such personal intentions in favor of an "objective analysis" of class realities hindering the revolution. Bishop Tutu, it would seem, is not in their company.

Although he could not be stronger in his public opposition to the "new dispensation," Tutu's privately expressed views are more nuanced. "I have a respect for Botha, I do not mind saying that. I respect him for his courage. When he took the steps that led Treurnicht to split the National Party, I sent Botha a telegram to encourage him. You cannot always be condemning. When somebody does something that is right, you should say so." Tutu tells me that Botha has done much that is right but has failed to follow through. "Botha has made some moves that must be described as revolutionary, I say that. The most revolutionary step he has taken is to declare once and for all that the future of South Africa will not be determined by whites alone. That is a sharp break from the past. But, after making such a revolutionary statement, then it is vitiated by excluding black Africans. So you see that Botha is paying the price for taking a revolutionary stand and then not carrying through. He's dithering, and there is a high price for dithering." At another point Tutu tells me that the government is only "playing marbles." "It is not reform that we want. That is, we cannot have real reform if it means keeping all the present structure and just making some adjustments. We want real change. It is not enough to have mixed sports and international hotels where apartheid is suspended. Suspending apartheid here and there is frittering away whatever time is left." I am reminded of Basil Hersov's distinction between "law by exception" and law by express determination and legislation.

In addition to the four changes mentioned above, Tutu believes real change would require a bill of rights. "The government talk about guarantees on paper, but I don't trust guarantees. They talk about 'entrenched clauses' in a constitution, but there was an entrenched clause that gave coloureds the vote and in 1953 the government removed it. So much for guarantees." What is needed, Tutu says, is "a bill of rights, not for groups but for individuals." Does that mean one person, one vote? "Yes, ultimately it must mean that. Maybe not right away but ultimately. Right away there must be a clear direction toward that." Is such a course politically possible for this government? "Why not? Botha has already stuck his neck out and has been stung by a blow. Why didn't he stick his neck out farther? It would not have hurt any more. If you're going to risk getting your head chopped off, does it really matter where the chop comes?" If Botha were to carry through, Tutu says, "the PFP would have no choice but to support him, and most whites would support him, and certainly all blacks would support him, and the West would whoop with delight!"

Instead of that, Botha dithers. While initiating "revolutionary" changes he also imposes reactionary and "draconian" security regulations. "The security system cannot work, it undermines itself. It is as if they never learned from their own history. I should think they would remember the Afrikaner's reaction when the English imposed draconian laws, but they don't." Draconian laws only undermine the law, Tutu declares. "Look at what we have here. A few years ago if a boy was caught throwing stones or something like that, that was a misdemeanor and there were laws about that. But now it comes under antisubversion laws, and then pretty soon it will come under treason laws. They will be able to hang people for it. This is absolute madness. There's that old saying that you might as well be hanged for a sheep as for a lamb, and it's true." The situation, according to Tutu, pushes dissenters into an ever more radical posture. "If you're going to be punished as a traitor for saying something that is not to the liking of the government, you might as well be punished for real treason. If you're going to be killed for what you say, you might as well be killed for killing. At least that's the way many of the young people are seeing it, and it makes our work harder, I mean those of us who are black leaders and want to be opposed to violence."

It comes as no surprise that there are clashingly different judgments passed on Bishop Tutu. The judgments offered by those on the right need not delay us here, since they turn out to be quite consistently what one would expect. Among South Africans devoted to comprehensive change, many agree with Mike Christie of the South Africa Foundation: "Tutu is a shrewd politician. He preaches revolution in order to advance reform, he demands 100 yards in the hope of getting 10." A Zulu minister of a predominantly white English church goes along with that, but offers a caveat: "We have no choice, we must support people like Tutu and Boesak, and I tell you I do admire them. But please do not misunderstand if I say also that they have it easier than some of us. They fly around all over and they have many connections, and if things get very bad here, then somebody will take care of them. . . . Some people say that Tutu soon will get a big position in Geneva or New York or some place. I do not think he leave us except they force him out, but people here feel better if they think he never leave, that he be finished with all this passport business. I think so."

Luci Mbuvelo is one of the most engaging people I met in South Africa. General secretary of the National Union of Clothing Workers, she is very black, very big, and brooks no nonsense from anyone. For four decades she has been a leading—some say the leading—black woman in public life. The term "grass roots leader" might have been invented for Luci Mbuvelo. Her somewhat tattered office is a hive of activity with assistants, mainly women, hurrying about, phones ringing, orders shouted and questioned, and a long line of people in the waiting room who have come, I am told, to see about funeral society arrangements, the funeral society being among the projects of the union. There are those who say that Luci Mbuvelo is "tainted" by virtue of being too close to the government.

"Ah, what nonsense that is!" she bursts out. "But I know they say it, also in some of the churches. And some of these new union leaders say that, but what do they know? It hurts me when church people say it, but they do not know about the true principles of trade unionism. They talk big about revolution, but trade unionism looks out for the worker. Sure, I speak out against oppressive laws, but if you have to work with such laws you always ask what is good for the worker." She does her duty, she says, according to the Bible. "The Afrikaner, no, he does not really believe the Bible, because if they believe the Bible then they would accept everybody. That is what the Bible says. Maybe only the blacks here believe the Bible. The whites they give us the Bible and then we believe it, and some church people say that is bad now, because of what the Bible says about bloodshed, it is all against it."

Leaders like Tutu and Boesak are appealing to the young people. "Many black youth today are moving away from the Bible. . . . They say Christianity wasted time for the achievement of freedom for the black man because it says you go to heaven and that is when you get yours, but everybody else is getting their good thing now." Does she think the Bible stands in the way of liberation? "No, I am from the old stock. I understand why young people say it, but I wonder if church leaders should encourage that. These young people, they would not walk as I did, three miles to the station just to get a train to come into town. Now they see the white boy has a motor car and they want a motor car. Ah, is it freedom or only more and more selfishness? I do not know, but maybe it cannot be helped. But when it comes, then maybe I will be gone, so it makes no difference. It is true, unless there are changes and changes very soon, then there will be bloodshed. Very big bloodshed."

What does she think of the comparison that Tutu and others regularly make between South Africa and the situation of blacks in America? "Ah, what nonsense that is. Have I not been to America? I have been there five times and I see that with American blacks it is very, very different. They have their whims, but they talk about oppression and persecution. Maybe there is discrimination, I do not deny that, but it is invisible discrimination. Here it is written in the law, it is the official system. . . . I understand why they make the comparison, because they need support from the U.S., but it is a big mistake to buy support by giving people the wrong idea of what is bad here and what can be done about it.

"To be black in South Africa, that is very sad. But that is just serving where God has placed me. But it is very sad.

Everything is dictated. Your whole life is dictated. We are all like women here. The men are like women, like minors, like boys. It is rotten, I tell you, it really stinks." But would she ever go into exile? "Oh no, never, never. I love to be South African. Such pride I have in being South African!" and she laughs an embarrassed laugh at the force of her expression.

"We have too many leaders," she says, "who ask people to die but when it comes time for the dying they will not be here." She has a brother living in Swaziland. "He says to me, 'Sissy, come with me now. You have no husband, come and live in Swaziland.' But I say, 'No, I love South Africa, I love Johannesburg.' " She is criticized for being too much a part of South Africa, for sitting on various government and voluntary boards with whites. "Why not? Why not? I ask you. Of course I go to multiracial meetings and I tell them what I think, I call a spade a spade. Some of these preachers who say that, why they say it you think? Because maybe they are jealous of my influence? Maybe. Because they want to be popular with young people, to look very radical? Yes, I think so. Me, I have to look out for my workers. I do not think they are second-class black people because they have to work so hard. Maybe some boss fire them and violate the contract and cheat them on their wages, then I must be there. What is this nonsense about black consciousness and not talking to whites and all that sort of thing? Who they think has the power in this country? . . . And I tell you another thing. If I do not go to these multiracial meetings then maybe the white man think that the black man is satisfied. I go to tell them that I'm not satisfied. And I speak up all the time for those black leaders who criticize me too."

I point out that her critics say there are other ways of letting the white man know that she is not satisfied. One could, for example, throw a bomb at them. "Oh yes, throw a bomb, maybe I could do that," she muses. "But I tell you, I think maybe the bomb would kill me first. I would not complain about that. These old bones are weary and I'm ready to go home to my Lord. But what would that do for my workers? Luci, we need this, Luci, we need that; my boss keep back my wages, where is my retirement money? No, they need me, so I think I wait until the Lord calls." She disagrees with Tutu's call for divestment. "I do not criticize him but I think he does not ask what it means for my workers. So they say Luci Mbuvelo has compromised herself. I do not think so, but compromise is not the most important thing, the most important thing is to help people. That is what the Bible says."

Yes, the SACC is in very big trouble. "It is not a strong organization, not like a trade union. My union is people and work and money but some church organizations they are mostly words, and then they can be blown away just like that." She illustrates with a great puff how they can be blown away. "This government, they are very stupid. They persecute Bishop Tutu and take away his passport and things like that, and then the blacks who are critical of him must shut their mouths, because he is a great man. And why is he a great man? Because the government persecutes him!" With this she seems to sense that she may have gone too far. She hurriedly assures me that indeed Bishop Tutu is a great man and will no doubt continue to make an important contribution to resolving the problems of South Africa. But one concludes that the gap between Luci Mbuvelo and Desmond Tutu is considerable. She is not in search of a constituency; for decades she has been claimed by a constituency. Her need is not for nimble footwork but for the strength to stand firm where she has been planted. She is not anxious about her critics, certainly not about those outside South Africa. She is solely dependent upon and accountable to her workers and her Lord. She is an extraordinary woman, at once a warrior and at peace.

C HARLES van Onselen is professor of history in the department of African studies at the University of Witwatersrand. "I am a socialist, and I agree with Eugene Genovese that my first obligation as a socialist is to be a good historian," says van Onselen. "A historian cannot be a worshiping Marxist. I do not think *Das Kapital* is the Bible. Marxism provides a general theory of history; it provides a theoretical basis that is extremely useful." Yes, there are many professed Marxists in the universities, "Many, many times more than in your American universities." He is amused by the ways outsiders misunderstand the nature of the oppression in South Africa. "They hear about the banning of books and think we must have pages scissored out in the text we use," he chuckles. "See all these volumes," he points to several shelves, "they are all banned. We use them regularly in our classes, all of us do." Once again it is law by exception. "Why don't the security forces move against us? Quite frankly, they wouldn't dare. These are their children in our classes. We're the safety valve for an oppressive system. And some of us enjoy being that, maybe too much." I should not take too literally the radical talk about revolution in the universities, he cautions. "It's a way of amusing ourselves in a dreadfully dull country." Then, somewhat gloomily, "I'd like to go. I've had enough of it."

But I came to talk about the churches, especially about the SACC and about Bishop Tutu. "Well, some of the churches are very close to their friends in England and America. To please American liberals, of course, they must be very anti-Reagan. What Reagan is doing may not be so bad, merely irrelevant. It might have done some good years ago, but not any more. . . . But liberals in the U.S., they think there will be hell to answer for if they have anything to do with South Africa. They have these stereotypes about blacks, especially African blacks, about black rage. Maybe they get them from watching Tarzan movies. So their attitude toward blacks is that you should be kind to animals lest they turn and attack you." One could be forgiven for thinking that Professor van Onselen is somewhat jaded.

The aforementioned Eugene Genovese, a historian of

the black struggle in America, argues that religion was an empowering force for liberation. Does the professor agree? "It doesn't fit into Marxist orthodoxy, but yes, that is true here too. It is amazing to me, the degree to which Christianity has gained the allegiance of blacks, especially given the lack of Christian practice in this society." Of course, he quickly adds, distinctions must be made between the several Christian groups. "I am not very impressed by all the talk about changes in the Dutch Reformed church. It is true that they no longer try to justify apartheid on biblical grounds, but you have something just as bad, which is the retreat of religion and ethics into the private sector of life. I don't mean the business sector but within their own private and family ethics, so that religion is quite compatible with supporting the National Party in the public sector."

As for the more liberal churches in the SACC, "They try to do good and maybe they do. But for whom do they really speak?" He is more impressed by what he thinks is the mushrooming growth of fundamentalist sects among whites, especially groups imported from the U.S. "You see all these new churches in the rich white suburbs. Oppression is good for the church business, and maybe even some of the older churches will experience something like a revival when things get worse. That's what happened in Rhodesia when the end was coming for white rule. I do not want to be unfair or to impugn the motives of these people, but you notice that these fundamentalist groups do not pose any challenge to conspicuous consumption and the so-called good life. Well, maybe that is unfair. There are worse things than turning to God when things get out of hand, and things are undoubtedly getting out of hand here." Then he muses, "It really is an amazing thing. Black and white are both turning to God as they turn against one another. It will be a civil war between Christians when it comes. Whether that means it will be less bloody or more bloody, I really don't know, and I really don't want to wait around to see."

S ALLY Motlana can hardly wait. Head of the Black House-wives League and very active in the SACC, she is, I guess, in her mid-forties and very angry. Her husband is a medical doctor and prominent member of the antigovernment "Committee of Ten" in Soweto. She has no doubt that the SACC and Tutu are in the vanguard of revolutionary change. "Not reforms, you understand, not reforms. I'm not talking about reforms, I'm talking about breaking the chains of our slavery." She thinks the charge that the SACC is the creature of Europeans and Americans is "absolute nonsense." ("Absolute" and "absolutely" recur with remarkable frequency in the talk of South Africans of all parties.) She believes "the struggles" in South Africa and America are quite parallel. The one exception is feminism. "Feminism the way you know it in America is not an issue here. Here it is a question of my man and myself fighting the oppressor together. Some nonthinking people try to promote American-style feminism, but the issue for us here is to free the black man. By 'the black man' we mean myself and all of us."

The Black Housewives League focuses on the devastation that apartheid works on black families. I mention that groups in the U.S. that call themselves profamily are often viewed as conservative. "The most radical thing you can be here is profamily," she responds. "This is the worst oppression for the blacks here—they cannot even have a normal family life. Influx control separates husbands and wives and parents and children. We have more and more divorces and alcoholism and everything that keeps the black man weak. Family and freedom go together. How can you be free if you can't even maintain the bonds of family?"

On the dependency of Tutu and the SACC on outside funds: "What do they expect us to do? We can go begging from door to door here [she illustrates knocking on doors], but they say there is no money. When they criticize us for taking money from overseas, I always say, 'You're right. Let's get our support in South Africa—beginning with you!' " The

League is financially supported by the SACC. "Tutu needs money. SACC needs money to defend itself from government attacks, lots of money. We can send out an appeal here and nothing happens, but Tutu writes overseas and then the money comes in." The critics, Sally Motlana says, are always asking big questions. "It is the little daily things that we need to be helped with. Look at education. Black education is not compulsory and it is not free. What education I got I got from the missionaries, so it is absurd to say that the church's dependence upon outsiders is something new. Then this government thinks it knows better and takes over the schools from the missionaries. But they do not give the money to black education. Black schools receive one eighth the money spent on white schools, and there are five times as many of us. So, yes, we go begging. Our people are in the streets begging for bursaries and, in addition to the bursaries, you have to pay for books and fees and everything else. Nobody likes to beg. Tutu doesn't like to beg. But we have no choice."

David Lewis also responds with an argument from necessity. He is a union organizer and we meet in a rickety second-floor office near Cape Town. His business is to organize the dockworkers, and it appears to be a frustrating business indeed. "We don't have many choices here. We have chaos and very little change. I am sure there will be more chaos. I hope there will be more change." Reluctantly, he dissents from Tutu's position on divestment. "The U.S. companies claim they are in the advance in bringing benefits to the workers and, all in all, that is true. . . . Even the government knows now that the unions are here to stay. They're not out simply to smash them, which was once the case. The problem is not that we need less dealings with U.S. business, we need more dealings with the U.S. labor movement. The government would be loath to see the American unions activated against this country. Imagine if the longshoremen in your country joined a boycott against South Africa!" Lewis quickly adds that he does not want to see that happen, but he does want closer ties between the labor movements of the two countries so that the threat of its happening would be more credible.

"The English-speaking churches are very important to labor. Not on a day by day basis, of course, but for their support in crisis when it comes to a real crunch. Maybe that's as much as the churches can do. They can't do the business of unions, but when we come into brushes against the government, then the churches can speak out. Tutu has been very helpful to us, along with many other church leaders. They are still listened to, even when the government condemns what they say." Very important, he adds, is that "the churches have a network of connections with the press." Does Lewis worry that the government might crush groups like the SACC? "To be sure, it would not be hard to do," he says, sitting beneath a poster picturing a young white medical doctor who had worked with Steve Biko and also died while in police detention. "They don't have to do very much, just declare the council an 'affected organization' and that cuts off all funds from outside. There is no doubt that would kill the council, but there would be an enormous outcry in the West and I don't think the government wants that."

What about the argument (I do not mention that Tutu has sometimes made this argument) that improving the conditions for workers is only delaying the necessary revolution? "That is absolute rubbish. We don't pay any attention to that at all. People who are paid to talk radical talk sometimes have very little sympathy for people who have to work to get paid. Even if I favored revolution, people don't fight on empty stomachs." The argument might make some sense, he says, "if in fact you had those masses of black workers out there with their nice big cars and satisfied consumer appetites, but that is not our situation." He allows that some of the better paid workers, such as those at Ford plants, might feel that they have a stake in the system so strong that they would resist significant change. "But I think that is unlikely. You can make a better case for saying that as people move up economically they will become more demanding about their political rights too. If people wanted to stop a black revolution, smashing the unions and crippling economic advancement would be a good way to do it." Although David Lewis is thought by some to be a dangerous radical and has had some scrapes with antisubversion laws, he would seem to be in essential agreement with Luci Mbuvelo when it comes to revolutionisms that are not in touch with the needs and aspirations of very ordinary people.

The prominence of the South African Council of Churches and its leadership both in and outside South Africa is matched by apparently unanimous agreement about their fragility. Delicately expressed but very substantive criticisms have arisen also from within the council. In June 1982, Joe Wing, secretary of the United Congregational Church, addressed the general conference of the SACC: "If there is a drawing together of the South African churches in the next twenty years, the role of the SACC must change. The council [must become] a vehicle for consultation, research, development, the pooling of resources and joint action. This would mean that the council would not do its own thing as an organization distinct from the churches, but would act on behalf of the churches in all matters of common concern and cooperative endeavor."

Such cautions have become more frequent in recent years, reflecting an unhappiness with an SACC that is viewed as a highly personalized political platform for figures such as Desmond Tutu and Beyers Naudé to act out their parts on behalf of "the international community." On the other hand, in a situation that is perenially declared to be revolutionary or prerevolutionary, questions about the "representativeness" of the Council of Churches may seem irrelevant. In this view, any platform, no matter how shaky, should be used for all its worth. Be that as it may, the questions about the SACC and what it does or does not represent go far beyond personalities and short-term tactics, as we discover in talking with David Bosch, undoubtedly one of the most respected analysts of religion and cultural change in South Africa.

CHAPTER SEVEN
RELIGIOUS WITNESS
IN DISARRAY

D AVID Bosch is an internationally recognized authority
in missiology, the study of the nature and practice of
the church's mission in the world. Within Afrikanerdom and
the Dutch Reformed church he is viewed as something of a
troublemaker. He is at the center of the *Stormkompass* group,
a loose alliance of Dutch Reformed theologians and other
leaders who have been challenging basic presuppositions of
the South African system. Although right-wingers despise
him and he has been charged with heresy from time to time,
Bosch is nonetheless respected. In part because he is one of
the very few Afrikaner theologians who have made a mark
in the larger world. In part because he is also one of the very
few who have remained on speaking terms with the several
religious communities within South Africa. And in largest
part, I suspect, because even his opponents recognize that
Bosch represents a way of substantive change short of the
revolutionary apocalypse.

Something of the complexity of the reformist Afrikaner's role is caught in David Bosch's testimony to the Eloff
Commission in 1983. The Eloff Commission was set up by
the government to investigate the South African Council of
Churches. At the time, many people agreed with Sally Motlana: "Of course they're out to destroy the council. The commission is judge and jury and, before it's done, it will be
executioner too. We all understand this." As it happened,

155

scandal and acrimonious divisions within the SACC did much of the commission's work, if in fact it was the commission's purpose to destroy the council. One staff member of the council explained to me, "It looks like the council is determined to self-destruct before it is destroyed." Yet at the end of 1983 the council was staggering but still on its feet. There are those who think that David Bosch's testimony played a part in persuading the Eloff Commission not to go in for the kill.

In his concluding testimony, the professor of the Dutch Reformed church is advising the government on what it ought to do when challenged by the churches. He has stressed that the church's witness is always "contextual"—that is, it speaks not only from Scripture and revealed truth but also in a way attuned to the particularities of its historical experience. Bosch points out to the commission that about 80 percent of the members of the churches in the SACC "hail from the less privileged sectors of South African society (the so-called blacks, coloureds, and Indians)" and that it is obvious that "their existential experience in the South African crucible will color their theological thinking." The white members of SACC churches have also since 1948 "become very marginal in matters political" and that affects the way they speak theologically. He pointedly adds, however, that "White Afrikaans-speaking Christians likewise theologise contextually"—the possession of power can influence religious witness as much as the absence of power.

In a conciliatory vein, Bosch allows that church leaders sometimes make "apodictic statements about social, political, and economic issues" on which they have no special competence, not to mention divinely revealed solutions. When the church "trespasses" on the terrain of civil authority— even if on the basis of Scripture it claims the right to do so— it may be "completely in order for the state to act against the church. . . . Whether it would be *prudent* for the state to act in these circumstances is, however, a completely different matter. . . . Where the church takes up the cause of those who have—for whatever reason—become marginal, it behooves a wise government to allow the church to become its conscience." Bosch continues: "A wise government would take even more care to listen if the ecclesiastical body that criticises it represents a segment of the population which does not have the same channels of expressing themselves politically as the rest of the population has. Though it may sound like wishful thinking, it should perhaps be added that wise government—even if it finds the church's criticism irritating—ought to welcome such a *critical* voice, even if it sounds radical."

Bosch's testimony is in the classic tradition of the "established" Dutch Reformed church "speaking truth to power." The novelty is that he is speaking on behalf of the nonestablished churches, urging that they not only be tolerated but be valued as contributing to the wholeness of Christian witness in South Africa. Implicit in his testimony—and this can hardly be welcomed by some leaders of the established religion—is that the Dutch Reformed church has failed in speaking for "the marginal" in society. Nonetheless, Bosch grounds his admonition in the historic self-understanding of the Dutch Reformed church: "The ecclesiastical tradition of the dominant group in this country happens to be the Reformed or Calvinist tradition. It is one of the pillars of this tradition that there is no area of life that does not fall under the scrutiny of the Word of God."[1]

Progressives in the Dutch Reformed church, such as David Bosch, privately indicate that they have no illusions about the lack of theological substance commonly found in the English-speaking churches. One of them refers me to a parody in Etienne Leroux's *Seven Days at the Silbersteins.* Leroux, a prominent Afrikaner novelist, has his disoriented hero, Henry, encounter some English divines at a party. "They were discussing an ecumenical conference in New Delhi with enthusiasm. One of them, with the help of an American grant, had attended it. They were ardently seeking formulas and patching dogmas together in the interests of greater unity. Thinking must be cosmic, the churches must be united, the territory must embrace economics, politics and all other aspects. The formula expanded; the clerics were excited about this, their greater field, and the program began to assume the appearance of a declaration of the principles of an international socialist movement. . . . The poorest would suddenly become strong, it was superior missionary work with all the appearance and adventure—nobody was being isolated any longer in a tiny parish where he had the care of only a few souls. It was Marxism in reverse. Who knew—perhaps, one day, the two extremes would be reconciled here. The poor Republic [of South Africa]! And they smiled. The poor Republic that lived in the illusion that the Almighty was well-disposed to it. A single nation did not matter, but all nations; not the individual soul, but souls. One had to learn to think big."[2]

In his spacious wood-paneled office at the University of South Africa, David Bosch, a very personable and self-confident fellow in his late forties, sits back to explain at leisure the shape of the world. His secretary has laid out for me in very orderly manner a number of his monographs which I should read for "background." (If I have not mentioned it, white South Africa is a very orderly society. At the movies your ticket is for an assigned seat. In a movie house seating about four hundred, the seventy-five of us in attendance were bunched together in one corner, all in our assigned places. In Johannesburg one afternoon a black man was shot dead while robbing a downtown store. There was considerable public excitement and the police roped off the area. At an open spot in the police line where the body could be seen sprawled on the sidewalk a long queue formed and people took turns at having a look. This is merely an aside and may have nothing to do with religion in South Africa. On the other hand, it may.)

The SACC has a serious credibility problem, says David Bosch. Nobody doubts that the churches in the SACC are concerned about black liberation, "but in another sense people wonder whether, as churches, they are concerned about black people. The member churches of the council all show declining black memberships." The independent churches, the Roman Catholic church, and the Dutch Reformed church all have strong missionary programs reaching out to blacks. "The churches of the council are essentially involved in maintenance programs rather than outreach." Does this mean that political involvement and missionary outreach are incompatible, as some scholars have suggested? "Incompatible is probably too strong a word, but I'm afraid there is some validity to the argument," he responds.

"Look at the growth of the independent churches. Sociologically speaking, they reach the less civilized and sophisticated elements of the black population, the so-called lower echelons. They deal with bread-and-butter issues. I know that people like Tutu don't like to hear this, but the independent churches appeal to first level rather than second or third level concerns. By second and third level, I mean the social and political concerns. These churches offer a home for people who all week long are bossed about by whites, it is a great relief, a powerful refuge, a place on Sunday where you can go that is entirely outside European control. To these people, the kind of religion and ideology that Tutu represents is suspiciously European.

"The Dutch Reformed church is very much involved in primary evangelism, and it is growing among blacks. In the nineteenth century the Methodists introduced evangelism methods here that made the Afrikaner very uncomfortable, but now, strangely enough, the Dutch Reformed church has taken over the methods that the Methodists have abandoned." But is not the Dutch Reformed church losing members because it is not sufficiently up front on the social and political issues? "That may be happening," Bosch says, "although we do not have very reliable data. I imagine that some of the top membership, the more educated, are leaving. But it is also my impression that we are not losing them to other churches. They are moving into various radical movements that are frequently hostile to all the churches."

There may be a "sociological law," says Bosch, that social involvement means membership stagnation or decline. "If there is such a law, however, it should be defied theologically. Sociological law must not be permitted to bulldoze the churches. We have to keep working at finding a balance, a creative tension between evangelization and social responsibility." David Bosch believes that the Dutch Reformed and the SACC churches have to be working toward that balance, although coming from different directions. Bosch says he agrees with Allan Boesak and other critics that this means the Dutch Reformed church must rethink the meaning of heresy. "They are right when they say we have to extend the notion of heresy to ortho-praxis as well as orthodoxy." (Remember Beyers Naudé's invocation of "by their fruits you will know them.") But Bosch also believes that it is wrong to let commitment or noncommitment to a specified political program be the determinant of what is heresy.

"I am not a typical Protestant in my understanding of the church," says Bosch. "Many of us in the Dutch Reformed have a very 'high' view of the church; it is not just a voluntary organization run by human rules. We are part of the body of Christ, and it is tragic if others in the body isolate us more and more." While sympathizing wholeheartedly with the campaign against apartheid, he strongly opposes efforts to drum the Dutch Reformed church out of the worldwide association of Reformed churches. "There is no doubt that we are failing miserably, that we are sinners, but there are still vestiges of deep Christian commitment in the Dutch Reformed church and you have to be extremely careful about excommunicating fellow Christians."

With some in the SACC churches, and with Allan Boesak in particular, Bosch says he has had many arguments about whether he, Bosch, should remain in the Dutch Reformed church. "Who can read his own heart aright? It may be, as they say, that my reluctance to leave is tied to group loyalty, ethnic solidarity, and so forth. But I do believe that I see in the Dutch Reformed church that more general, more catholic, Christianity which holds my primary allegiance. I am not ready to give the Dutch Reformed church over to the devil." Bosch points to the existence of groups like that associated with *Stormkompass*, "and this is only the beginning, there are more dramatic statements of dissent to come." In fact, says Bosch, "I will not be entirely surprised if in the next two or three years you will see a very different situation. What is now called dissent may very soon become the dominant direction in the Dutch Reformed church." We have already noted the election of Johan Heyns as moderator of the Northern Transvaal. In the fall of 1983 the Dutch Reformed church in the Western Transvaal was passing resolutions critical of separate development and calling for an open church in which all races and national groups would be welcome. In short, Bosch's hopefulness is not unsupported by empirical evidence.

David Bosch does not put it this way, but he obviously resents the way in which the SACC and its member churches tend to posture as "true Christianity" in South Africa. "You have to look where Christian vitalities are to be found. If the Dutch Reformed church is weak in addressing social injustices, and it is, that is something we have to work on without overlooking the other vitalities in the church which are not so evident in the English-speaking churches." From his viewpoint change is too slow, but it is nonetheless impressive. "Ten years ago it was not uncommon to find people who would use a biblical text like the Tower of Babel to justify apartheid in a fundamentalist way. But in 1974 the Dutch Reformed church officially repudiated that kind of fundamentalism. To be sure, there are still defenders of apartheid or separate development in the church, but now they use pragmatic arguments, not theological arguments. For example, they take a page from your American 'church growth movement' that says evangelism requires homogeneity of population, and that sort of thing."

Bosch has been charged with heresy, and there have been attempts to "discipline" him for his insistence that church membership must be entirely open. "Believe me, it would be very easy for me to do as Boesak and Naudé and others say, and just resign and walk away from this. These disciplinary measures would immediately evaporate and, I can assure you, I would be quite happy in a black or coloured church. But I am sorry, I think that would be self-indulgent. Quite frankly I see a more enlightened view on the ascendancy in the Dutch Reformed church. Politically, most of our people support P. W. Botha in the hope that he really is leading, step by step, toward a society that is more morally defensible."

Bosch admits that a legitimate question of heresy can be raised about the Dutch Reformed church. "When people talk about some peoples being necessarily irreconcilable, that approaches heresy, and when it is said in the church, it *is* heresy. The most basic principle of the Protestant Reformation is that God through Christ accepts all people unconditionally. Now the government may feel forced to set up certain restrictions, certain requirements for citizenship. Every government in the world does that. But the ethics of the government are not the ethics of the church. It is simply not possible for the church. Here is where the inescapable crunch comes for the church, on church membership. It is impossible, it is heretical, for the church to set up any other criteria other than the acceptance of Jesus Christ, Lord and Savior."

In South Africa, as elsewhere in the Christian world, the

argument is made that the important thing is the "invisible" or "spiritual" fellowship of Christians. That, it is said, is a given gift of God, and therefore visible or organizational unity is not so important. "Oh, we hear that all the time," says Bosch. "Of course I do not deny that spiritual unity of all Christians, but you have to ask whether in fact we believe it when in all too visible practice we contradict it. Here there is much nice talk about the 'Reformed family of churches,' but as far as real fellowship within one church, it is nothing more than nice talk. For example, the ordination of a minister in the black church is not recognized in the white church. A black minister cannot become a pastor in a white church. Also, membership is not transferable, a white minister or layman can transfer to a black church but not vice versa. Practices like that contradict everything we say about how much we believe in the real 'spiritual fellowship' of Christians."

I comment that in some respects it sounds like the situation prevailing in the U.S. in the 1950s. I mention a white Lutheran congregation in Detroit which was surrounded by black communities. Each Sunday ushers waited on the church steps and, if a black showed up, supplied him or her with taxi fare to the nearest black Lutheran church. Bosch laughs and says, "I haven't heard of anything quite like that happening here, but I would not be surprised. But you must understand that, if we're dealing with problems you had in the 1950s, that's great progress for South Africa." In South Africa there have been ugly and much publicized incidents in which blacks have been turned away from funerals, weddings, and other church events. In 1982, at a funeral of a white who was much respected by blacks, a dominee ordered the church cleared of nonwhites before he would go on with the service.

"In my own congregation it is more sophisticated. The policy is that, if you're going to bring a nonwhite to worship, you are supposed to call up the pastor or the executive committee of the church and get approval. But it is not a very strict policy. A few months ago we had some nonwhite students visiting with us and I called up the church to tell them—not to ask for approval but just to tell them—that they were coming to worship. I am told there was a letter or two of protest, but in general this is acceptable practice. But I have to say again that the question of admission to worship is not so important as the question of membership." As mentioned earlier, one of the smaller Reformed bodies, the one thought to be most liberal in theology, is the only one that actually has "whites only" written in its constitution. "That," says Bosch, "is heresy."

Bosch says that he resists facile comparisons between race relations in the U.S. and in South Africa. "But here there is a real comparison. I think there is an almost inevitable movement toward a more open society, and an open church can contribute to that. The people who resist it are like the die-hards in the American South; they are clearly on the defensive. One by one, they've had to give up their moral and theological arguments. Now it is clear to anyone who has eyes to see that it is only color prejudice that supports these discriminations. They know they are fighting a losing battle." But all this does not make Bosch entirely sanguine.

"I have a very great worry that we may end up doing the right thing for the wrong reason. In politics people like Botha are pragmatic, and that is good. But in the church there should be more than pragmatism. . . . In the council [SACC] churches you can smell the secularization in the air; it is like a dilution of any specific Christian or biblical rationale for action. I don't want to be unfair, but I wonder if they aren't paying too high a price for trying to be in the political vanguard. . . . Change must come in the Dutch Reformed church, it is coming, but it must come much faster—and it must also come in a way that is responsive to biblical truth and not just to pragmatic and secular trends. . . . When we really and finally become an open church, I pray it will be because we are finally taking seriously the Reformation principle of God's unconditional acceptance. I confess that my chief concern is not that we be more respectable in the eyes of the secular world. I am not contemptuous of that, but that is not the main thing. The main thing, ultimately the only thing that counts, is that we become more fully the church of Jesus Christ."

W. Esterhuyse is professor of philosophy at Stellenbosch and adds an intriguing angle in understanding the role of the SACC and of religion in general in South Africa's cultural and political change. "It is in some ways an unnatural development," says Esterhuyse, "that the council and the English-speaking churches have come to be viewed as the opposition to the status quo. I mean by that that opposition was historically the role of the Dutch Reformed church. . . . Religion was the central power in the Afrikaner's struggle, and then, when we seized power in 1948, very suddenly the Dutch Reformed church had to take on a role for which it was not at all accustomed, of defending and legitimating the new status quo. And I must say we were not very good at it. We were much better at being in opposition to the establishment." But did not the Dutch Reformed church in fact succeed in providing a religious rationale for apartheid? "Succeed? No, not really. At least it was a very limited success. For a brief time in the 1950s people thought the rationale was firmly in place, but then there was Sharpeville [1960] and everything that has happened since then, and fewer and fewer people really believed what we were saying."

Esterhuyse agrees with Bosch that those still standing by the apartheid rationale are die-hards and know they are on the defensive. In this view, then, the SACC temporarily filled a vacuum created by the Dutch Reformed church's abandonment of its oppositional role. "It may be," says Esterhuyse, "that groups like *Stormkompass* and all the other things we see happening mean that the Dutch Reformed church is returning to its historic posture." He thinks the worries about secularization are excessive. "It is still the case, and I do not see this changing very soon, that Botha and other politicians have to frame their policies in Christian terms. That is because of personal reasons too, of course. I know Botha, for example, is a very committed Christian. I have his children in my class. But it is more than personal; it is the whole ethos of South Africa. And I don't mean just the Afrikaner, I mean the black too. Whatever happens, I am sure that in a very important sense South Africa will always think of itself as a Christian society. The question is who is going to provide that Christian content and direction. I have no objection if groups like the SACC were to do that but I don't see how they can. They simply do not have the people, whites or blacks."

Esterhuyse has been a strong public critic of government and church policies and, like Bosch and many others, has received a good deal of negative attention from the authorities. But he is quite hopeful. "I do not believe in resigning from anything. They have to chuck me out." He says he has great respect for his friend and colleague Nico Smith who had a while back resigned from the Dutch Reformed church. "But it's the old inside-outside question, isn't it? I don't know if there's any general answer to that, beyond acting on conscience, but I would like to think there is a complementary relationship between those who work on the inside and those who work on the outside." He says he hopes for the day when South Africa will be less pervasively politicized than it has been in his lifetime. "In the church, in the university, everywhere it's politics. I believe it is true to say that there is no country in the world in which academics play such a big political role as we do here. I see academics in the U.K. and America wanting to be involved in politics, and sometimes I would like to change places with them. I'm not a politician, I'm a philosopher."

At the same time, Esterhuyse acknowledges that the political temperature is not likely to fall any time soon. "I get discouraged. For example it was very unpleasant a couple of years ago when Vorster was here and gave a speech in which he attacked for forty-five minutes my book on apartheid. I could really live quite well without that notoriety, thank you." But he repeats, "I do not resign from anything." He will not resign from the Dutch Reformed church, nor from the Broederbond, nor from his university posts. "If I resigned I think it would appear that I was resigned to the other side winning, and I'm not. We may just be on the verge of Afrikanerdom coming to its senses."

Pierre Roussouw, ecumenical executive of the NGK, the largest of the Dutch Reformed churches, had told me that the opponents of change in Afrikanerdom, such as Treurnicht and his conservative breakaway group, "are increasingly seen as infantile." Esterhuyse says that is true. "They are like little children in their refusal to see the difference between responsibility and guilt. If you say that racial discrimination is a cancer and a sin, which I try to say very forcefully, they complain that we are trying to induce them into some kind of guilt complex. That is their standard response. But in fact we are simply calling them and all of us to a sense of responsibility for our history and the consequences it has had for ourselves and others. . . . Of course there is also guilt in that history, but we claim to believe in divine forgiveness. I sometimes wonder if their great fear of acknowledging the guilt is because they finally do not believe in the possibility of forgiveness."

Esterhuyse claims to see signs of the acceptance of responsibility, beyond finger pointing and mutual recriminations. "If that happens, the Dutch Reformed church will come into its own as a loyal but critical opposition, addressing the word of God to the powers to be. In that case, I think it is possible that the recent prominence of groups like the council and, earlier, the Christian Institute will evaporate. Please don't misunderstand, I don't say this against people like Naudé and Tutu. If they really care about all South Africans, and I want to believe that they do, I should think they will be very happy if the Dutch Reformed church resumes its moral responsibility. Certainly the outsiders will have played an important part in bringing that about, if it happens."

I T is not evident where the Roman Catholic church fits, if it fits, in the inside-outside imagery. Some years ago in what was then Rhodesia, a English Jesuit explained to me, "You can be sure of one thing: the Catholic church will always come to terms with the barbarian." From the Visigoths to the communist regimes in Eastern Europe today, he said, the church's single concern is to protect its own mission, regardless of who is in power. Although to my knowledge no Catholic leader has said it publicly, many undoubtedly agree with the Christian Institute slogan "the future is black." Under a leadership that is mainly white and foreign, the Catholic Church has made enormous evangelistic inroads among black South Africans. A Dutch Reformed dominee told me, "The Catholics are very cautious, very smart. We Protestants are with Martin Luther. We say, 'Here we stand, so help us God.' The Catholics say, 'Here we stand—and here, and here.' " He enjoys this immensely, so I do not tell him it is an old quip about the difference between Luther and Erasmus. His point is evident enough: "The Catholics look out for themselves, whatever happens."

There are about 1.5 million black Catholics and a little under half a million whites, many of the latter being recent Portuguese and Italian immigrants. So Catholic leaders must address a diverse constituency. In addition, Afrikanerdom has been inculcated with a deep fear of the *Roomsgevaar* (the Roman danger). Nonetheless, since the Nationalist victory of '48, the Catholic bishops have consistently and often boldly criticized apartheid. At the same time, because of the traditional Catholic investment in education, the church has also had to negotiate with the government over schools. There have, for instance, been testy moments over the Catholic insistence, contra apartheid doctrine, of maintaining "mixed schools" (an insistence more important for its principle than its practice, since in fact there are very few schools that are racially mixed). In addition, the church must always contend for its right to be involved in the educational field, a right that has sometimes been threatened by the government's "socialist" propensity to monopolize education, among other things. Yet its essentially critical posture toward the government has not led the Catholic church into unqualified alliance with the English-speaking churches of the SACC.

To the extent the Catholic church is getting ready for a black future, its "point man" is Archbishop Denis Hurley of Durban. Almost everyone is much impressed by Hurley, and your reporter is no exception. Hurley is a big man, over six feet tall I should think, and military in posture and manner. His bearing is that of the bishops we remember from before Vatican Council II; his views are distinctly post-Vatican II. In the 1960s he led the way in exposing the sufferings of people who had been removed to the homelands that could never be home, places that often offered not even barest subsistence. He speaks of a visit to Limehill, a resettlement village for "discarded people." There was an epidemic and one afternoon he counted the graves of ninety children. Hurley has protested the brutality of the pass laws, and along with the conference of bishops, has challenged the fundaments of apartheid, such as the Group Areas Act and the Race Classification Act. Hurley also prompted his church to assume "observer status" with the SACC.

Archbishop Hurley speaks movingly about the injustices of South Africa, and modestly about the church's ability to provide the answers. "It's fine to be prophetic and throw stones at the government, but we have to look at the beam in our own eyes," he says. He points out that the several churches that are so critical of racial discrimination, and rightly so, have not done very well in promoting interracial community or in advancing blacks to leadership positions within the churches. (Peter Butelezi, a black, is now Catholic archbishop in Bloemfontein, the capital of the former Orange Free State and, as it is sometimes said, the "heart of Afrikanerdom." Archbishop Butelezi is much criticized by some for being an Uncle Tom. As one supporter of the African National Congress, a Catholic, told me, "He's the worst white bishop we've got." Archbishop Butelezi, one suspects, understands the strategy of the Catholic church in South Africa.)

On one critical issue Archbishop Hurley has dramatically distanced himself from Tutu and the SACC. He has refused to endorse the campaign for divestment. He is on record as saying, "Foreign disinvestment in South Africa would be a disaster. It would precipitate a conflict that will go on for twenty years and end in total devastation for the country." Although he does not mention Tutu by name, he says, "We bishops are babes in the woods when it comes to economics." He nonetheless has an economic bias and it is in favor of "economic evolution which will also result in a greater sharing of wealth."[3] When I first met Hurley in 1971 I pressed him on why the Catholic church did not ally itself more publicly with efforts like those of Beyers Naudé and the Christian Institute. He said then that he was very sympathetic, and had often said so in public, but that the sufferings of South Africa were so enormous that they required many different approaches. After listing a large number of Catholic efforts with and on behalf of black South Africans, Archbishop Hurley paused and with a knowing look said very deliberately, "You must keep in mind that the Catholic church intends to be here a very long time." I infer that he is not so sure that the same can be said of institutions and personalities that may one day end up on the venerated memorial list of radicalism's lost causes.

If the Catholic church's cautious attitude toward the SACC is ecumenically nuanced, the attitude of some of the independent churches might be described as relentlessly candid. Bishop Elijah Mokoena, who once spent five years in prison for supporting the African National Congress, heads up the Black Reformed Independent Churches Association. The association claims to represent about 900 independent churches and more than 2.5 million black Christians, but nobody is keeping very close count. In fact, people connected with the SACC tell me that the claims of the association are wildly inflated, and therefore a certain skepticism is in order.

The bishop's group has joined the Southern Africa Theological College for Independent Churches in assaulting the SACC and Bishop Tutu in particular. The college claims to represent more than two million black Christians, so, if the claims are anywhere near reality, we have groups representing close to five million blacks challenging the claim of the SACC that it represents the blacks of South Africa. (A painful irony here is that the Christian Institute and the SACC both contributed substantially to bringing the fragmented independent churches into cooperative association.) Bishop Mokoena's group has resolved: "We totally reject the statements and activities of Bishop Desmond Tutu and the SACC as not being representative of the Black Christian community. We are particularly distressed at the arrogance of the SACC in suggesting that many Black Christians consider those recently condemned for high treason as heroes [this was in 1981]. We Black Christians reject violence as the solution to our problems or as a means to achieve our aspirations. Treasonable activities are a violation of the Word of God."

The independent church groups have also complained that Tutu and the SACC have not spoken out in condemnation when blacks are tried without trial and executed in, for example, Marxist Mozambique, and they have frequently declared their opposition to divestment. The government, not surprisingly, has expressed appreciation for the independent churches' devotion "to a philosophy and policy of constructive and peaceful participation in resolving the issues confronting our country and Southern Africa."[4]

R IVAL claims about who speaks for black South Africans should be received with lively skepticism. Competitions among political clerics are frequently as volatile as they are unedifying, with enmities and alliances in a constant state of flux. I have been treated to a number of "behind the scenes" explanations of who is trying to do what to whom today for doing what to whom yesterday. The point at hand is that within South Africa it is easy to see how the SACC, Desmond Tutu, and others can be portrayed as very marginal actors— marginal to the power structures and marginal to the "marginal people" (the majority of South Africans) for whom they would speak. This does not of course discredit the analysis they offer or the solutions they would advance. It does serve as a caution against reading the realities of South Africa exclusively through their eyes.

Within the SACC the criticism is frequently heard that it is not a council of churches at all but simply an inchoate cluster of ill-managed programs and a personal platform for figures such as Naudé and Tutu. The observer must try not to let the voices of the disgruntled few dominate his perceptions; yet the disgruntlement within and around the SACC is particularly acute. In these last pages we have talked with figures in various communities, especially within South African religion, and the purpose of that was not only to understand the place of Tutu and the SACC, as important as they are in Western perceptions, but also to convey something of the range of opinions and passions in South Africa today. Add to this somewhat confused picture, then, the difficulties that Bishop Tutu has had in relating to sundry political organizations within South Africa, both black and white. Most important of these perhaps is the running feud with Chief Gatsha Buthelezi of the Zulus and Buthelezi's political organization, Inkatha, which claims one and a half million members.

It is said there is an element of personal chemistry contributing to this feud, and in listening to each discuss the other I have come to believe it. A couple of years ago the

172

American civil rights leader and erstwhile presidential candidate, Jesse Jackson, was in South Africa and tried to heal the rift between Buthelezi and Tutu. As an aide to Buthelezi tells me, "It was an absolute muck up. Jackson came in with a squad of retainers, there were television cameras and reporters all over, and after it was finished we saw that the Chief and Tutu could have talked better on the telephone. It was what they call a big PR event for Jesse Jackson." But the difficulties between Tutu and Buthelezi are not merely personal by any means. Buthelezi deeply resents what he views as Tutu's efforts to monopolize the attention and money of Western churches and other institutions. Tutu, who is not a Zulu, is suspicious of the "tribalism" that is the base of Buthelezi's leadership and that, he believes, is an obstacle to black unity.

Obviously, Bishop Tutu does not need more enemies. Among other things he did not need were the ugly internal scandals and divisions which erupted in the SACC during his term in office. For a long time there was uneasiness among those working for the council and those sympathetic to it. The uneasiness was vaguely related to money—there was so very much of it and it was so very unclear what was being done with it. It was inevitable that when the government set up the Eloff Commission to investigate the council it would demonstrate a lively interest in the monies. Had the commission focused simply on the "subversive activities" of the council, that could unify the council and its supporters who would, as usual, condemn the government for red-baiting. Money, the love of money, the insidious entanglements that money weaves—here was a much more fruitful line of inquiry for the commission.

The nature and scale of SACC financing was set forth by the commission in a 246-page financial report in 1982. It showed that the council had an income from 1975 to 1981 of 20,296,166 rand. Of the twenty million, less than 1 percent came from within South Africa. By far the largest overseas donor was the Evangelical church of West Germany, which is the beneficiary of a church tax collected by the government that produces monies far in excess of what is needed by the church in Germany. Denmark and the Netherlands were next on the list, with church groups in the U.S. and the U.K. each contributing about 3 percent of the SACC's budget. The scale of the financing helped many South Africans understand the unhappiness of Chief Gatsha Buthelezi and, most particularly, of the independent churches. The independent churches have even called upon the government to declare the SACC an "affected organization" so that it will not be able to receive further funds from overseas, a measure that the government could yet impose. According to some independent church leaders, they have the black people while Tutu and groups such as the SACC have only the money. As one independent bishop told me, "Take away Tutu's overseas money and put us on an equal footing and then we'll see who speaks for the blacks of South Africa." (Other, and perhaps more objective, observers believe that most independent church leaders are not all that interested in "speaking for blacks" on political questions. At the moment they may be portrayed as supporting the government, but, according to these observers, "come the revolution" and the independent churches will switch sides with remarkable facility.)

Having a lot of money is not necessarily a scandal, however. The scandal came with the revelation of what was done with the money and how the council reacted to the revelation. John Rees is a Methodist layman, a white, and Tutu's immediate predecessor. From 1968 to 1978 he was general secretary of the SACC. Few people were more revered by blacks and liberal whites in South Africa. He left the council to head up the South Africa Institute of Race Relations, the organization once led by the late Fred van Wyck, one of the cofounders of the Christian Institute. In June 1983, John Rees was convicted on twenty-nine counts of having misappropriated more than 275,000 rand of council money. Many believe the amount involved may be much larger since more than 500,000 rand went through more than fifty personal bank accounts Rees had set up, some of them after he left office in 1978.

The claim that the conviction was part of a pattern of government persecution was given little credence. The judge in the case was manifestly sympathetic to the SACC and bent over backwards to distance himself from the activities of the Eloff commission. There seems to be no dispute about that. The dispute is over the meaning of "trust" and "solidarity" in the small liberal world of the SACC. Rees had gained personal control of such enormous funds on the basis of trust. For years, and much more following the 1976 Soweto troubles, money had poured in for the support of the families of those who had been killed or detained. Rees contended, and the council leaders apparently agreed, that the doling out of these funds had to be handled with highest confidentiality, since many of those aided were vulnerable to government retaliation. Some staff members were uneasy about the huge wads of money Rees carried on his person and about the large checks he would write on accounts unknown but, as Sally Motlana told me at the time, "If we can't trust one another in the struggle, who can we trust?"

If, as it seems, John Rees betrayed that trust, it would be bad enough for the morale of those supporting the SACC. Adding to the damage in the view of many was Bishop Tutu's reaction. He refused to testify on Rees's behalf and, according to some critics, provided damaging information to the prosecution. A story widely credited among white liberals is that Tutu was intimidated by a police threat that he would be prosecuted as a codefendant unless he cooperated. According to this version, Tutu was vulnerable because the SACC's bookkeeping had not been entirely put in order during the years of his stewardship. More than that, Bishop Tutu had accepted from Rees approximately 15,000 rand to renovate his own home in Soweto. At first Tutu said it was his understanding that this was a no-strings-attached gift from the council, but when the flack began to fly Tutu announced that he was repaying the "loan." Most debilitating, however, is that the whole affair had taken on very unedifying racial overtones. Whether or not, as critics claim, Bishop Tutu introduced the racial element, pretty soon it had turned into an acrimonious debate over whether whites can trust blacks, and vice versa. In criticizing him, Tutu said, whites were rallying to their own. "Blood is thicker than water," he declared.

In fact probably as many blacks as whites—especially the blacks in Rees's Methodist denomination—were disillusioned by Tutu's role in the affair. It was altogether a depressing period for the liberal community in South Africa. Peter Storey, president of the SACC, felt forced to resign. He is John Rees's pastor and was distressed by the way Rees had been treated by Tutu. Bishop Tutu held on to his position, but Lutheran bishop Manas Buthelezi took over as president in the hope that he could put the pieces back together. Meanwhile, it is feared, the Eloff Commission watched with grim satisfaction as the courts, John Rees, Desmond Tutu, and white liberals did their work of discrediting the South African Council of Churches. On the other hand, were the SACC to be destroyed, the government must know that those millions of dollars expressing the international community's outrage at South Africa would surely create some new instrument by which to advance their purposes. From the government's viewpoint, therefore, it might be preferable to leave a severely tarnished SACC in place. "Better to deal with the devil you know," as one Nationalist member of parliament said to me with a wicked smile.

As the Rees scandal (or the Tutu scandal, as some would have it) was breaking, I talked at length with a church executive who heads an SACC-related program and whom I will call Adams. "I have no doubt that the government is out to destroy the council. They see it as nothing more than the arm of the WCC, and as far as they're concerned that's being in bed with the communist archenemy," Adams says. "I doubt if they're going to use bannings or put anybody in jail at this point; they don't want to create more martyrs." Adams believes the long-term government strategy is to more and more use black leaders to discredit those who claim to speak for blacks. "It's the homelands idea turned upon the churches and liberal institutions, and it could be very effective. I know that there are many blacks who disagree with me. They like the homelands idea, they support separate development, after all they benefit from it. I mean all those people who are leaders in the homelands, they owe everything to the government—their positions, their cars, their airplanes, everything." Adams notes that there are also many black church leaders who benefit greatly from the homelands arrangement. They too like their cars and titles. In the fall of 1985, P. W. Botha was suggesting that blacks in the homelands could be offered "dual citizenship" which would make them citizens of both the independent homeland and of South Africa proper. This, according to critics, would intensify the seductiveness of the government's grand strategy. Pretoria is proposing, that is, that these blacks can have their cake and eat it too, hanging on to homeland leadership privileges while, at the same time, seeming to be "integrated" into a unitary South Africa. If in fact that is the government's design, it fits neatly into the framework of what has been termed Pretoria's "politics of stealth."

According to Adams, the government's goal in dealing with groups such as the SACC is to magnify "the gap between the leadership in the churches and the people in the pew." "The people in the pew have no investment in the council and they have no loyalty to it," he says. Its support base is "artificial" and this makes things like the Rees scandal almost inevitable. "The council has honestly tried to be trusting, especially toward blacks, but sometimes this leads to naivete," he explains. He gives the example of the SACC's program to train blacks in accounting. It turned out that some of the people trained in the program were involved in "out-right embezzlement" of about 30,000 rand belonging to the council.

"When they were caught, they said, 'If you act against us, we will sing and then it will become known that we're not talking about 30,000 but about 250,000 rand or more that has been misappropriated.' " In Adams's opinion, the council, with the best of intentions, made the mistake of defending those who had embezzled. "That's where the trouble started because then it was not just a criminal procedure, but the government set up this commission and it was gazetted with much wider powers to look into every aspect of the council's work." The government's legal rationale, he explains, is that the SACC is a public institution, that the funds of the public are involved, and therefore the government has an obligation to see that the funds are used the way they are supposed to be used.

"We have to face the fact," says Adams, "that most of the member churches do not feel in any way that the council represents them. It is in that sense an alien body. For in-stance, there is almost no support for the program to aid the dependents of people who are in jail. In some of the white member churches especially the people refuse to pray, never mind to pay, for this program. If someone's in jail or under suspicion they say, 'Where there's smoke, there's fire,' and they keep their distance. So it is the Europeans and the Americans who really have an investment in council pro-grams like that."

Adams believes that Tutu has done a good job of "calling the bluff" of the white churches. "In some ways groups like the council and the Christian Institute let the churches off the hook. 'Oh well,' they say, 'we don't need to get involved because the council is doing that.' But now Tutu is saying to the white churches, 'Look, you have your chaplaincy for "our boys" in the South African military; now how about chap-laincy and support for those on the other side, the ANC or

SWAPO [South West Africa People's Organization] or whatever?' " According to Adams, Tutu is saying to the white member churches, "It's your turn to carry the can on this program." And are they starting to carry the can? "No," Adams says sadly.

"Some of us have thought all along that perhaps it would have been better if we had not aimed at building the South African Council of Churches as a massive empire. That is what Steve Biko was always telling us, that institutions are no good unless they belong to the people involved. A smaller council, more closely related to the Christian communities, might have been more effective. But then there was all that money. I don't mean that people acted out of the love of money, although maybe that was there too, but you could see the needs and they were so immense, and then people said here's the money to meet those needs and . . . well, I have no doubt we've made a bundle of mistakes."

Adams discusses the anguish of being a white liberal in South Africa. His own son is a deserter, refusing to answer the military call-up. The government has recently declared, although not yet acted upon, a conscription that would include men up to the age of sixty. "I know I would not answer if the call-up came. It's a matter of witness; so much that we do here is a matter of witness, and you almost have to resist the temptation to ask whether it all does any good." What visibly hurts Adams is the thought that much of the work in which he has been involved has not advanced his most cherished hope for interracial understanding and trust. "It's frightfully complicated," he says in tones on the edge of despair. "How do you avoid being paternalistic, even when you know paternalism breeds resentment? The fact is that in the black community there are not enough trained people to manage their own projects, to manage or to monitor them. And over the years, beginning perhaps in the sixties, there were these progressive white forces and they had access to outside money and the feeling among whites is that they should trust the blacks to whom they give the money. So you don't ask for very close accountability, after all these people are just getting started and we can't expect them to manage a program the way we would, and that too is a kind of paternalism. From the black side, the feeling is that it doesn't matter if a little money is wasted, or even a great deal of money, because, after all, there is plenty more where that came from. And so it went on and on, and here we are."

Battered though it may be, the South African Council of Churches will continue to be a factor in that country. Were it to happen that the council is declared an "affected organization," another organization would be raised up. Raised up, some would say, by God, and that may well be the case. But raised up also by the sheer financial and institutional force of Western opposition to the government of South Africa. Progressive forces in the West can and do support outlawed revolutionary organizations, such as the African National Congress and the South West Africa People's Organization. But they also, and quite understandably, want to channel resources to "change agents" within South Africa. Considering the range of nongovernmental groups within South Africa, the choices are very limited.

A political party such as the Progressive Federal Party cannot receive money directly from foreign sources. Helen Suzman can accept any number of honorary degrees, but she does not need and could not afford to accept money from her admirers abroad. In addition, international progressivists need an institution in South Africa that clearly poses a moral, preferably a religious, challenge to the government. There are, as we have seen, restless and rapidly growing forces within the Dutch Reformed church. But in the view of the World Council of Churches, for instance, the Dutch Reformed church is beyond the pale. Equally important, any suspicion that they are instruments of overseas designs would be fatal to those in the Dutch Reformed church who are working for substantive change. And it would almost certainly be impossible to strike a deal with nine hundred or three thousand or however many there are of the independent churches.

As for progressives in business leadership, they do not need the money and, in any event, it is inconceivable to most antiapartheid activists in Europe and America that corporations could ever be on the side of justice. There are the unions, of course, especially the rapidly growing black unions. But the white unions tend to favor aspects of apartheid, especially "job reservation" for white workers. And the black unions are looking, as David Lewis says, to solidarity with the labor movement in the West. To the extent that tie increases, the determined anticommunism (some call it cold warism) of groups such as the AFL-CIO in America would preclude close association with antiapartheid groups devoted to "the global liberationist struggle." So who is left?

Chief Gatsha Buthelezi is left. He is clearly antiapartheid and obviously in opposition to the present movement. He and his organization, Inkatha, have numerous uplift and development programs which progressives in the West might want to support. But he is also very much his own man, an unreliable instrument for the purposes of others. His accountability is less to a global design than to a constituency of millions of blacks in South Africa, and that cannot be changed. In addition, he has been known to say positive things about free enterprise and the value of a market economy, and he is very negative on divestment and economic sanctions. If that is not enough, he is also suspected of being open to negotiating the full enfranchisement of blacks through some kind of confederation rather than in the standard model of a unitary state. Finally, and perhaps most devastatingly, he is so very and unfashionably tribal. Gatsha Buthelezi is an unlikely recipient of the benison of the progressive West. So who is left now?

The South African Council of Churches and Bishop Desmond Tutu, it would seem—or those institutions and persons raised up in their place.

CHAPTER EIGHT

COLOURED AMBIVALENCE AND THE POLITICS OF REFUSAL

THE category of coloured seems odd to Americans. It is odd. It refers to the more than two million South Africans of "mixed race." In America "colored" was once a polite term for blacks. Our oldest civil rights organization is still called the National Association for the Advancement of Colored People. For a long time in this century "Negro" was the preferred term, before it was succeeded in the late sixties by "Black" with a capital B. If we employ South African terminology, the great majority of blacks in America are in fact coloured.

Nomenclature can be ideologically loaded and most people who write about South Africa are in something of a quandary over what terms to use. Those devoted to the "black consciousness" approach incline to sticking with "black and white." The merit of that usage is that it keeps our eye on the essentially black/white or white/nonwhite dichotomy that dominates South African life. The problem with it is that it obscures very significant differences—culturally, religiously, politically—within the categories of black and white. For ideological reasons one might want to obscure the differences, but it does not make for an acute appreciation of the realities of South Africa. Some writers refer to blacks as "Africans," but that leaves the problem of what to do with the Afrikaner white. Others write about "blacks" and "browns"—meaning by "blacks" all nonwhite tribes (Xhosa, Zulu, Tswana, etc.)

183

and by "browns" the coloured and the Indians (the latter, until recently, also called Asians or Asiatics).

There is no happy solution to the problem. It would be nice to refer to all people in South Africa simply as South Africans, but that is a sentiment that obstructs analysis. If or when it becomes possible to refer to all South Africans simply as South Africans, people will be writing about a dramatically different South Africa. My nonsolution to the problem is to employ the nomenclature most commonly used among the various groups in South Africa. Thus we speak of the coloured.

The coloureds are, as the demographic jargon puts it, a "closed population group." That means that, at least since 1948, few blacks have been classified as coloured and few coloureds have been able to "pass" as white. There is an official Race Classification Board that attends to these matters. Such a monstrosity is required for the maintenance of separate development with its Group Areas Act that designates, according to race and tribe, where people are permitted to live. The coloureds are the "between people" and the line between being black or being white is often genetically elusive. Readers of James Michener's *The Covenant* recall its concluding scene in which a young woman is demeaningly probed by officials checking shade of skin, shape of cuticles, and kinkiness of hair. At the Legal Resources Center in Johannesburg I was told about cases in which children born in hospitals were classified as belonging to a different race from their mothers, and about husbands and wives being denied the right to live together because one or the other had been "reclassified." It is agreed that such bizarre and cruel instances are rare and that they usually get corrected in the end by the plodding bureaucracy. But that they happen at all is a sharp reminder of why so many people view the apartheid idea as a species of madness. In 1985 laws prohibiting sexual relations and marriage across color lines were rescinded. While this was viewed as another step away from apartheid ideology, it was not clear how such "mixed" unions would fare with the mishmash of other racial regulations.

On the origins of the coloured, a government publication says this: "Like the Afrikaners, the Coloured population is indigenous to South Africa, the result of intimate contact between Whites, Khoikhoin and Malayan slaves." That phrases it very delicately—"the result of intimate contact." Today there is almost no cultural link between coloureds and their Khoikhoin roots. Some "black consciousness" proponents might want to revive such a linkage but are at the same time reluctant to accent a tribal connection that might get in the way of the more inclusive category of blackness. In any event, the great majority of coloured people are culturally Afrikaans and are sometimes referred to as brown Afrikaners. (About 6 percent of the coloured belong to a group known as Cape Malays and are mainly Muslim.) As might be expected, the tendency of coloureds is to identify as much as possible with the privileged class, which in South Africa, of course, means to identify with whites. This, in turn, means that a definite prestige is attached to lighter skin. There is no doubt that coloureds, who are predominantly urban, are generally better off than blacks in South Africa. In the western part of Cape Province, coloureds are the largest population group and, until the Nationalist takeover in 1948, often thought of themselves as "almost white." But the triumph of the apartheid idea could not abide that illusion. Several coloured students who now insist upon calling themselves black explain to me with evident passion that they have not turned against the whites, it is the whites who have turned against them. "Forty years ago the whites could have had us as allies, if they had accepted us as part of them, but now it is too late," says Rudi. So much in South Africa is said to be too late.

Unlike all the other population groups, no ethnic memories tie the coloureds to any place other than South Africa. In this sense, they are the archetypical South Africans. At the same time, the large majority of coloureds speak Afrikaans, worship in the Dutch Reformed church, and share with the Afrikaner memories of the frontier and the treks. In this sense, then, the coloureds are disinherited Afrikaners. "The worst of it," a school teacher tells me, "is that we are supposed to like it and to teach the children that." She shows me a section of a primary school text titled "1948—The Dawn of a New Era for the Coloured and Asian People." There is no mention of race classification, group areas, or laws against intermarriage and other "immoralities." There is a note critical of General Smuts because he "revoked his promise," declaring war on Hitler and putting some Nationalist leaders in internment camps. "Of course we don't want to teach this rubbish," she says, "but when they are examined the children must know the 'correct' answers."

Marcia is a successful junior executive with a business firm in Cape Town. In the heart of town she shows me the notorious section called District Six. World-wide publicity made it notorious when in 1966 the government started removing coloureds from District Six because it was in a "whites only" area. "My parents and grandparents and great-grandparents all lived here," Marcia says. "There were more than sixty thousand coloured here, going back to the beginning of the last century. There were whites too, and we always got along." (The government says there were only 800 whites in District Six.) "Then we were told that we had to be removed and they offered my father three thousand rand for our house, a very nice house with three bedrooms," she says. Her father protested and appealed and finally received seven thousand rand for the house but that, Marcia says, was "pitifully inadequate." There was much protesting in connection with the removals, much sitting in front of bulldozers and the such, many wounds, and a few deaths. Marcia and her family now live in Athlone, a flat and dull coloured area outside Cape Town, in a house that "is not nearly so nice."

"What you hate is that people can push you around like

that. District Six belonged to us, not to them," she declares with considerable feeling. "And it's not only apartheid. Apartheid is only the excuse. We lived there twenty years after the Nats came to power, but then somebody had a big development scheme and was going to make a great deal of money, and that's when suddenly we were in the way and had to be removed." The sources of Marcia's bitterness are complex. "I say I am black, but I don't spit on being coloured. I am a coloured person who insists she is black." Some of her friends, who are also in their late twenties or early thirties, tend to discount the coloured dimension too much, Marcia believes. "We are the real South Africans, more than anyone else. We carry the culture and the blood of the two main streams in South Africa. I think that is why the Afrikaner became afraid when we got too close. Apartheid is his way of assuring himself that he is different after all." One resists the temptation to easy psychologizing about love-hate relationships, compensatory aggression, and the such, but conversations with coloured South Africans frequently reveal a palpable and painful ambivalence toward the Afrikaner. Many Afrikaners took it as an ominous sign that coloured youth from Athlone joined wholeheartedly in the petrol bombings and other violence of 1985.

If the bond is irrevocably broken, Marcia has faced up to the consequences. "I am not afraid of revolution. I do not say I want it, but I am not afraid of it." Some of her friends criticize her for being co-opted into the business world. "I tell them that *I* do not take money from the government. Some of them are teachers, and they do. And the students, they receive government money. They say they're doing big things for the revolution, but I tell them they don't *have* to be teachers in government schools." Marcia believes that everybody can help the cause in their own way, no matter how close they are to "the system." "They say I have such a nice car, and I do, but I would be willing to give this car to the revolution if that were necessary. But I don't want them just to expropriate it. I mean they should take into account that it *is* my car. I bought it with money that I earned. I didn't steal it, for goodness' sake!" Marcia tried working in England for a little more than a year. "In London I was discontented all the time, always thinking about South Africa. What if the great thing, the revolution or whatever, happened and I wasn't there!" She confesses that she doesn't know what is going to happen. "I really don't." And then with a great grin, "But I know I want to be on the ground to see how all this unfolds."

If the coloureds are ambivalent about the Afrikaner, the feeling is fully reciprocated. One is frequently told by English speakers that the Afrikaner has more positive feelings toward the coloured than toward the English. Because the coloured are blood cousins, that is one reason given. Because the coloured pose no threat, that is another. Related to the second reason is the fact that the coloured have never defeated and humiliated the Afrikaner. It is not the coloured but the English who will have conquered once again if the Afrikaner is forced to change against his will.

"Although a great deal has been written on the Anglo-Boer war," John Chettle of the South Africa Foundation writes, "one suspects that non-Afrikaners still fail to measure its full impact. It was the Afrikaners' holocaust. It resulted in the death of perhaps 20 percent of the total Afrikaner population of the Transvaal and the Orange Free State, most of them women and children. It ruined their farms and their country. It brought a pastoral unsophisticated, and very private people into contact with the outside world in the most bitter way. Jan Smuts, then a young Boer general, wrote in a letter to his wife in 1901 as Britain tightened its hold on the two conquered Boer republics: 'Our future is very dark—and God alone knows how dark. Perhaps it is the fate of our little race to be sacrificed on the altar of the world's Ideals; perhaps we are destined to be the martyr race.' "

According to Allan Boesak, undoubtedly the most public coloured in South Africa today, the government's new dispensation means simply that "they want company in their dying." As coloureds felt betrayed by Afrikaners after 1948, so now it is the turn of Afrikaners to be betrayed by coloureds. "This is what has hurt many of them," says Boesak, "they thought there was a special relationship between us and now they find out it 'ain't necessarily so.'" In other words, the coloureds have joined up with the world's Ideals on whose altar Afrikanerdom is to be sacrificed. At least that is one version.

It is said that P. W. Botha has a very deep and passionate feeling about the special relationship between Afrikaner and coloured. In a speech in the spring of 1982 promoting the new dispensation, Botha was interrupted by a white heckler who accused him of selling out the Afrikaner to the coloureds and blacks. "If you are not prepared to change places with a coloured person," Botha responded, "you have no case." He continued, "If it is true that whites need the black people and the coloured people, then the converse must be equally true. That is, that the black nations depend upon the stability of whites, and coloureds need the survival of whites to secure their own future. This brings us to the reality of South Africa. We have a choice between the path of prosperity based on cooperation and the path of poverty and regression which will lead to eventual collision." Note that the black nations (plural) need the stability (power) of whites, while, it is implied, the futures of white and coloured are somehow one. It is not very likely that Botha would have told the heckler, "If you are not prepared to change places with a Xhosa, you have no case."

Addressing a National Party congress in Bloemfontein in July 1982, Botha underscores that coloureds "belong to the four Afrikaans religious denominations and 2.2 million coloureds are Afrikaans speaking." (The others speak English.) "The coloureds are not a 'people' (*volk*) in the cultural sense of the word and consist partly of developed, sophisticated communities and partly of still developing communities.

... But these 2.5 million coloureds do not have any political rights—not on any level of government. It is a fact. Whose fault it is, is at this moment not relevant. Blame may be laid on various instances over many years." Determining whose fault it is is not as difficult as Botha implies. As a young Nat politician, Botha himself agitated for withdrawing the franchise from coloureds. But his point today is that coloureds are part of the core reality of South Africa in a way that blacks are not. Here and on numerous other occasions Botha is arguing against his conservative opponents who would create a separate homeland for the White Tribe—and for everyone else, including the coloureds. Botha has frequently called the idea of a coloured homeland "impracticable"; others say it is simply ridiculous.

The reason given for the enfranchisement of coloureds within one South Africa is both moral and pragmatic. Morally, a sense of responsibility is acknowledged for these separated cousins. The *Sunday Times* editorially inquires, "Is Afrikanerdom a biological concept; that is, must membership be confined to those of one particular hue? Or is it a cultural one which can be enlarged to embrace those who sprang from Afrikaner loins, who speak the same language and generally worship the Almighty in the same way, but who in this country are defined as coloured?"[1] A politician who is said to be very close to Botha told me: "The prime minister has always felt very strongly about the coloureds and has often expressed himself on this subject. I don't say there is a guilt feeling about the coloured but there is a strong sense that they have been wronged. . . . He has said that in the long-term there will have to be a dispensation that satisfies the political aspirations of the blacks, but that is not his appointed task. In the years left to him he wants to establish a formula for including the coloureds, and whoever comes next can extend that formula, or find some other formula, for the blacks."

The new dispensation, however, does not only include the coloured, it also includes the Indians. In its first report the constitutional committee of the President's Council that drew up the design said, "The Committee regards the political interests of Whites on the one hand and Coloureds and Indians on the other as reconcilable within a single political system." This logic has been seized upon by critics of the new order. David Bosch, it will be recalled, suggests that the idea of communities that are "necessarily irreconcilable" is incompatible with the gospel, and Allan Boesak makes much the same point. At the same time, the Conservative Party objects to the implied equivalence between coloured and Indian. In the 1983 referendum campaign Treurnicht protested the idea that Indians, who are overwhelmingly Hindu and Muslim, should be part of the government. "We cannot accept that nonbelievers should rule over Christians in a Christian land," he declared.

The inclusion of Indians, it may be argued, gives the lie to the proposition that the new dispensation is much influenced by the Afrikaner's sense of moral responsibility toward the coloured. However deep and complex may be the "special relationship" between Afrikaner and coloured, the new dispensation is, on this view, nothing more than a desperate effort at consolidating forces against the *Swartgevaar.* The Indians feel, perhaps with reason, that they have much to fear from black rule. For the coloured, identification with blacks is a reversal of the historic aspiration of coloureds to identify with whites. For "the people between" it poses the threat of being dragged down—unless, of course, blacks are on a course of inevitable ascendancy to power. Moral considerations aside for the moment, the choice posed by the new dispensation is something of a gamble for coloureds. Put somewhat cynically, do you deal with the devil you know or take your chances on the devil you don't know?

Which is more likely, another twenty or fifty years of white control or black majority rule within, say, ten years? If coloureds do join whites in the new dispensation and then blacks come to power by whatever means, the consequences

191

could be dire for coloureds, as we have heard Bishop Tutu remind his coloured brethren in rather unsubtle manner. On the other hand, the government is able to go ahead with the new dispensation with or without majority coloured support. What does a coloured person have to lose by opposing the new system? If he has political ambitions, he may be denied a seat in parliament or cushy public appointments. But political ambitions can also be satisfied, perhaps better satisfied, in the communal politics outside the formal polity. In any event, opposition carries no great price since during the interregnum one can count on the special relationship between Afrikaner and coloured and, come the black revolution, one has been certified in advance as a friend of the new regime. Such are among the considerations expressed and implied by coloureds in South Africa today.

Andre Brink, the South African novelist, sees irony in the Afrikaner-coloured connection. Brink has great respect for the Afrikaans language. "It's a remarkably exciting language, it's so young and vital. It should represent much more than a political ideology, but Afrikaans has been so inextricably tied to an ideology that when the one goes the other will probably follow." But the coloured also speak Afrikaans. "That would be the only guarantee of the survival of Afrikaans, if either blacks or coloureds went on speaking it. Blacks can be ruled out at this stage. . . . In '76, when the students at the University of the Western Cape [a coloured university] joined in the upheaval, there was a total rejection of Afrikaans there, as the language of the oppressor. But, during the strikes and boycotts in 1980 and last year, there was a marked return to Afrikaans—using it as the language of the revolution! It would be the supreme irony if that was the way it survived."[2]

I N a black country that is ruled by whites, many of the ironies of being coloured are embodied in the person and career of Allan Aubrey Boesak. Born in 1946, Boesak is about five foot seven, light complexioned, a handsome and energetic man with only slight worries about becoming overweight. His manner is engagingly urgent and I find I am not the first to remark that in appearance and bearing he is a little like Andrew Young, the American civil rights leader, UN ambassador, and now mayor of Atlanta. Boesak smiles ruefully at this since Andrew Young is not among his favorite people. "Andy Young did more harm than good when he came here. He talked, talked, talked when he should have listened, listened, listened."

Boesak is student chaplain at the University of the Western Cape. The job he gets paid to do, however, is only a small part of what Allan Boesak does. He is second in command of the large coloured "mission church" of the Dutch Reformed church. In 1982 he was elected president of the World Alliance of Reformed Churches. In Amsterdam, London, Geneva, Stockholm, and New York he is next only to Bishop Tutu in carrying the can, as they say, for international protest against apartheid. (The caustic remark is several times heard that Boesak's problem is that he wants to play Tutu but Tutu insists upon keeping the part for himself.) In South Africa Boesak is a sparkplug of the United Democratic Front, a broad coalition of coloureds, Indians, blacks, and some liberal whites in opposition to Botha's new dispensation. Ed Huenemann, an official of the Presbyterian church in the U.S. who coordinates things African, tells me, "I would not be at all surprised if Boesak turns out to be the first nonwhite prime minister of South Africa." There are some in South Africa— not many but some—who do not find the idea outlandish.

Boesak and I agree to meet at his university office. This is a coloured university, of course. The physical difference from a white university is comparable to the difference one often finds in the U.S. between a major campus of a state university and a campus in the community college system. The University of the Western Cape has the appearance of being built in a hurry, the grounds are unkempt, the faculty offices are small. In sum, it has the feel of being an afterthought on the part of the government. And that, in truth, is what education for nonwhites has often been. Boesak virtually bounces about, introducing me to his colleagues, exchanging niceties with students in the halls. The atmosphere is one of hurried bonhomie mixed with deference, an atmosphere that frequently surrounds a celebrity, and Boesak is undoubtedly a celebrity in the student world of coloured South Africa.

Over these two days I see at least a few of the many sides of Allan Boesak. In an introspective mood, he talks about the hurt he and other coloureds have experienced in being rejected by whites. "I grew up believing that I was really white, and it was only because of some temporary confusion in the laws that this fact had been overlooked." Only the racialist intransigence of white South Africans helped Allan Boesak to understand that the whites were right—Allan Boesak is a black man. He allows that most coloureds have not yet come to this understanding, but he thinks most of the students have, and they are the "wave of the future."

To a meeting of about four hundred students at the university Boesak speaks about democracy. He speaks in Afrikaans with a high-pitched voice that tends to squeak when he becomes impassioned. He passionately affirms a society that is "free and open, joint and just." That expression occurs several times in the course of his half-hour oration. The same Allan Boesak, addressing a white university audience, is asked what he would do if he had the power and he mischievously responds that he would set up an apartheid constitution that would reverse white and black. "Where it now says 'white' I would put in 'black,' and vice versa." It is meant less than half seriously, but the questioning student shouts, "That's what I thought you would do!"

The fact is that Boesak seems uncomfortable when it comes to the specifics of what should be done in South Africa. Those are "insider's questions," he feels, and Boesak does and does not want to be an insider. One side of this ambivalence is spelled out in a speech he gave in Johannesburg against the new constitutional proposals (part of which finally ended up on the Op-Ed page of the *New York Times*): "One ought not to play around with evil. Working within the system for whatever reason contaminates you. It wears down your defenses. It makes easier those rationalizations for staying in. It makes you susceptible to the hidden and not-so-hidden persuasions that are at work in every system. It whets your appetite for power.... What you end up calling 'compromise' for the sake of politics is in actual fact selling out your principles, your ideals and the future of your children."

With the possible exception of the reference to children, it is an expression reminiscent of the student radicalisms of the sixties in America. The question is how to have both purity and power. I ask Boesak if in fact he is not trying to exercise power to dissuade coloureds from cooperating with the new dispensation. "It may be, but it is only the power of persuasion. Of course if you're involved in politics you're dealing with power in some sense, but our politics is the politics of refusal." The phrase "politics of refusal" recurs frequently in Boesak's conversation. It would seem, however, that there are limits to the politics of refusal. Boesak is aware that coloureds might very well refuse his politics of refusal and take part in the new dispensation proposed by the government and overwhelmingly ratified by white voters in 1983. Talking at a time when the government proposals had come out but before they were ratified, Boesak said, "If in fact the coloureds broke with the black community and accepted a role in this system, then I must say that I would in conscience have a very hard time staying in South Africa." Much has happened since then.

As Boesak knew all along, the government is playing with a very strong hand. The political party of coloureds is the Labour Party. While it is scorned by radicals and students who identify with black consciousness, Labour has a solid base in working class and rural coloured communities. Much to Boesak's disgust, Labour endorsed the new dispensation and is now involved in encouraging coloureds to participate in the new system. As Boesak said, "The government can do what it wants, really. They can decide quite arbitrarily what level of participation in the poll signifies coloured acceptance of the new system." He refers to other instances in which the government has recognized black "puppets" who were elected—with less than 6 percent of the black people going to the polls.

In other ways too, events are outstripping the politics of refusal. Given the religio-political mix of South Africa, Boesak's new prominence within the World Alliance of Reformed Churches and within his own church is a power base of significance. In addition, the growing repudiation of apartheid in the Afrikaner churches—a repudiation which it is thought will be ratified officially at the next General Synod in 1986—may make attacking apartheid not very radical, perhaps not even very relevant. Boesak has pondered these contingencies and confesses to being uncertain about what his role should be. He says there is a danger of his "playing to a Western audience" and of coming to believe what that audience wants to hear, but he is determined not to lose touch with what is actually happening in South Africa. In our conversation he remarks almost glumly, "I don't know what I'm supposed to be doing or what people expect of me. I know that I'm not a politician and I have no intention of becoming a politician. But I also know that I am not simply speaking for myself. . . . People ask me to speak for them, the unions ask, the students ask, and I don't see how I can say no."

The unique evil of South Africa, according to Boesak, is not that it is racist. "There is racism in many places around the world. The uniqueness of apartheid lies in its claim to be based on Christian principles," says Boesak. I press him on this. After all, the clearly ascendant view within the Dutch

Reformed church has publicly repudiated the linkage between apartheid and Christian principles. On this view, apartheid must stand or fall purely on its political merits; it may be a stupid and unjust system, as a growing number of Afrikaners also agree, but if no one tries to legitimate it with theological reasoning the question of "heresy" does not arise. To this Boesak responds that the viewpoint which I describe may be on the ascendancy, but it is not so *clearly* on the ascendancy as some people have told me. "We are not just talking about viewpoints and ideas," he says, "we are talking also about praxis." Then, like Naudé and Tutu, he cites the passage, "By their fruits ye shall know them."

As a form of racism, Boesak explains, apartheid continues to be unique because, even if they do not claim to base it on Christian principles, they are Christian people who cannot divorce their practice from their principles. The explanation may seem strained, unless one understands how Boesak and others sympathetic to various forms of liberation theology put together principle and practice. As Boesak has said and written on many occasions, "reconciliation means liberation." Those who are not engaged in the praxis of liberation are in fact engaged in the praxis of oppression. Or, as it was said some years ago, if you are not part of the solution you are part of the problem. It is not enough for whites to say that apartheid is unjust and is unjustifiable by Christian principles. "They must refuse to be part of the system and join others who are liberating themselves from the system," Boesak says with finality.

How liberation is to be achieved and what it might look like when it comes—these are questions on which Boesak tends to be reticent. Violence may be necessary, he believes, "but the question of violence can only be addressed by black people." "Whites have lost the right to talk about violence or nonviolence, except for maybe a very few like Beyers Naudé." Boesak criticizes those who take what he considers a cavalier attitude toward violence. For instance, on the American black

197

liberation theologian Joseph Washington, Boesak writes: "His understanding of people and the nature of violence lacks depth if he holds unreservedly to his premise that a violent revolution in which 'thousands of whites and perhaps millions of blacks' will be killed is the 'quickest and cleanest' way to end racial hatred and effect reconciliation."[3] Boesak is also critical of those who have called for a black Christian nationalism that is, he believes, simply the mirror image of Afrikaner Christian nationalism.

On the second day we are eating at the Mount Nelson in Cape Town. Boesak is the only nonwhite guest I have seen there and he is the object of some veiled but unmistakably hostile stares. He says he rather enjoys that. "In situations like this I always feel like a teacher helping them to be accustomed to the reality of South Africa." We pick up on what liberation might look like. "It must be a totally new social order," he says with feeling. A totally new social order is, of course, a big order. As he elaborates, however, it becomes apparent that a totally new social order is also very ancient. "We have to recapture what was sacred in the African community before the white man came. We have to recapture real community, solidarity, respect for life, all the things the modern world has destroyed."

I ask if there are in the modern world models of what he hopes for. He is not sure, but he mentions Nyerere's experiment in "African socialism" and the Chinese revolution as instances "where the people have really participated and everyone has benefited by change." I mention that I believe there is something of a scholarly consensus today that Tanzania under Nyerere has been a disaster, going from a food surplus nation to one of the most bitterly impoverished in the Third World, and that in China even the government acknowledges that under Mao millions died by starvation and political brutality. Boesak says he has not heard that, but he is not surprised. "There are so many schools of thought about economics and I try not to talk about it in a detailed way," he explains. "What I have said many times is that we have to find our own way, and it has to be an African way. It can't be the capitalism that oppresses people here or the system you have in the U.S. where only the elite benefit from the wealth and it never reaches the masses."

A close friend of Boesak remarks that he has often been worried by Boesak's vagueness when it comes to the specifics of a just social order. "He tends to speak in cliches at times, and I think the fact is he's not very interested in political theory or economics or social structures. I sometimes tell myself that I certainly hope that behind Boesak and others are some boys in the back room doing the homework on the details." The friend says that he is not alarmed by Boesak's sometimes sweeping political pronouncements. "You have to know him—he is truly a loving person." Referring to the fact that Boesak dresses somewhat nattily, the friend says with a smile, "The revolutionary rhetoric may be extreme at times, but you can be sure that Allan is not one of the brown tunic fellows." And I did find it difficult to envision Boesak in the brown tunic of revolutionary fever.

Allan Boesak obviously feels himself to be on more solid ground when he talks about the spiritual and psychological wickedness of apartheid. "In the Christian view, the very essence of love is to overcome separation. But in the apartheid ideology—whether they still say it this way or not—love serves alienation and separation. That means the white person can be a neighbor to the black, he may even sincerely believe that that is his obligation. But the black person cannot really be a neighbor to the white. He does not have the human quality of someone who can help, he is always the object of someone else's help. Being a neighbor, being a helper, is 'for whites only.' " This, it would seem, is Boesak the preacher, not Boesak the politician. That Boesak is not one of "the hard men" of the revolution does not mean that he is soft, only that he intuitively distrusts the extent to which politics can bring about the "totally new social order" for which he yearns.

He knows that the partisanships required of the political actor can too easily overwhelm that healthy distrust.

In Boesak's own experience partisanships have at times imperiled those bonds he wants to affirm. He offers harsh criticism of Dutch Reformed theologians involved in efforts such as *Stormkompass*. They have not gone far enough. He has publicly charged Bishop Tutu with compromise when Tutu says that efforts at dialogue with the Dutch Reformed church should not be abandoned. You do not dialogue with heretics. And, while he has some kind things to say about Chief Gatsha Buthelezi, it is also the case that "Buthelezi is the most dangerous black man in South Africa." That is because Buthelezi wants to revive Zulu nationalism and such a revival undermines "the unity of black consciousness that is necessary to the struggle."

But Boesak the politician allied himself with Buthelezi, Tutu, and some white liberals in campaigning for a No vote in the referendum on the constitutional reforms. A standard argument made was that the new dispensation would "entrench apartheid in the constitution of the country." It was not mentioned that apartheid could hardly be more solidly entrenched than it had been in the old constitutional order. And it was not mentioned that the new dispensation "entrenched" the participation of coloureds and Indians, however inadequate the degree of participation. Even in the unlikely event of a right-wing victory by the Conservative Party, the nonwhites could not constitutionally be removed from government without their consent—a consent it seems they would have no reason to give.

As Boesak made the standard arguments against participation in the new dispensation, I recalled our conversation in the Mount Nelson. "One reason I do not think I could be a politician," he said, "is that politics is very hard on truth. Maybe you have to choose between speaking truth and wielding power, and in that sense I hope I will always be outside the system."

K NOWLEDGEABLE South Africans of diverse persuasions question me sharply on why I pay so much attention to figures such as Tutu and Boesak. There is a strong feeling that they are marginal to the forces that are, for better and for worse, bringing about change in South Africa. As we have seen, Boesak himself says he is determined to remain an outsider even as he works hard at expanding his influence. People such as Boesak and Tutu may be doubtfully significant political actors in South Africa, but attention must be paid because they are so large in the West's perception of South Africa. And the perception of the West is itself such a major political factor in South Africa, thus giving to those who shape that perception an indirect political influence that they are not seen to possess at home. In addition, to the extent that church and politics are interlocked in South Africa, Boesak as churchman becomes also an agent of political change.

"If we break apartheid in the churches," Boesak says, "the whole system must inevitably collapse." This I take to be hyperbole, but there is little doubt that the "moral delegitimation" of apartheid is also potent politics. Boesak's depiction of apartheid as being theologically legitimated by the Dutch Reformed church is, I suspect, mainly for export abroad. When abroad, for instance, he cites Professor Carel Boshoff's theological arguments for apartheid as representative of the Dutch Reformed church when Boesak well knows that Boshoff, whom we met in an earlier chapter, is representative only of the increasingly marginal die-hards in Afrikanerdom. Perhaps this is necessary to sustain the standard international perception of South Africa and, as Boesak says, he is not immune to the temptation of playing to foreign audiences. There is no play-acting, however, in the direct influence that Boesak brings upon the churches in South Africa.

In 1979 Allan Boesak told *Time*, "Black Reformed Christians are tired of being associated with an apartheid church. In four or five years we will have a united church following the tradition of Reformed churches around the world, rejecting all forms of ethnic separation."[4] The announcement may turn out to have been remarkably prescient. In 1977 Boesak had published a book, *Farewell to Innocence*, in which he details his disillusionment with reformist measures. In 1982 Boesak was elected head of the world Reformed movement and returned to South Africa to be defeated only by the slimmest of margins in his bid to become moderator of the coloured *Sendingkerk* (mission church). The person who won by a few votes is in fact the first coloured moderator of the church, and it is said that he was elected because the church wanted to take one big step at a time. Electing a coloured person as moderator was change enough, some thought, without making that person the "radical" Allan Boesak. In addition, there may have been some backlash to a challenge raised to the voting rights of some white ministers. Just a few years ago such a challenge would have been unthinkable, since it was assumed that the *Sendingkerk* was a mere child under the tutelage of the "mother church" in the Dutch Reformed family.

Boesak had made no secret of his determination to have apartheid declared a heresy and to merge the nonwhite churches into an open and multiracial communion. Nonetheless, he was elected assessor, the position of second influence in the church, and it is generally assumed that Boesak's actual influence exceeds that of the moderator. Boesak supporters dominated the synod meeting and succeeded in having the "mother church" accused of "heresy and idolatry" for its support of apartheid. Unless "Mother NGK" formally repudiates apartheid at its 1986 general synod, it would seem that the *Sendingkerk* must break its last ties and go independent, all according to Boesak's plan.

These developments set off a tremor within political Afrikanerdom. They came, after all, precisely at the time when the government was trying to put together a white-brown coalition that could take the lead, allegedly, in moving away from apartheid. Now the *Sendingkerk*, the most venerable and previously reliable institution defining white-coloured relations, was in rebellion. The success of Boesak's plan thus poses a serious problem for the government's grand design. According to Peter Collins, political scientist at the University of Cape Town, that design is "to get together the 'cwichets' with a view to including the 'prurbs' in a coalition able to deal with the problems of South Africa." CWICHET is Collins's acronym for Coloured-White-Indian-Chinese-Et alia. PRURB stands for Permanent Resident Urban and Rural Blacks. If that is the design, Boesak's ecclesiastical strategy could undercut it at its starting point, the coloured-white connection. To be sure, at the beginning of 1984, it appeared that the government could secure coloured support—at least what the government defines as sufficient support—for involvement in the new dispensation. But if at the same time coloured religion is rejecting every vestige of separate development, it cannot help but cast a moral shadow over those sitting in a separate parliamentary chamber labeled "coloured."

A number of white leaders of the Dutch Reformed church tell me that the coloured church will not finally make the break. Pierre Roussouw, ecumenical officer of the church, explains that coloureds and blacks would have too much to lose in dissociating from the mother church. Ministers within the Dutch Reformed "family," for example, receive substantially higher salaries than do coloured and black clergy in other churches. "And, since we don't give theological support to apartheid at present, I believe our synod [in 1986] should be able to make a statement that puts to rest this 'heresy' business once and for all." Professor J. B. O. Oberholzer, the Old Testament scholar, explains to me at his home near Pretoria that complete separation "would be the worst possible thing for coloureds and blacks." "Having separate churches," he says, "was for their sake and is in keeping with the Reformation principle that the gospel should be preached and people should worship in their own language and culture."

But Oberholzer and others are talking about an originating rationale that is, it would seem, no longer in tune with the thinking of nonwhites in the Reformed family.

Boesak has heard all these arguments and gives them little weight. "They are afraid," he tells me, "because they know that a new church could in fact be larger than their own. If the black [including coloured] Reformed and maybe the Indians and a significant number of whites came together, we would be *the* Dutch Reformed church in South Africa, and we would be recognized as such internationally. And here it would be a clear statement—a political statement too—that Reformed Christians have nothing to do with the whole idea of some people being irreconcilable." Boesak may not end up as prime minister, but there are some people who think he would be a logical choice as moderator of *the* Dutch Reformed church in South Africa.

By the time of "the troubles" of 1984–85, Allan Boesak had been established as a very major actor on the South African scene. Serving as a "patron" of the United Democratic Front, he was also the UDF's chief spokesman. UDF is a loose affiliation of some six hundred organizations, ranging from substantial unions to block associations with ten members or fewer. It is generally viewed, by both critics and supporters, as the instrument of the outlawed African National Congress within South Africa. In fact, and as may be necessary with an organization walking the fine line between reform and violent revolution, nobody seems to be quite clear about how UDF makes decisions, or if indeed it has anything like a decision-making body. At least on some occasions it appears that Allan Boesak *is* the leadership of UDF.

UDF was the banner under which Indian and coloured opposition to the new dispensation was most visibly advanced. As mentioned earlier, the government did not need to ask the Indian and coloured communities whether they wanted to participate in the new three-chamber parliament. Rather, the government simply called an election for Indian and coloured members, with the idea that anyone who voted was in fact approving of the new dispensation. As it turned out, only about 20 percent of the eligible Indian and coloured voters took part in the election. Needless to say, this did not prevent the government from going ahead with the implementation of its design. But the very low vote greatly enhanced the status of UDF and Allan Boesak who were then positioned as the authentic opposition to the minority that had elected to "collaborate" with Pretoria.

Boesak's star was briefly dimmed when he was accused of a sexual liaison with a white coworker. Evidence supporting the charge was disseminated by the police who, it is said, saw a golden opportunity to discredit Boesak. Boesak himself did not deny the accusation and, for a time, this seemed to throw into question his ministerial status. After a process of hearings, however, the church reaffirmed Boesak's ministry, and today his standing as a political actor, if not as an ecclesiastical leader, is greatly enhanced. "No matter what he steps in, Allan always comes up smelling like roses," says a friend approvingly. A critic of Boesak in the PFP puts it differently: "There's something about Boesak that fascinates people, precisely because he doesn't fit into the categories. He's always crossing the lines. It begins with his being coloured, then the business of sex with a white woman, it all fits into the way he provocatively violates the way South Africans think the world should be ordered."

In August 1985, Boesak announced that he would lead a mass march on the prison where Nelson Mandela is incarcerated. Shortly before the march, Boesak was arrested by the police, and thus his name is added to the long roll of imprisoned martyrs. (After three weeks he was released, but his legal status is still very much in question.) The same friend remarks, "Allan loves the high wire act, and the more he pushes the possible to its limits, the more people love him. Four years ago, even two years ago, I would not have said that Allan or any coloured man could have gained this degree of influence. But I've been wrong before, and in this case I think it's not despite the fact that he's coloured but because he's coloured. It all gets back to the ambivalent feelings that Afrikaners and coloureds have about each other."

ALLAN Hendrickse is a Congregational minister and a leader of the Labour Party. A big, swarthy, affable man with flowing black hair, Hendrickse has very mixed feelings about Boesak and about the choices open to coloured South Africans. "We had Allan speak at my church and there were more than a thousand people there. We had to bring in chairs. I've told Allan many times, this is where his audience is, not overseas and not in the political arena." Hendrickse has reason to be unenthusiastic about Boesak's involvement in the political arena. Labour came out in support of the new dispensation and as a consequence became the object of Boesak's wrath. "I know what Allan means when he says he is black, we're all black here, all of us who aren't white. But," Hendrickse continues, "we're also coloured and I don't think we should even try to forget that. It is a matter of history, of personal relationships and experiences. I have an uncle here who passes for white. That doesn't make him or me any better; that would be racism. But it isn't racism to say it matters, to say our experience in this way is different from that of the blacks. But it is almost impossible to say that to some people without being misunderstood, and I'm afraid Allan sometimes panders to the people who want to promote misunderstanding."

Hendrickse is skeptical about "the politics of refusal." "Our people have been working at protest politics for decades," he says, "and now it's time to go beyond that. . . . We live in a massively unjust society, and we'll never live in a perfect society, and as long as it's not perfect there will always be a market for people who have nothing to say but no, no, no. But I'm not one of those people," Hendrickse declares. He knows it is possible to be compromised by "working with a changing system to change the system more." When the President's Council that framed the constitutional proposals was formed Hendrickse was one of the first people asked to serve on it. "Someone from Botha's office called and the first thing he told me after asking me to serve was that members would get 2,400 rand per month. I was deeply offended by that and I refused." (The salary of a Congregational minister, he says, is about 300 rand per month.) "But I am not blind to the fact that politics is about benefits—not just benefits for leaders but for the groups that make them leaders. There's nothing immoral about a group advancing its own interests if it doesn't hurt anyone else. I know Allan looks at it differently, but I wonder if he doesn't forget that the students at Western Cape and the World Alliance do not represent the coloured people of this country."

And so we are returned to yet another variation of the debate over the relative merits of working "inside" and working "outside." Coloureds are once more experiencing the pains of being "the people between." One argument is that the new dispensation offers obvious benefits for the coloureds. Usually joined to this is the argument that coloureds who work inside will be able to press aggressively for opening the system to blacks as well. ("Tell me you're going in to work for your own people and I'll respect you; tell me you're going in to fight for blacks and I'll call you a hypocrite," a black told Franklin Sonn, the coloured leader.) Against participating in the new dispensation is the argument that it really offers coloureds nothing more than they had until 1953 when the franchise was taken away from them. "At the very best, it puts us back to square one," a coloured teacher told me. While the new dispensation is designed to assure white control, the difference from 1953 is that now there are coloureds who believe that black rule is coming, and coming sooner rather than later. It could be a fearful thing to be caught on the wrong side of the revolution.

Allan Hendrickse and other members of the Labour Party

have now taken their seats in the coloured chamber of the new parliament. Allan Boesak remains outside practicing the politics of refusal. The inside Allan, it is said, has been co-opted. The outside Allan, it is also said, still has not bid "farewell to innocence." It is hard to be a people between.

> ## *"Economics is the engine, politics the caboose."*

CHAPTER NINE

THE INDIANS OF NATAL

WE have already sampled something of what it is like to be English in Durban, the urban center of the province of Natal. In his brilliant *Waiting for the Barbarians,* South African novelist J. M. Coetzee has his easy-going imperial agent on the frontier come up against a brutal no-nonsense colonel sent out from the capital to deal with an alleged onslaught from the barbarians. The agent-narrator comes to realize that "I was not, as I liked to think, the indulgent pleasure-loving opposite of the cold rigid Colonel. I was the lie that Empire tells itself when times are easy, he the truth that Empire tells when harsh winds blow."[1] In the view from Afrikaner Pretoria, the English of Natal can indulge the lie of easy empire. The Afrikaner, on the other hand, must deal with the harsh winds of a civilization under attack. In Natal, according to this version, it is possible to play around with sundry speculations about how to accommodate competing sectors in a pluralistic society. In the rest of the republic, however, accommodations take second place to confrontations of life-or-death consequence. That is one version.

In Natal one gets a different story. This story is that the winds are not necessarily less harsh in Natal, nor is empire easier, but there may be flexibilities that enable Natal to "model" patterns of change applicable to all of South Africa. These flexibilities result from the peculiar mix of populations in Natal and, most particularly, from the special relationship between Natal and the homeland of Kwazulu. "Natal-

Kwazulu" is the term commonly used in speculations, proposals, schemes, and dispensations for this large part of the Republic of South Africa. During the American constitutional period it was said that every citizen went about carrying in his hip pocket his own constitutional design for the republic. It is a little like that in South Africa today, and most especially is it like that in Natal. There is a "Lombard Plan" for Natal-Kwazulu and there are the proposals issued by the "Buthelezi Commission," an enterprise set up by the Kwazulu legislature, and there are numerous variations on numerous variations. Our attention at the moment is not on the details of the possibilities debated but upon the peoples of Natal-Kwazulu, with particular attention to the Indian population. Later we will focus on the blacks there, looking very closely at their remarkable leader, Chief Gatsha Buthelezi (who has already entered our narrative at several points—so unavoidable is his presence in any serious discussion of South Africa).

There are about 5.8 million people in Natal-Kwazulu. Of these more than 4.2 million are Zulu speaking. So Zulus make up 74 percent of the population. With 670,000 people, the Indians are the second largest group. There are 653,000 whites in the region and 70 percent of them are English speaking. Afrikaans-speaking whites account for 2.7 percent of the total population of the area, so it is understandable that they feel somewhat lonely. Moreover, Afrikaners tend to be on the farms near the edges of Natal-Kwazulu and in some of the dispensations proposed for the area it is suggested that they might feel more comfortable if they are counted in with the neighboring areas of the Transvaal or Orange Free State where Afrikaners predominate. There is also a relatively small number of coloured in Natal-Kwazulu, and of course in the 1983 Botha dispensation their political fortunes are closely tied to the Indian population.

In sum, the quest for a social and political "accommodation" in Natal-Kwazulu is essentially a process involving a large Zulu majority and very sizeable minorities of English-speaking whites and Indians. The numbers are important of course. Also important are the enormous social and economic disparities between the groups. For example, more than 90 percent of the whites and 85 percent of the Indians are fully urbanized. Only 22 percent of the blacks are urbanized—and that chiefly on the margins and at the lower economic rungs of the white-Indian establishments.

The great majority of Indians in South Africa live in Natal, and mainly in the metropolitan area of Durban. That makes this part of the country unique. The great majority of whites are English speaking. That adds to the uniqueness. Almost all the blacks are Zulus and identify themselves as such under the leadership of Gatsha Buthelezi. That clinches the uniqueness. In this light we can understand why some claim that Natal-Kwazulu is the laboratory in which South Africa might find a "breakthrough formula" toward a democratic and nonracialist society. By the same token, others say that any plan that might work in Natal-Kwazulu would be largely irrelevant to the rest of South Africa.

To complicate matters a bit more, still others say that Cape Province, especially Western Cape, with its coloured majority and White English political culture, also represents an opportunity for some breakthrough formula. But the Cape does not have a black population unified as it is unified in Natal-Kwazulu. Further, when one hears people talking about how Natal-Kwazulu and the Cape are both "exceptions," it is usually an English white who is talking. And the implication, one suspects, is that the problems of the country could readily be resolved were it not for the Afrikaner's South Africa with its doubtfully legitimate government in Pretoria. But enough of such complexifying. Our concern at the moment is with Natal-Kwazulu and the Indians there.

Sometimes the term Asian is used rather than Indian. That is because there are a few Chinese in South Africa. But the usual term now is Indian and for all practical purposes Indian means people from the Indian subcontinent. They came from 1860 to 1911, the first group as indentured laborers to work the sugar fields of Natal and the second group as merchants and entrepreneurs. Indians whose ancestors came with the second and more "respectable" migration still remind you of that fact today. Since all Indian immigration was stopped by South Africa in 1913, almost all Indians living there today are native-born South Africans. Indians are the majority population of Durban and are viewed, especially by blacks, as very affluent. The government reports that there are more than 12,000 Indians who make more than fifty thousand rand per year (compared with 83,000 whites and 32,000 coloured in that income category). One is not as frequently reminded that, although there is a large middle class, there are also many Indians who are very poor. Nonetheless, even the very poor Indian is likely to be better off at present and in prospect than are the majority of rural blacks in the surrounding areas of Kwazulu.

The relationship between Indian and black is delicately described as uneasy. In 1949 racial rioting broke out in Natal and 138 Indians were left dead. The scar has never healed. Amichand, a student radical of the Natal Indian Congress is eager to have me understand that "It was not a thing between the blacks and us."

In this telling of it, 1949 was but one of many instances in which the white oppressor stirred up one sector of the oppressed to attack another. "It is the same thing they always do," Amichand says. "It is what the government want us and the so-called coloureds to do for them now."

Many Indians may not share that view of how it happened but they do not forget what happened in 1949—black wrath turned on the Indian. Nor will it be forgotten that in the summer of 1985 it happened again. The consequences were not so lethal, and some blacks from Inkatha opposed others who were attacking Indians and their property, but 1949 nonetheless seemed very contemporary. "We never forget that underneath they hate us. We have it and they want it," an Indian small businessman tells me in a tone suggesting that he is stating the self-evident. Whatever may be the usual resentments of the "have nots" against the "haves," an additional reason for black resentment of Indians is that the Indians, unlike the coloureds, are living on land that once belonged to blacks. Between blacks on the one hand and whites and coloureds on the other there can be and is a lively debate about who was where first. With respect to Indians there is no such debate; however mean their circumstances when they came, they have clearly established themselves in an area that had been traditionally black.

1949 retains its ominous symbolic importance also because Gatsha Buthelezi and other Zulu leaders have from time to time reminded Indians of their vulnerability. When, for instance, Buthelezi says that Indian support for Botha's constitutional reforms would have "grave consequences," he does not need to become more specific; the Indian ear hears "1949." In truth, Indians do not require such regular reminders in order to feel a bit queasy about the prospect of black majority rule. They are painfully conscious of what has happened to Indians elsewhere under black rule—in Nyerere's Tanzania and, most particularly, in Uganda under the bizarre and bloody reign of Idi Amin.

Students of Third World development have frequently remarked the similarity between Indians in Africa and the overseas Chinese in places like Hong Kong, Singapore, and Indonesia. As the overseas Chinese have been called "the Jews of Asia," so the Indians are often referred to as "the Jews of Africa." It is an acknowledgment of their industriousness, but most Indians seem not to welcome the compliment. "Whatever goes wrong," the same small businessman tells me, "we will be the lightning rod for all the anger. It is certain that nobody has cause to love us except ourselves." (It strikes me that I have heard from leaders of every group in South Africa the same statement, namely, that they perceive themselves as resented and unloved by members of other population groups. We should not be surprised perhaps, but it suggests something of the sadness of South Africa. In conversations with Afrikaners and blacks it is implied that in being feared there is some compensation for not being loved.)

Indians have not passively gone along with apartheid. At the beginning of the century Gandhi acted on his dream here in South Africa and today the Natal Indian Congress claims to be his heir. A cluster of small buildings, called the Phoenix farm, is maintained as a memorial to Gandhi. It is now sandwiched between a large Indian township on one side and a black township on the other, and when people refer to Phoenix they do not mean Gandhi's experiment in interracial harmony but the ranks upon ranks of two-story cinderblock houses that make up the Indian township. In the violence of the summer of 1985 the small building which had been a shrine to Gandhi was smashed and the pieces carried away by black youths. The desecration was a powerfully depressing portent of things to come, or so many feared.

Jayaram N. Reddy represents the spirit of those who are not about to give in to depression. Reddy is an energetic, almost frenetic, man, determined to come across as a no-nonsense realist. In the new dispensation there will be Indians and coloureds in the national cabinet, and Reddy is sometimes mentioned as a likely candidate. He has been known to mention the possibility himself. He is chairman of the New Republic Bank, an institution which others tell me was set up by English whites in order to solicit the business of Indians. He also has his own shipping agency, and we meet in the modest offices of that firm. Reddy begins by noting that I have undoubtedly been hearing an awful lot of rot about South Africa and he implies that he is just the man to straighten out the misguided critics of that besieged land.

"You hear all the time about politics, but economics is the engine. Politics is the caboose. We've got it exactly the wrong way in South Africa, and that is a large part of our problem," says Reddy between sniffs of snuff picked from an elegant box. Reddy is of a darker hue and refers to himself and other Indians as "black," only occasionally using the term Indian. "Is there injustice? Yes, surely, but who agrees on what justice means? We have a situation in which the white man makes one rand and the Indian makes 80 cents and the black makes 25 cents, but at least everybody is making something. Would it be better if we destroyed the whole system and then nobody would be making anything?" Reddy declares himself for change, however: "The argument for change must be based on economic common sense. The National Party should not argue about what justice demands and so forth. No, it should appeal to the logic and interest of whites. They need a reliable and expanding labor market as much as other people need work. So the Nationalists should say to the whites, 'Look here, if you're building a house and the chap is not there to bring the bricks, or if you're making bricks and the chap is not there with the cement, or if you're making cement and the chap is not there with whatever you need—well, somewhere down the line, if you run out of labor, nothing can be done and you're not going to have your house.' "

At one point Reddy says there is not much difference between the English and the Afrikaner, "They're all whites." But then it becomes clear that he thinks the English have a much greater respect for what he calls common sense. The English let groups interact pretty much along the lines of economic interests, "But then the Afrikaner said, 'Now we have to put things in order. We'll show you how it should be done.' And so we got all these laws and rules about group classification and group areas and other things that are contrary to economic common sense," Reddy explains with some passion. Even then, however, the Afrikaner could have done it differently. "If Verwoerd had moved with real decisiveness and speed, they could have set up the homelands and the apartheid scheme and South Africa would be home free today. But, no, they dithered and compromised. Part of a homeland was somebody's farm, so he got to his member of parliament and they chopped that part out, and this was repeated a thousand times and the whole program was in a shambles, and now it is too late."

Reddy so admires decisiveness that he seems almost to regret the failure of Verwoerd and the Nationalists. Not really, however, for as much as he admires decisiveness he admires the free market more. He talks about a meeting of the International Monetary Fund where he saw "the humiliation of black nations who came with their hats in their hands, looking for another handout." "I have no political ambitions, but if I can help it that will never happen here," he says with considerable force. "We have a First World economy, a world class economy, but we have a Third World geography and we could end up with a Third World economy. If I were minister of finance, we would only spend what we had to spend. These other countries, they spend and they spend and then they look around to see where they're going to get the money." I comment that Reddy and Reagan would get on well together, and he thinks that is probably true.

Like many businessmen in South Africa, Reddy believes that the West will finally not back violent change toward majority rule because the West does not want Southern Africa to become another "economic basket case" with fifty million or more people added to the global dole. Interestingly, some blacks who endorse violence as a legitimate way to majority rule assured me that the same consideration works in their favor. That is, the West and powerful economic interests within South Africa will effectively restrain those reactionary whites who would, Samson-like, destroy the country and themselves rather than give in to black rule. So "economic common sense,' as Reddy calls it, can cut in several directions.

Reddy believes that if or when it comes to black rule, the Indian can still prosper. "The black man is basically a capitalist. Why else would he get three wives so he can buy a house?" Another doubtful evidence offered for the allegedly capitalist propensities of blacks is that black merchants are notorious for "shortweighting" their customers. This is an interesting charge in reverse since it is commonly said by non-Indians that the Indians have grown rich by short-weighting. Maybe in a more serious vein, Reddy says that the Indians will not be kicked out the way they were from other countries under black rule. "Here we are not all in business. There are many Indians—many, many—who are workers, lorry drivers, even sweeping the floor. And then too, remember that we are not the primary objects of resentment here the way the Indians were in East Africa. The black man may resent the fact that an Indian has a building of five stories, but then he quickly looks next door and he sees the whites have a building of twenty-five stories." Reddy makes the additional point that has become familiar in conversations with Afrikaners—"We have nowhere to go." I mention that it is said of some Indian leaders that they have one foot in South Africa, one foot in India, and their bank account in Switzerland. "That might have been true for some people of the previous generation," says Reddy, who is about fifty years old, "but for us both feet are in South Africa." Not only his feet but also his heart and mind, as he makes clear in discussing with pride the economic and military strength of South Africa.

While on the question of generations, he has strong views about student radicals. "Why should we be upset? Maybe it is the business of students to be radical," he shrugs his shoulders in a show of tolerance. "They are just out of high school and they don't know. Pretty soon they will realize that they are not going to solve all the problems of the world, certainly not as students. And when they stop being students, they'll be as interested as anyone else in making money." I allow that that may have been his own experience, but are there not now some genuinely new factors, such as the foreseeable prospect of majority rule? He responds that indeed the situation is rapidly changing, but in his view the changes are positive. Indians and coloureds will now wield power within the central government, thus correcting an "absurd exclusion" of long standing. There is no doubt, he believes, that the new dispensation is provisional and that "if the interests of the several groups are safeguarded" black participation and even a black head of state pose no great problem. We end where we started: "If the political caboose stays on the track and follows the economic engine, this country will be the hope of Africa. It already is the hope of Africa."

THIS evening there is a dinner at the gracious home of Mr. E. M. Moosa. The house is somewhat sprawlingly situated on a hillside looking down on the lights of the Indian township and what I am told is a fragment of Kwazulu. Physically it is Californian, but the feel is unmistakably Natal. Mr. Moosa is the head of Trueart Furniture Sales (Pty.) Ltd. According to the firm's letterhead, the directors are E. M. Moosa, I. E. Moosa, and A. E. Moosa. I am informed that Indians are very family oriented. Trueart also controls Francisco Investments (Pty.) Ltd., Haven Properties (Pty.) Ltd., Investrite Investments (Pty.) Ltd., Nuera Stores (Pty.) Ltd., and a half dozen other enterprises. Mr. Moosa is not embarrassed to have it known that he is doing rather well. The house is approached by a winding road and at the gate is a private guard in khaki. He is black.

In addition to the extensive Moosa family, there are other guests, including a medical doctor, an Indian member of the President's Council (the group formally responsible for the constitutional reforms), and a professor of Islamic studies from the university. All are Muslim, although the professor is the only one who makes a strong point of the matter. Mr. Moosa presides with palpable self confidence and pride, both as paterfamilias and as a figure in the community. Yes, he says, the Group Areas Act and other aspects of the system are an abomination. Because of racial restrictions on residential areas he has had to move three times and each time "my good fortune has been diminished." But he explains this with an apparently tolerant spirit. "If you work hard you can do well. I have not been doing too badly," he says with a sweep of his hand around the comfortable living room.

At table Mr. Moosa favors us with his views on what might be done about the blacks. "They are really not good at business, not good at all, they have no head for it. I believe that what we must do is help them to concentrate on farming; they are very, very good at agriculture," he says. In an act of seeming temerity, another guest interjects, politely, that this is not the case at all, that it is well known that the Zulu in particular detests farming, believing that it is work barely fit for women. Mr. Moosa takes this with good grace, saying that he was not aware of that but was glad to stand corrected. I am astonished that an obviously intelligent man who has lived sixty or more years in the heart of Natal could be ignorant of what everyone agrees is an elementary cultural fact about the Zulu nation. (I had been similarly astonished in an earlier conversation with a well-known Afrikaner writer who asserted with confidence that most blacks in South Africa are Roman Catholic and that blacks almost never speak their tribal languages when white people are around. I wonder to myself how he could be so ludicrously wrong. Instances such as these underscore the closed nature of life within the several population groups and make one exceedingly skeptical about the claim frequently made that "we understand our situation best.")

At Mr. Moosa's table the mood changes. The professor of Islamic studies opines that America will be of no help to the Indians, no matter what happens. The reason is that "America is always on the wrong side in any issue involving Muslims." This is true in the Middle East, Ethiopia, Indonesia, and everywhere else. Mr. Moosa suggests that the Indians will have to be like the Jews and look out for themselves. "The Jews have a good nose for trouble, they sense when the storm is coming, and many of them are getting out now." This he believes is particularly true of the young men who face the prospect of being conscripted, and it contributes to what everyone present agrees is a "braindrain" from South Africa.

As to Indians and conscription, I am told that there are five or six hundred Indians in the South African navy and some who are fighting on the borders with the army. There is no agreement among the guests as to whether this is a good or bad thing. "It shows that we're part of South Africa and willing to do our share," says one. "Why should we fight when we do not have all our rights?" asks another. (Remarkably enough, there are also tens of thousands of blacks in South Africa bearing arms in the military and police force. They take an oath of allegiance to a country in which they technically are not citizens. A radical black student tells me, "It's simple, they are mercenaries," but their status strikes me as being rather more ambiguous than that.)

Mr. Moosa and his friends are, like Mr. Reddy, dismissive of student radicalism in the Indian community. "I hire people to be salesmen or managers or engineers; nobody hires somebody to be a radical. So you see they get out and make money like everybody else," says Mr. Moosa. He has a great affection for the common sense of Jews. Years ago, when his father began the business, the whites would advertise that whites should do business with whites, not with Indians. But the Jews, he says, looked for the best deal and today he does 80 percent of his business with Jews. "There are some stupid Indians," he says with disgust, "who think there is more prestige in buying their furniture and other goods from whites." On other scores too, Indians might learn from the Jews. The Jews, for example, understand that change can work in their own interest. "Some people are alarmed by the unions, especially the black unions, but I say we should not worry. Now you see union leaders driving their Mercedes, and soon they will have to be keeping out the unemployed in order to protect their union jobs, so everybody has a stake in doing business," he concludes with a chuckle of satisfaction.

There are different views on how Indians should calculate what is in their own interest. The member of the President's Council relates a meeting with former prime minister John Vorster. "He told us, 'I will give you power sharing where it counts, in the cabinet.' " This, Mr. Moosa's guests are told, is important because the cabinet in fact has more power than the legislature; the cabinet determines what will be proposed and what will become law. "I asked Vorster if this meant an Indian could be state president, and he said that would be no problem at all," we are told. I listen as this Indian politician goes on at some length about his dealings with Pretoria and am struck that blacks are not mentioned in this discussion. Indians and coloureds, mainly Indians, are talked about. There is nothing said about excluding blacks, it is just that they are not mentioned. (I raise, gently I hope, Allan Hendrickse's point about some members of the President's Council serving because of the money involved. This Indian member says the salary is about thirty thousand rand, plus a number of perks, "But I make three times that much in my business. I don't need the President's Council. Politics is taking time away from making money.")

If or when "the crunch" comes, with whom will Indians be aligned? Mr. Moosa says right off, "With the whites, of course, not with the blacks." Others say that should be qualified, that every effort should be made to reach some accommodation with the blacks, or else it will be "1949 multiplied by a hundred." Nonetheless, all agree that Indians feel much safer with whites—even if it means being under whites— than they would with blacks in power. The evening has been long and the conversation has ranged over myriad topics. One is left with the impression of a courteous group of people with enormous good will, who chiefly want to be left alone to attend to their families and their business. There are indications of ignorance about others and of indifference to the plight of others, but there is no maliciousness in it. Mr. Moosa and his family and friends seem quite innocently pleased with themselves. They want to exhibit their successes, not their wounds or their anger, yet at the same time they want it understood that they are not at all satisfied with the present system. There is particular dissatisfaction with the Group Areas Act that restricts Indian residence and owning of property. I do not mention to this group that white and black critics of the bourgeois Indian community claim that the only reason Indians are so opposed to the Group Areas Act is that it prevents them from buying up all kinds of white land and making a bundle out of it. Had I mentioned it, however, I suspect that Mr. Moosa and his friends would not have been offended. They seem to agree with Dr. Johnson that a man is never so innocently employed as when he is busy making money.

O NLY about 20 percent of the Indian population is Muslim. About 70 percent is Hindu and 10 percent Christian. At least those are the standard figures given. A young Hindu lawyer who says he has strong leanings toward Christianity tells me that the Muslims are more pragmatic, more open to compromise. The Hindu, on the other hand, must do what is morally correct since he believes that he could jeopardize his place in his next incarnation. Others propose a theory almost opposite to that, saying that the Hindu is less interested in moral justice since this present life is but the ephemeral appearance of reality. Professor G. D. L. Schreiner of the University of Natal served as chairman of the Buthelezi Commission and has overseen extensive survey research on the attitudes of various groups. He is not convinced that the Hindu-Moslem-Christian factors are very pertinent to Indian political attitudes. He is convinced by the evidence that Indian students are more radical in their attitudes than other students. How important this may be is another matter.

Schreiner is a great bear of a man with a magnificent white beard. In our discussion we are joined by several of his colleagues at the university, and it is evident that Schreiner is the most liberal of the group. But his is a liberalism of a complicated sort. He believes, for instance, that it would be a mistake to overestimate the impact of Indian student radicalism. He agrees that the Indians "are a tightly knit community." Radicalism of various types is nothing new, but it tends to be short lived. "Culture, family, career—all these things soon draw the students back into the mainstream of the community," he says. A more important finding, according to Schreiner, is that students of all groups tend to be more radical the more education they have. He notes—and I take it he is troubled by this—that Zulu students with more schooling identify themselves less as Zulu and tend to be much more critical of Gatsha Buthelezi. The Buthelezi Commission Report is seven volumes and well over a thousand pages chock full of such survey research data which are, needless to say, amenable to myriad interpretations.

One interpretation that attributes more to the "religious factor" is offered by Professor Gerhardis Oosthuizen of the University of Durban. Oosthuizen has been studying religious and cultural change in South Africa for decades, and his picture of the Indian community indicates much more transition and turmoil than Mr. Moosa and his friends would suggest. The Group Areas Act, says Oosthuizen, is hardly just a slight inconvenience; it has had a profoundly disruptive effect upon the Indian community. For instance, more than 300,000 Indians were uprooted and relocated in the Indian township of Chatsworth, twenty-five kilometers south of Durban. The disruption has been especially severe for Hindus. His studies indicate that the Hindu percentage of the Indian population has dropped from 72 to 62 in just the last ten years. In the same period, the percentage who are Christian has jumped from 8 to 12.5. "There are almost no Muslim converts to Christianity. In all my experience, I do not think I could document more than seven Muslims becoming Christian. If you say 120 times a day that there is no God but Allah and Mohammed is his prophet, it makes you disinclined to convert."

The Christianization of the Hindu population is dramatic and, he believes, growing still. In the original nineteenth-century Indian immigration, 2.5 percent of the Indians were Christian. In 1960 it was 7.6 percent. "So today's 12.5 percent means that in the last few years there has been as much Christian growth among Hindus as took place in the hundred years that went before that," says Oosthuizen. "The growth is almost all in the Pentecostal churches, not in the so-called classic churches. Anglican and Methodist membership among Indians has actually declined and the Dutch Reformed spend substantial amounts on missionary work but have little to show for it, perhaps two thousand Indian members."

Why the Pentecostal growth? "Their version of the Christian message is so very simple. 'Jesus Saves,' 'Jesus Heals,' and so forth. There is secularization, uprooting, the breakdown of the family, all these things, and the Hindu finds powerful compensation in these tightly knit Pentecostal churches," he explains. A big factor, he believes, is that Hinduism is so very complex and very few of its putative devotees understand much about it. In any event, communal disintegration is a fertile climate for fundamentalist Christianity. He notes the similar development among some Afrikaners, even in the affluent white suburbs. While the Afrikaner Pentecostals are associated with the Apostolic Faith Mission which has its roots in Denmark, the Indian Pentecostals are more along American lines, according to Oosthuizen.

"The Muslim is semitic and more straightforward, just the opposite. Hinduism is *ahimsa* and *dharma* and a host of other complexities, not only of religion but of culture, and it seems to suggest that all is illusion. In addition to all that, I suspect that many people, especially the young people, are thinking it doesn't work very well," Oosthuizen says. "If you go to the great Hindu festivals, and I do, there is a conspicuous absence of young people between fifteen and twenty-five. These festivals have the tone of something in decline, dying, trying to hold on to the past." Yet Oosthuizen notes that Gandhi and other Indians who have "taken hard stands for what they believe to be justice have almost always been Hindu." "You do not find many Muslims in that category," he adds. He is not sure why that should be.

As for student radicalism among Indians, "the parents tend to be more relaxed about it." "For the blacks that kind of radicalism has a more immediate crunch point—it may mean their children are going over the border to fight on the side of the liberation forces against South Africa. That kind of consequence is not there for the Indian; his children are not going to go across the border." As we have heard the coloured described as "the people between," so Oosthuizen and others also describe the Indian. "The black man has a powerful sense of direction. No matter how long it takes, blacks believe, rightly or wrongly, that the future belongs to the black man. I think many, maybe most young Indians think that too. So the Indian has to play all sides. He wants to compensate for the privileges of Indians in the past, and he may feel so uneasy about that that he overcompensates. But most of all he wants a certificate from the blacks that he was on the right side before the revolution came. Getting a certificate from the blacks—that is mainly what student radicalism is about in this country.

"For the Indian this is terribly important. He cannot forget what happened to Indians in other parts of Africa when the revolution came. He knows that blacks here call him 'the black Englishman,' that his long hair and English language are conspicuous. He tells himself that in Uganda the Indians were 1 percent of the population and controlled 18 percent of the economy while here Indians are 3 percent of the country and control about 3 percent of the economy, but that's little comfort if you make the comparison with the black situation. And the Indian knows that that's the comparison blacks are making."

Oosthuizen thinks there is a correlation, however complicated, between growing radicalism and growing Christianization. "The government may see the radical new order coming from the communist East, and maybe it is, but to many of the young people revolution is a Western phenomenon. Christianity and the worldview that comes with it is seen as a stepping stone to the Western world. They want to be part of that. Their Pentecostal churches are closely linked to Americans, and American Pentecostalism is not political, but here, in a strange way, it takes on a more political form. I don't mean that the churches act like political parties, but they are part of that larger and essentially Western community of faith and vision, they provide a sense of community and direction that is seen as the future."

The declining influence of some of the more traditional churches, such as the Catholic, Methodist, and Anglican, comes because they are *too* Indian. At least Oosthuizen thinks this is part of the reason. "The established churches are enclaves and very emphatically Indian—you are an *Indian* Catholic or an *Indian* Anglican. They are turned in upon themselves. You have cases such as processions in which Indian Catholics cannot take part with Zulu Catholics." In terms of missionary method, it is implied that the traditional churches put too much stress on the indigenous.

The Hindu students know that in those places in Africa where Indians were brutally expelled the Indians involved "had never left India." They were temporarily in Africa, but their hearts and homes were in India. A declining number of English whites still talk about "taking the gap" and going "home" when the harsh winds blow. That is not an option for these Indian students. They, and probably their parents, do not know India as home. To be Indian—just that and nothing else—in South Africa is to be frighteningly vulnerable. Yet, at the same time that the Pentecostal churches provide a link to the West, they are not perceived as being institutionally dependent on the West the way some of the traditional churches are. They are self-starting, self-supporting, and self-directing, and as such they provide a sense of community and strength to a threatened people. It is not a community with India nor merely with Indians; it is community with a larger world from which, in one form or another, the future will come. That, plus a certificate from the blacks, might see them through the storm.

P. W. Botha and his cabinet ministers appeared at public rallies and campaigned hard for Indian support for the new dispensation. Counterdemonstrations were organized by the Natal Indian Congress and the United Democratic Front (in Natal, it is said, the UDF is the Natal Indian Congress). As mentioned earlier, something less than 20 percent of eligible voters cast a ballot for members to sit in the Indian chamber of parliament. Clearly, not everybody is as enthusiastic about cabinet seats for Indians as is Jayaram Reddy. Some observers claim that in the Indian community, and to a lesser extent among coloureds, the dividing line was between parents and their more radicalized student children. In any event, the ambivalence of the Indian community continues, and was intensified as a result of the anti-Indian rampages of black youth in 1985. In relation to the government, the Indian posture is a mix of participation and protest. Participation is for the short term, while enough protest continues to signal to blacks that Indians are not withdrawing their applications for the certificates that will be so necessary when "the inevitable" happens. It may be that one reason Indian elders seem so undisturbed by the radicalism of their young is that they hope the protest of the youth will keep Indian applications in the active file of the coming revolution.

Once again, it is not easy to be the people between. It seems everybody in South Africa professes to be part of a people between. There are the Indians. Then the coloured who are between black and white. And the English who are between the Afrikaner and everybody else. And of course the Afrikaner who understands himself to be between onslaught from abroad and apocalypse at home, between communism's conquest and liberalism's seductions, between, in short, multiple manifestations of the devil and the deep blue sea.

But it only *seems* that everybody is part of a people between. Partly pushed apart and now partly standing apart from the mainstream are the blacks. They are the main story line of South Africa. As all stories are told in relation to their endings, so the stories of all others in South Africa are told in relation to black South Africans. Almost everyone knows—many with trepidation and many more with hope—that at the end of the day the future is black. In all that we have been hearing so far we have been hearing, directly or indirectly, about black South Africa. We cannot forget that that is the "basic definition" of the country's present and future. And that brings us to the leader who, perhaps more than any other, might be the instrument of that future's becoming, Gatsha Buthelezi, chief of the Zulus.

CHAPTER TEN

THE ZULUS AND THEIR CHIEF

T HE city hall of Durban is an elegant remnant from the days of empire. Inside, the tastefully lighted marble and polished oak auditorium is packed with four thousand people, mainly blacks. Another two thousand who could not get in listen to the proceedings on loudspeakers set up outside. This very public event is illegal in South Africa. It is an interracial political rally sponsored by Gatsha Buthelezi's political organization, Inkatha, and the Progressive Federal Party. Because this meeting is illegal, it is billed as a "symposium," for the law says nothing about interracial symposia. When it comes his turn to speak, Buthelezi refers to the meeting as a seminar, and then as a discussion, and then as a debate— he is obviously taunting the enforcers of apartheid rules. Whatever the meeting is called, it is generally agreed that it is unprecedented.

The meeting is also very long. It begins with a choir of 150 black children and teenagers, the girls in blue school dresses and the boys in English school uniforms with ties, and the songs in Zulu. There is a hymn sung in English, and I catch references to Jesus and a couple of "Amens" in the Zulu songs. Buthelezi is a very serious Christian and a lay reader in the Anglican church. The stage is dominated on one side by his picture and the banner of Inkatha; on the other is the banner of the PFP and a picture of its leader, van Zyl Slabbert. The songs are to warm up the congregation before the entrance of the principals. Through the intervention of a

Buthelezi aide I have a front row seat in a section reserved for dignitaries. The West German consul is on my right and remarks on how few whites are in the audience. He notes also that the Zulus present are disproportionately women and girls, with most of the men being middle-aged or older. This he takes as evidence that it may be true, as is often said, that Buthelezi is losing his hold on the young men of Kwazulu.

Chief Buthelezi, with an imposing entourage, makes his entrance from the rear of the hall and the meeting comes alive. There is much cheering and applause and the undulating shouts of tribal salutations. It is a "hail to the chief" that a U.S. president might envy. That Slabbert is entering with him seems quite incidental. Buthelezi moves slowly to the front, finally taking the stage and sitting at a desk that is floodlit front center. The undulations continue for some time and Buthelezi peers around, almost shyly, at the excited crowd. At last he raises his hand, holding the rod of chiefdom, and the audience is silent. He looks very young, more like a prince than a king. Some of his lieutenants and some in the audience wear the Inkatha uniform, khaki banded by stripes of green, yellow, and black, which are also the colors of the African National Congress. Buthelezi himself wears a navy blue jungle suit with simple epaulets, a blue ascot spotted by white, and a fez-like cap of blue trimmed with white.

Lawrence Schlemmer kicks off the evening's program with a detailed commentary on the report of the Buthelezi Commission. Schlemmer was the chief research person for the commission, which began its work in the fall of 1980. His earnest manner conveys the impression of a party ideologue, but the substance of his message is all moderation. Like most of the members of the commission, Schlemmer is white and he underscores the symbolic importance of the commission as an evidence of interracial reasonableness. He cites the results of a recent poll that indicates most people of all racial groups would favor a "healthy power sharing" that also included blacks. Even two-thirds of the National Party members polled would support that, he says. The genius of the Buthelezi Commission, Schlemmer believes, is that it builds on hopes rather than fears. In addition, it is a black initiative which defies those black intellectuals who say that the injustices of South Africa were created by whites and therefore it is up to the whites to find a resolution. According to Schlemmer, the commission underscores that blacks must be full participants in the search for a more just dispensation.

The commission tried to give sympathetic consideration to the most favorable possible interpretation of the government's homelands policy—and found it wanting on six scores. First, the business community opposes it because it makes no economic sense. Second, it does not advance economic equality but rather increases inequalities. Third, it is a formula for increased alienation between white and black. Fourth, it is not a policy supported by the consent of the people involved. Fifth, Kwazulu and Natal are in every respect—economic, social, ecological—inseparable ("There are no visas for cholera," observes Schlemmer). And sixth, the consolidation and independence of Kwazulu would preclude Inkatha's playing its role as a national political movement for blacks. These six arguments—elaborated in detail in the formal report of the commission—constitute the case against Pretoria's homelands policy. Even if one credited the government's stated intentions to build up the homelands as viable independent states (and there is little reason to believe the government can or will do that), the case is devastating. And so it seems to the Buthelezi Commission.

Schlemmer addresses at length some of the key ideas in what emerged as P. W. Botha's constitutional reforms. Particularly unsatisfactory, he says, is the idea of "segmental autonomy" or "segmental authority." This is the idea that public policy can be segmented into "general" concerns that involve the whole community and "own" concerns that are relevant only to particular population groups. It is an idea embodied in the three-chambered parliament of whites, coloureds, and

Indians in the 1983 new dispensation. Segmental autonomy is a bad idea, say Schlemmer and the commission, because it locks in the racial factor; it makes every conflict a racial conflict.

Apologists for the new system disagree with Schlemmer, claiming that his is a too formalistic assessment of the arrangement. In fact, they say, with different racial groups in the cabinet (where the real power lies) there will be the normal political wheelings and dealings among members of the parliament, and this will cross and temper racial lines. Whether that will happen cannot be known until the new order has been in effect for some years, if it lasts that long. But to Schlemmer and many others the very structuring of the polity along racialist lines is anathema. In addition, and although Schlemmer does not say it this evening, the new structure can hardly accommodate black aspirations. That is, blacks, who are more in number than the other three groups combined, are not going to be content with another, fourth, chamber in the parliament.

The proposal of the Buthelezi Commission, Schlemmer continues, is "open consociation." In such an arrangement Natal-Kwazulu can take initiatives, emphasizing local options about how people should interact, but all within the context of one Republic of South Africa. Natal-Kwazulu would be headed by a "balanced executive" that would at first have to take race into account but would structurally anticipate a nonracialist basis in the future. So also there would have to be proportional representation in elections. "It cannot be a question of winner take all," says Schlemmer. The reason it cannot be is that whites and Indians would never agree to a system in which they would be "swamped" by blacks. The commission would not oppose the creation of regional jurisdictions, so long as the lines are not drawn upon the basis of race. And all this, concludes Schlemmer, would work; it would "stick" because everyone will be involved in the negotiation of the new arrangements.

The proposals of the Buthelezi Commission have a very uncertain status. Some say they are a blueprint not only for Natal-Kwazulu but for all of South Africa. Others look upon them as a speculative "what if" exercise that may contribute to a new design when the political climate is right in some indeterminate future. The New Republic Party, which is small in South Africa as a whole but big in Natal, did not participate in the commission and has little use for its report. Pretoria almost pretended not to notice, presumably because the government did not want to distract attention from its own proposed dispensation. By 1985, however, when it was obvious that the current form of the new dispensation was not going to appease internal and external protest, Pretoria was emitting vague signals of interest in the recommendations of the commission. Complicating all this is uncertainty about Buthelezi's own attitude toward the commission.

"What does Buthelezi really want?" a cabinet minister asked me, and then answered, "He wants power, you can be sure of that. I do not blame him for that, that's what all political leaders want; it's what they must have if they are to continue as political leaders." Like many others, this politician thinks Buthelezi believes that he is sitting in the catbird seat. Pretoria supplies him with the position and resources that go with heading up a homeland, and then he skillfully uses position and resources to undermine Pretoria's policies. "Buthelezi can toy with his options for a time, if he thinks time is on his side," I am told. In this view the Buthelezi Commission is but one option with which the chief is toying. "I do not doubt he would like to be chief of all South Africa. But if and when he realizes that is not possible, he will settle for less. Will he settle for being president of an independent Kwazulu? No, I do not think so, although he might sometime take independence. But he would not call it independence, he would call it something else. And he would want more than Kwazulu. He wants South Africa and, if he can't get South Africa, he'll settle for Natal." In the view of this cabinet member, who is reportedly very close to the thinking of P. W. Botha, the Buthelezi Commission is important mainly because it is Buthelezi's tentative probe toward establishing a backstop position in the event that his national ambitions are frustrated.

But back at the rally-symposium-seminar-discussion-debate in Durban it is Buthelezi's turn. He reads from a prepared text, much too quickly, stumbling over lines, swallowing phrases. He is quite obviously nervous. This is to be a grand tour of Buthelezi policy. It takes an hour and a half, and then another twenty minutes to recapitulate the main points in Zulu. When he speaks in Zulu he becomes much more animated, gesticulating and maintaining contact with the audience. But for most of his address the people manifest patience more than enthusiasm. Many of the points are familiar, some are new, but all are endowed with a certain earnestness by this context of an unprecedented public gathering sponsored by major black and white organizations. Inkatha is undoubtedly the largest black political organization in the country, and the PFP is, after all, the official opposition to the government.

A strength of the Buthelezi Commission, according to the chief, is that it takes self-interest into account. He stresses that there is nothing immoral about self-interest as such, but explicitly moral considerations must be brought to bear also. Quite apart from how self-interest is to be calculated, apartheid is evil: "The bus of apartheid must be stopped, and everyone who accepts my leadership agrees not to climb on the bus of apartheid." Cooperating with Botha's constitutional reforms, he makes clear, is an instance of climbing on the apartheid bus. Key to Botha's scenario for reform is the distinction between urban and rural blacks, and this is entirely unacceptable to Buthelezi. It is unacceptable, he says, because in any conceivable dispensation there will be heavy dependence on migrant workers who will not have political rights in accord with their economic contribution. What he does not say in his speech, but is recognized by almost everyone, is that the rural-urban distinction goes to the jugular of Buthelezi's political power. That is, it divides Zuludom down the middle, with the possible result of leaving Buthelezi as leader of the mainly rural and most deprived population of Kwazulu. In that case his position would be worse even than that of a leader of an independent homeland under the old dispensation. The urban half of his people would be politically accommodated in a system entirely outside his control.

Buthelezi insists that more is at stake than the economic development of the homelands, even if that development were encouraging, which it is not. "Economic development is not enough, unless it is supported by the participation and consent of the people." This is central to the work of Inkatha, he says. "From the beginning I refused to limit Inkatha to Zulu membership, even though the government pressed me to do that." He does not mention that there are no hard figures on how many non-Zulus belong to Inkatha; it is assumed that their number is at best token. This touches on Buthelezi's critical dilemma: how to be, at the same time, the leader of the Zulus and the leader of all the blacks of South Africa.

He refers several times to commerce and industry as "the breadbasket," and asserts that no political arrangement should be permitted to destroy the breadbasket. But the crucial thing now, he says, is to get "the idea" of a new politics, knowing that many details will have to be negotiated later. The blacks of South Africa may not be denied citizenship, "but they are denied the rights of citizenship, and that is a very hard thing." He is not opposed to "the idea" of regionalization and consociation "so long as it is not based on racism." This line of argument is later seized upon by some observers as further evidence that Buthelezi is prepared to "settle for Natal."

Buthelezi then launches into a long polemic against various critics. A frequent criticism of Buthelezi is that he is hypersensitive, that he overworks the printing presses of Kwazulu by answering in great detail every critical word said about him, no matter how inconsequential the source. Allan Hendrickse of the Labour Party tells me about having Buthelezi at his church. "The place was filled and people wanted an inspiring speech. Instead, Buthelezi spent two hours belaboring the errors of a journalist who had said something unkind about him that week." We are in for some of that tonight. Tonight the targets are the African National Congress and the New Republic Party, especially the latter. He refers by name to "narrow politicians" who do not respect his vision. The audience is for the most part very patient, although I notice some whites looking about the hall, snoozing, and otherwise making no secret of the fact that they are bored, and maybe embarrassed for Buthelezi.

That over, Buthelezi moves on to questions more ominous. Those in Pretoria who refuse to explore the ways to needed change "are the true advocates of violence." "We must have conversation, for the only alternative to conversation is the destruction of everybody concerned." "I am not threatening, but I am warning. There are people like myself who are now prepared to be reasonable, but even a small spark could set off a conflagration and then reason would be cast out the window." (There are a couple of Indians present and I recall the remark to the effect that "whenever we listen to Buthelezi, we hear '1949.' ") In Buthelezi's remarks about potential violence, there is a teasing, titillating, and threatening tone. He affirms his devotion to nonviolence, but, if nonviolence fails, "the consequences will be too ghastly to contemplate." (That is a phrase used also by Botha and by Vorster before him; in fact it is something of a cliche in South African conversations—probably because it is true.) One thing Buthelezi wants understood: "Never again will Zulus be crushed by might." This is joined to reminders about the warring traditions of the Zulu nation.

But then he returns to the theme of being a reasonable man. It is not easy to be a reasonable man. "There are times

in which I feel I should just pack my bags and let the ava-
lanche take place." (*Après moi le déluge.*) "I need to be given
more hope." "I am not encouraged." Much of the speech
comes across as a plaint on not being appreciated. But this is
more than a personal grievance. "If the proposals and offers
represented by the Buthelezi Commission are thrown back in
our faces, then know that never again will blacks in this
country be ready to undertake such a study that tries seriously to take into account the interests of other groups."
Buthelezi presents himself as—and he probably is—the best
chance that white South Africans have for negotiating with
a "moderate" black leader. He knows that this posture has
alienated more militant blacks, also within the Zulu nation;
that is the price he has paid, and he believes that is not appreciated by the Nationalist leaders.

This evening he emphasizes that the President's Council and its new dispensation are the antithesis of what he and
the commission represent. Because it excludes blacks, the
President's Council is no more than a "forum for racism."
But then, somewhat confusingly, he goes on to say that the
needed answers will not come so long as people are thinking
in terms of left and right. The imperative is to "think anew."
"If left and right feet stink, you don't want either one." This,
presumably, is a criticism not so much of the President's
Council as of his more-radical-than-thou detractors within
the black world. Buthelezi's alternating attention between
white establishment and black insurgency is a constant in
his conversation, writings, and pronouncements.

On a later occasion I ask him whether it is accurate to
see his role as being similar to that of Martin Luther King,
Jr., during the late sixties when King's leadership was challenged by "black power" advocates. He says it is very accurate
indeed. I take it that part of that role requires balancing af-
firmations of nonviolence with assertions about the horrible
consequences of violence—assertions that others might interpret as threats. Another part of it means addressing his
audience as "Ladies and Gentlemen" at times, and as "Friends

and Comrades" at other times. This is designed to say to the black militants that Buthelezi is really much more radical than he is prepared to say in public. To the white establishment it says that, if they refuse to deal with the good Buthelezi, there is a bad Buthelezi ready to take his place. Of course I do not know if this is Buthelezi's conscious intention but my impression is that he knows very well what he is doing. If I am right, it may say less about personal duplicity than about political sagacity.

After Buthelezi has recapitulated his main points in Zulu and has received prolonged ovation, it is thought the main business of the evening is over. Slabbert has yet to speak, however, and it turns out that his address is as brief and inspiring as Buthelezi's was long and laborious. Slabbert acknowledges that the proposed new dispensation is a limited advance in that "this is the first white government that has acknowledged it cannot govern with whites alone." He also thinks it a "positive factor" that the government seems to recognize that any new constitution needs the support of all groups. But whatever is positive is negated, he says, by the exclusion of blacks. With great rhetorical effect, he says, "I challenge any member of this government to stand on any corner of Johannesburg or of any of our other great cities at noon hour and say out loud, 'This is white South Africa.' If you can say that three times, you are clearly certifiable." This brings an appreciative roar from the audience, and then Slabbert concludes with a peroration obviously drawn from Dr. King's "I have a dream" speech of August 1963. The crowd is on its feet acclaiming a white man who has demonstrated his ability to communicate with blacks in public—an ability, I cannot help but think, much greater than that of Gatsha Buthelezi.

A ND now the proceedings have come to their end. An elderly white gentleman who is serving as chairman properly thanks the ladies and gentlemen for attending and wishes them a very good night. But that is clearly not enough of an ending for Chief Buthelezi. In high good spirits he takes over the microphone and starts leading the crowd in a hymn-fest. His singing voice is a fine tenor, and the crowd joins with enthusiasm in several hymns and what I take to be Inkatha anthems. At last there is an announcement that people should stay in place until the leaders on the platform are able to make their way to the back, but it is a greatly expanded Buthelezi entourage that starts down the aisle in an atmosphere of jubilant chaos. The Buthelezi aide who is attending to me takes me by the hand and leads me behind the chief, out of the city hall and across the way into a hotel where Buthelezi and I are to have our first discussion. All the way we are mobbed by an excited crowd, the women and young girls jumping and waving their arms and ululating in a quite remarkable manner. The loud ululation is not one of mournful keening; it is more of a high-pitched chirping, and it is obviously much enjoyed by Buthelezi and those around him. At the hotel the doorman remarks to Buthelezi, "I wish I had all those women chasing me," and the chief thinks this very good, repeating it to several people who come up to congratulate him in the hotel lobby.

Buthelezi is much more impressive in person than on the platform. A thin man of medium height and delicate manner, the impression he makes is a far cry from the fierce Zulu warrior he sometimes dresses up to be in publicity photos, with lion skin, spear, shield, and intimidating glare. In talking with Buthelezi there is almost always a slight smile. A smile of friendliness and goodwill, but also of derision when speaking of his opponents, and also of apparent uncertainty and self-consciousness. We sit facing one another across a small coffee table, with five or six aides and Kwazulu cabinet members sitting around us and sometimes pitching into the conversation. From time to time, someone is admitted to the circle to offer congratulations to the chief on his evening's performance and he seems almost boyishly pleased by these compliments. "Did you really think it was good? I am so glad. Thank you so very much." The demeanor is boyish, and yet distinctly aristocratic too; it is pleasure in being praised and it is also gracious acceptance of homage due.

Buthelezi is not king of the Zulus. Someone else is that, and Buthelezi pays deference to him on appropriate public occasions. But Gatsha Buthelezi is unquestionably of Zulu royal lineage, the recognized leader of the Zulu people, and the executive head of Kwazulu. We have noted the ambivalence this creates when it comes to his aspiration to be the premier black leader of South Africa. He is always vulnerable to being accused of promoting "tribalism," a bad word in contemporary Africa. He rejects the charge with vehemence. "The Zulus have a colorful history. They are a warrior people. So some say I am trying to dominate with a Zulu imperium, because they fear our past reputation. But we are not a tribe. The Zulus were the mightiest *nation* here in the nineteenth century. And I am the great-grandson of King Cetshwayo, who defeated the British at Isandhlwana, and the grandson of King Dinuzulu on my mother's side. My mother was Princess Constance Magogo Zulu. ANC was founded in 1912 by a Zulu, Pixley Seme, who was married to my mother's sister, Princess Harriet. We Zulus have the best case for wanting independence. But we do not see a Zulu destiny. We see a common destiny, not only for all blacks, but for blacks and whites in one nation."[1]

In this typical statement two critical points are being made. First, that Buthelezi is committed to a unitary, modern, democratic South Africa, a South Africa beyond tribalism. The second point, however, is that, to the extent that tribalism continues to be a factor, Buthelezi is in a unique position to benefit from it. A leader who openly espouses tribalism in Africa today loses all credentials as a progressive. But any leader who ignores the perduring force of tribal identity will not likely be a leader for long. Blacks in South Africa express a sharp awareness of what happened, for example, in Zimbabwe where Robert Mugabe easily displaced Joshua Nkomo because the latter had the much smaller tribal base.

At the end of the day, after all the talk about political theories and dispensations, no one doubts that, if and when the black majority is politically empowered, tribe will continue to be a determining factor in South Africa. That is one reason why it is commonly acknowledged that "there is no way of going around Buthelezi."

It is commonly acknowledged but not universally so. Marius Jooste is former director of the South African Bureau of Racial Affairs and now an ideologist of the right-wing Conservative Party. He is part of the small group that espouses apartheid in all its purity, including the creation of a white homeland that would not be dependent upon or threatened by the black majority. He tells me that, if Buthelezi were offered a greatly expanded and consolidated Kwazulu, he might well "take independence." "And if Dr. Buthelezi does not go along," he says with a conspiratorial smile, "we have found in setting up the other independent states that chiefs are not indispensable. We have been successful in going around chiefs before and we can do that again. Dr. Buthelezi is not forever." But his is a distinctly minority viewpoint. Also in a distinct minority is the Indian member of the President's Council who has created a row by publicly referring to Buthelezi as "this vicious, overrated little black man." Even Afrikaans editorials and politicians felt this was going too far and made public noises affirming their respect for—albeit respectful disagreement with—the chief of the Zulus.

Buthelezi is both insider and outsider. Denis Worrall, who headed the constitution committee of the President's Council, says, "For the time being the President's Council is the only exercise in inter-group dynamics where the future of South Africa is being negotiated, and Buthelezi is not there." In this sense Buthelezi is an outsider. But, as Worral and others readily admit, everything turns upon that "for the time being." The time being may not be very long, and undergirding the President's Council's deliberations is the assumption that a future dispensation will have to deal with all those living within "the traditional boundaries of South Africa," or, as it is alternatively stated, "all those born on South African soil." In this sense Buthelezi is the inescapable insider.

Buthelezi is not alone in playing what some call the insider-outsider game. For example, President Lucas Mangope of the "national state" of Bophuthatswana is frequently mentioned as a figure who will likely play a major role in the period that follows "the time being." The leaders of the other homelands that have to date "taken independence" (Transkei, Ciskei, and Venda) are deemed less promising. Buthelezi has given careful thought to the "independence option," to the idea of formally going outside the system in order to work against the system. His comments on Mangope are sharply critical but not derisory. He also knows there is an element of truth in Pretoria's claim that the "independent states" are, in terms of size and resources, better off than many of the countries in the United Nations, and the people are more prosperous than perhaps most of those in Africa (which is to say they are not quite so miserably poor.) But Buthelezi also knows that independence for Kwazulu would let South Africa "off the hook," opening the way for other homelands to take independence, and resulting finally in South Africa's black majority becoming a black minority.

"We single-handedly have made certain that South Africa will remain a black nation," he tells me with considerable feeling. "I am criticized for accepting the leadership of a so-called homeland under the apartheid system, but if I were not here and some other leader accepted independence for Kwazulu, then the struggle would be lost, there would be no hope for a national convention, for a negotiated future for South Africa, and the whites could do whatever they wished forever." In sum, according to Buthelezi, his remaining an ambivalent insider is the best insurance against all blacks becoming eternal outsiders.

Buthelezi is ambivalent also about the connection between principle and power. We have seen this in the alternation between the commitment to nonviolence and the threat of violence. Similarly, he does not know how much weight should be given a shared Christian faith between white and black. "Of course religion is important and I try to let it rule the way I deal with people. But how can you do that when you are dealing with a government like this? Pieter Kornhoof says he is a Christian and in our discussions he has even opened a Bible and says that we are brothers in Christ, and then he says that it is a proper Christian thing that our Kwazulu land should go to Swaziland. Now how do you talk to a Christian who says it is his Christian duty to steal your land?" The reference is to Pretoria's minister of cooperation and development, and the story it touches on is revealing of the curious relationship between Buthelezi and the South African government.

In June 1982 Pretoria proposed to meet some dubious land claims by the elderly King Sobhuza II, leader of Swaziland, the nation neighboring Kwazulu. A big chunk of Kwazulu, plus the whole of the Kangwane homeland, controlled by an ally of Buthelezi, was to be given to Swaziland. The administrators of the Kangwane homeland were locked out of their offices, their official cars were taken away and Pretoria gave every indication of intending to treat Buthelezi in the same peremptory manner. In conservative Afrikaner circles it was rumored that all this indicated that P. W. Botha's government had "written off" Buthelezi and had set out to humiliate him, thus demonstrating that he is not nearly as indispensable as he and others claim. It was further said that the government intended to build up the Zulu king, Goodwill Zwelithini, who has been very much in Buthelezi's shadow. Part of Pretoria's design was to transfer with the land a population of more than one million blacks who would thus become statutory citizens of Swaziland. In a successful struggle that powerfully reinforced his claim to be South Africa's premier black leader, Buthelezi fought back.

Many liberal whites, including some Afrikaner Nationalists who had little taste for the gross unfairness of tyrannical government, publicly protested. There were interracial rallies. Most important, Buthelezi went to court and won. He won in the Natal supreme court and, when the government appealed, he won on appeal. By the end of the year King Sobhuza had died, the government looked dismally inept as well as unfair, and Pretoria, having no stomach for further battle, gave up, even agreeing to pay court costs.

It is the kind of incident that tends to confirm Buthelezi in his understanding of how change is effected. "You cannot depend on people doing the right thing for moral reasons. I wish you could, but that is not my experience. I do not mean that morality is unimportant, but there are other things, like self-interest. The churches do not understand this, and the ANC does not understand that. No they don't, not most of the time. The churches make moral pronouncements and the others talk about revolution, and they both think that if you say something is so then it is so. But that is not so. You have to look at the other side and see what their interests are and what their fears are and who has power and what kind of power they have, and then you try to make a settlement that is as close to just as you can get." "You see, I do not think that is immoral," he concludes with a great smile, "I think that is a better morality."

Frequently encountered criticisms of Gatsha Buthelezi are that he is vain, in ill health, and has surrounded himself with sycophants. Of course our few hours together could not confirm or disprove any of these points. He claimed to be in good health and in our spirited conversation he gave evidence of great mental and physical vitality. As to sycophancy, I received rather the opposite impression from the aides present at the Buthelezi conversation and in my talks with some of them individually. While obviously they are the chief's men, they seemed at ease and did not hesitate to jump into the conversation, never flatly contradicting Buthelezi, but at several points offering additional information and amendments to what he had said. I have seen much more demeaning diffidence among faculty in the presence of the university dean, or among corporate vice-presidents in the presence of the chief executive officer.

Vanity is harder to measure. Judged by the vanity par among U.S. senators, for example, Buthelezi is the model of self-effacement. But there is no doubt he is thin-skinned, and his voluminously detailed responses to critics are embarrassingly excessive. A professor who served on the Buthelezi Commission thinks it a measure of vanity that Buthelezi named the commission after himself. "It really wasn't his work at all," he says; "all he did was help initiate it and give some testimony." He thinks that naming it the Buthelezi Commission weakened its impact, since it distracted attention from the inclusive process of consultation that went into the commission's recommendations. When I raised this question with Buthelezi aides, however, they said that it was not Buthelezi's idea to name the commission after himself. "We did that in the Kwazulu legislature as a measure of respect for the chief. Our people would have thought it an insult if we did not name it for him." They also suggest that, while Buthelezi's active role in the commission may have been small, he was closer to its deliberations than others indicate. In any event, I am told, Buthelezi never expected that the commission's report would be the last word. What is important is that a series of probes and explorations be identified with his leadership, so that people of all races will be looking to him for signals about the future.

"No, I do not think I am too thin-skinned," Buthelezi says good-naturedly. "What criticisms should I not answer? If I do not correct these lies, then someone says, 'Aha, it must be true. Buthelezi did not deny it.' You cannot know which criticisms are important. Something very small that is said by somebody very small can become very big. So I cannot stop answering. I cannot say 'Stop the world, I want to get off.' You have to keep going round and round, sometime on the same subject, or else you are not seen as a leader, and if you are not seen as a leader then maybe you are a little less a leader." He chuckles and says, "Maybe it's crazy sometimes, but this is a crazy country, and please remember that I did not invent this game of political leadership."

But what of the charge that he has surrounded himself with weak people who are little more than sycophants? This arouses one of his aides: "Yes, we have heard they say that. When they stand together they call it solidarity; when we stand together they call it sycophancy. We must build an impregnable base here in Kwazulu. Impregnable. Impregnable. The chief is the cornerstone of that, but no matter what happens in South Africa, and no matter what even happens to the chief, Kwazulu must be a base for fresh and independent initiatives." This is said with some heat and is seconded by murmured approvals from Buthelezi and his cabinet. There is some additional discussion about how much easier it is to talk about leadership from the safety of London. The reference is obviously to the leaders of the ANC. Later I put the question of excessive vanity to Gibson Thula, a Buthelezi lieutenant whom I had first met in Johannesburg. He smiles gently, taps my hand that is resting on the table, and says, "If you were chief of six million Zulus, wouldn't you be a little proud of it? Our people would be disappointed if the chief were not proud of it."

I may have transgressed in saying so much about Buthelezi's alleged personal failings, but I am impressed by how frequently the subject arises in South Africa. Perhaps it is not so different elsewhere in the world. When analysis is too demanding, the conversation turns to gossip. Within the several population groups, talk about Gatsha Buthelezi is often marked by a note of pettiness.

W HERE Buthelezi actually stands in the affections of his countrymen is not easy to determine. In South Africa, too, the pollsters are busy maintaining public interest in real or imagined horse races. The question of who is ahead and who is behind in terms of black support is a constant one. If early popularity polls in the interminably drawn-out U.S. presidential campaign are unreliable, polls of black leadership standings in South Africa are thought by some critics to be almost surreal. An implicit question they are designed to answer is: If blacks were enfranchised in an election held tomorrow, who would be the first black leader of South Africa? Of course such an election may never take place, or, if it does, it may be held ten or twenty years from now when some of the current actors are no longer around. Nonetheless, the question of black leadership standings is as inescapable as it is, in large part, unanswerable. It is inescapable because of simple human curiosity and, more important, because it has some bearing on the political and moral question of who speaks for whom in South Africa.

According to survey research by Lawrence Schlemmer and others, the tribal factor may at times be predominant in how blacks rank their leaders. The government and those to the right of the government emphasize this finding, using it to bolster the claim that black South Africa is in fact a mix of quite distinct nations. And the findings do support the claim that the leaders of the independent homelands, for instance, have considerable popular backing in the tribal groupings upon which the homelands are based. Yet among what might be called the "politically attentive" sector of the black population the picture is somewhat different. Among the politically attentive who focus their attention on all of South Africa and the future of black leadership in it, only a few names seem to command much allegiance. Dr. Motlana of Soweto, whom we have met, shows up in the polls, as does Bishop Desmond Tutu. But just two names in the polls consistently dominate the debate among political activists: Gatsha Buthelezi and the imprisoned Nelson Mandela. As the turbulence of 1985 intensified, there was little doubt that, at

247

least in the opinion polls, blacks viewed the imprisoned Mandela as their number one leader.[2]

Buthelezi makes no secret of his resentment of the African National Congress and the ways in which it uses Mandela in absentia to undercut his own role. "If it were not for us, nobody would be talking about the ANC in South Africa. It is against the law to talk about the ANC or quote its views. I am the one who broke that by talking openly about my agreements and disagreements with the ANC, and they [Pretoria] could not silence me, so now everyone is talking openly about the ANC." But the ANC is not grateful for Buthelezi's help in giving it more open currency, and Buthelezi says he is not surprised by that.

"Those who criticize us from outside, those who want to discredit me, they have already decided on revolution. You must understand that. Everything that we are trying to do to advance solutions other than violent revolution is counter-revolutionary in their view. I understand their position, but I am convinced they are wrong. I have been very clear, very public, in saying that maybe there will have to be a violent revolution. But there is no way, no way at all, in which it is possible in the next fifteen or twenty years to envision any circumstance in which blacks could confront this government with violent force and have any hope of success." Buthelezi is emphatic about this.

"I sometimes wonder if they're interested in South Africa or in the blacks of South Africa. They speak so casually about the need for people to die. Maybe they are caught up in some grander designs." This is too obvious an opportunity to ask his opinion on the alleged communist domination of the ANC. The ANC itself does not disguise the fact that it has prominent communists in its leadership and aligns itself with the Soviet bloc. Over the years this has been a cause of divisiveness within black radicalism, resulting in black organizations and movements bitterly opposed to ANC. For example, the late Steve Biko's "black consciousness" movement was in part a protest against ANC's alleged subservience to whites who define the South African situation in terms of class, rather than race, struggle. Buthelezi chooses his words carefully. "I do not say that ANC is a communist organization. That is too simple. But if you ask me whether in fact the people who are really calling the plays in ANC are puppets of Moscow, then the answer is yes. I do not hesitate to say that. I am convinced it is true. I know these people and there is no other way of explaining their behavior."

Buthelezi's view is sharply challenged by many activists. Allan Boesak, for example, says, "I am sorry, talk about communism is unreal to me. Maybe there are communists and communist conspiracies, but that's all we hear about here and it's always the language of reaction and racism." In Boesak's eyes the important thing is that ANC has the loyalty of "the people." He points out that joining Inkatha is quite legal and, if one is a Zulu, there might even be considerable pressure to sign up.

Boesak's views of Buthelezi are commonly expressed in a sector of opinion marked by a certain political sophistication. "Buthelezi," he says, "is a man of vast potential influence for good, but also for evil. I believe Buthelezi is the most dangerous black leader in South Africa. He seems to be bent on reviving Zulu nationalism, and that is contrary to what we need, to black consciousness and the common struggle." In this perspective, Buthelezi and ANC are seen as incompatible; the test is between Buthelezi on the one side and, on the other, Nelson Mandela as the symbolic, albeit disengaged, head of ANC. "More and more," says Boesak, "we see the people coming out for ANC. I have presided at funerals where people wear ANC T-shirts and sing ANC songs. That would have been inconceivable a few years ago. The people make way for the ANC delegation. And you never know how deep the ANC tie is. For example, an old man died and nobody was even aware that he was political, but after he died it develops that he was a key person in ANC and thousands of people showed up at the funeral for this unknown old man." The suggestion, against Buthelezi's argument, is that in an open contest with legal inhibitions removed, the popularity of ANC and Mandela would swamp that of Inkatha and Buthelezi. To date, of course, it has been impossible to put that suggestion to the test.

Alex Boraine, the PFP parliamentarian, speaks more sympathetically of Buthelezi. "Buthelezi has the problem that he has never been arrested, but if he were in the business of being arrested he wouldn't be able to have the other kinds of influence he has." According to Boraine, "If Tutu were arrested you would see real fireworks and the creation of a popular hero beyond the status of any black today. But if Buthelezi were arrested, I really think the whole country could blow up." Boraine's own son was detained by the security forces and received stacks of letters, including one from Nelson Mandela, and black tributes making him a "Son of the Soil" and so forth. "In an oppressive situation like ours there is a powerful mystique to being in prison. Militant blacks say to Buthelezi, 'You say we live under oppression and you're right. But if the situation is so oppressive why aren't you more oppressed?' " Boraine thinks it is almost impossible to answer that kind of question to the satisfaction of most militants. "Buthelezi says he is not involved in protest politics, that he's working for real change, but that assumes that real change can happen without violent revolution, and so everything comes back to that. Political talk in South Africa always starts and ends with that—revolution, how to prevent it, whether it should be prevented, whether it can be prevented, and on and on. Buthelezi's difficulty is that he wants to talk about something other than revolution."

We talked earlier with Sally Motlana and heard her angry impatience with persons and programs that would distract attention from the central question of "breaking the chains of the black man in South Africa." Her opinions about Buthelezi and his competitors for black leadership seem to be representative of many who belong to the community of the self-consciously radical. "Buthelezi is a leader of the Zulus. We need a leader of the blacks. He is a good leader, I do not deny that. He has superb ideas and real capacity for power with Inkatha. But how many non-Zulus do they have in Inkatha? Very few, I tell you. At the beginning they did not even let non-Zulus in. If I joined Inkatha, I know I would feel like an outsider there." (There is considerable dispute about how exclusively Zulu Inkatha has been. As we have seen, Buthelezi says membership has been open to all from the beginning, but until recently there were no non-Zulus in the upper leadership levels of the organization.) Sally Motlana believes Buthelezi could become a great figure, but he cannot do that by "sitting up there in Natal and expect everybody to recognize him as their leader." (Buthelezi protests that he has held frequent meetings, including huge rallies, in Soweto and elsewhere, and that he will continue to do so. "The same people who say I isolate myself in Natal also say I am speaking out too much on issues all over the country," he says, with a shrug of his shoulders and a smile of resignation. "There is no pleasing them.")

Nelson Mandela was once Buthelezi's leader in the ANC youth organization and, according to Sally Motlana, that is where he learned much of what he knows about leadership. So even the merits of Buthelezi are a product of ANC. Is she bothered by the allegation that the ANC leadership is dominated by Marxists? "Oh, I don't know anything about that," she responds with evident impatience. "Maybe it's true, maybe not, but what difference does it make? All I know is that we are all children of South Africa and that the struggle will have to involve all of us." Talk about communism, she suspects, is another way in which "the whites are always trying to divide us." "Black-white, that is the only question in South Africa. All these political theories only get in the way of our liberation." Nonetheless, she does have some political ideas of her own. "America used to be a model for me. Not anymore. I have been there. I have seen the Indian reservations in North Dakota and the way that blacks live in Atlanta. Do they have freedom? No. That is not the way we want to go here. I don't understand why Buthelezi wants to talk that way about communism. If the communists happen to be in favor of the freedom that we're struggling for here, what's wrong with that?"

Sally Motlana's husband is the Dr. Nthato Motlana of Soweto who is regularly mentioned among the top three or four black leaders of South Africa. They are reportedly separated, but their views on Buthelezi's role are very close. Dr. Motlana has an ambivalent attitude toward "tribalism." He does not think that people should despise "what American blacks call their roots," but neither does he think blacks should follow the Afrikaners in "building a cult around tribe and language." In urban areas like Soweto, he believes, the significance of tribe is fast declining and therefore black solidarity is on the ascendancy. "I shall not deny that in 'purer' communities, like Kwazulu or Lebowa or Botswana, where the Tswana have not met the Zulu, there would be that natural resentment you would find anywhere about a strange people you do not know. People do not naturally like strangers. But we reject efforts to build this into a cult, or into a way of life, and reject attempts to structure all our schools and townships on ethnicity."

In the riotous rebellions that flared in Soweto and elsewhere in 1976, much of the violence was black-on-black. Zulu workers were frequently in the lead of angry mobs that turned upon the student and other protestors favored by political radicals. This is yet another anxiety expressed about the prospect of Zulu dominance—and Buthelezi dominance—in the future of black South Africa. But Dr. Motlana declares: "This is another myth spread by whites, from Prime Minister Pieter W. Botha down. It is not true! In any case, when liberation comes and we have a black government, the Zulu will only constitute five million people out of a population of well over twenty million. Five million Zulus alone can never dominate all other blacks against their will. But, if the Zulu should somehow be dominant, even like the Afrikaners are today, I will not mind."

"Let me explain," he continues. "If we had a 'one man, one vote' unitary or federal system, with a constitution accepted by *all* the people, and if a predominantly Zulu party were freely supported by the overall majority and then managed to form a government, I certainly would not mind. After all, the ANC leadership was almost entirely Xhosa, and I accepted that. In any case, the Zulu are not racist like the present establishment." Here again the question of the elite and the masses crops up. It is almost as though Dr. Motlana, who is undoubtedly a member of the elite, is preparing himself and others to accommodate to the "prejudices" of the masses.

He allows that it is "a natural tendency" for people to support leaders like Buthelezi who are part of their tribe and speak their own language. "But, when people become more sophisticated and come to discuss and understand the issues and principles involved, then they will not support a man simply for ethnic reasons. Even now, many younger and politically sophisticated Zulus do not support Buthelezi. . . . I am willing to concede that the mass of the people might be swayed by such irrelevancies as tribal affiliation—for example, the fact that Buthelezi is a Zulu. Obviously he influences a lot of ethnic Zulu in Soweto—the migrant workers and so on—to support him, even when he talks nonsense!" The masses are clearly in need of reeducation, Dr. Motlana and others seem to be saying, but, just in case the reeducation doesn't take, we are not going to burn our bridges to the beneficiaries of mass ignorance, such as Gatsha Buthelezi.[3]

Internal black leadership conflicts erupt in unpredictable ways and sometimes leave lasting scars. One such incident was the funeral of Mangaliso Robert Sobukwe, the leader of the Pan African Congress which was formed in opposition to the white and Soviet elements in ANC. (Many major black events happen in connection with funerals. One reason is that black leaders frequently do not live very long. Another is that funerals are among the few events entirely under black control.) The Sobukwe funeral was in 1978, but it is still a lively subject of debate. Buthelezi, who says he was an old friend of Sobukwe, was invited to make an address but was prevented from doing so by stone-throwing radical "thugs" (his term). As he was effectively driven from the meeting, shots were fired and Buthelezi narrowly escaped being stabbed in the back. He believes that his opponents staged the violence as a demonstration against him and Inkatha, and he most particularly resents Desmond Tutu's speech at the funeral "in defense of thuggery."

Bishop Tutu says: "All that I said at the funeral was said without condoning the action those young people took. I tried to quiet them down, but at the same time I did express my understanding of their feelings. They represent a widely held view—opposition to the Bantustan policy. . . . They see the Chief as a collaborator. That incident was a nasty thing to happen to anybody. But I believe that if the Chief were to step out of the Bantustan policy, he would be acknowledged by all blacks as their leader. God has given him leadership qualities. And I've been trying to set up a meeting for rapprochement. But the Chief refused to meet with me."[4]

"First," says Buthelezi, "I do not refuse to meet with people." He then recounts again the abortive "reconciliation conference" arranged by "your friend and mine, Jesse Jackson." Then, Buthelezi wants it known, "you do not make speeches of 'understanding' for thuggery and mob violence. You condemn such things. I'm afraid my friend Bishop Tutu tried to quiet the mob by agreeing with the mob." Moreover, he professes not to understand how people expect him to "step out" of the apartheid system. "Should I take independence for Kwazulu? You know they would then condemn me as a quisling, just as the other independent leaders are condemned. Should I resign and let someone else be the chief executive of Kwazulu? How would that help the struggle? No, my friend, I am sorry but I do not believe these people who say they would acknowledge my leadership if I gave up my positions. Without Kwazulu and without Inkatha, they would turn around and say that Buthelezi is nothing."

Buthelezi's own analysis often comes through most lucidly in his addresses to Inkatha loyalists. There he takes on, sometimes in tedious detail, the criticisms lodged by ANC and other black leadership circles. In a recent presidential address to Inkatha he declares: "We can be quite assured that the whites of South Africa do not regard Inkatha as a tame, sell-out political movement. Those vociferous little cockerels who crow about their purity and our contamination have no significant role in the central political process towards democratic rule in this country. We must not step into the trap of their self-importance. We cannot design our constructive engagement in the politics of South Africa by seeking to appease the views of those who have failed." (The use of "constructive engagement" by Buthelezi predates the Reagan administration's use of the term to describe its policy toward South Africa.)

Or again, "After June 16th, 1976, [the start of the Soweto riots] there were many little cocks crowing on political dunghills that the events of Soweto were the death knell of Inkatha and my involvement in politics. During the six months which followed June 16th, Inkatha's membership doubled. . . . At the height of the unrest, when black killed black, it was I, as president of Inkatha, who had to go to Soweto to defuse the black-black confrontation. There is a hunger amongst people for a disciplined organization which attends to the hard work of constituency building." Then comes a typical appeal that might be described as populist and is aimed against "politically sophisticated elitists." "It is the ordinary people who have confounded the prophets of doom. The ordinary man in the street, the ordinary worker, the ordinary peasant, yearns for an organized and well-run political home." There are those who are always trying to exploit "flashes" of outrage, but they must learn that "a sequence of revolts do not necessarily make a revolution. A

revolution begins with hard work in which discipline dominates over personal ambition. This is a point which many
bandwagon black politicians that have emerged in recent times
have all missed."

In personal conversation Buthelezi speaks with feeling
about how much he is hurt when "outsiders"—notably some
churches in the West and the World Council of Churches—
depict him as a sell-out or collaborator. "They define liberation, and their definition of liberation determines for them
who is and who is not a Christian brother. White Europeans
and Americans decide what is a 'Third World viewpoint.'
White people say that Gatsha Buthelezi is not a Third World
leader. Why can't they see how arrogant that is, how absurd
that is? I am sorry, but I do not think they can care very
much about Third World people, the oppressed people. I am
of the Third World. How can that be denied? How can they
close their eyes to the fact that we are engaged in a revolutionary struggle and I am the acknowledged leader of millions
of people in that struggle? But no, they pretend it is not so,
and then they send large amounts of money to set up rival
leaderships. I am afraid they do not care about the revolution
of Third World people. They want to use Third World people
to export their own kind of revolution. I admit that this infuriates me, but I honestly say that most of all it hurts me
when they say that I am not a Christian brother engaged in
the struggle."

In a presidential address to Inkatha he asserts: "It is not
only arrogant to pontificate to us who are the authentic leaders of Black people and who are not, but it is also divisive.
This is not only just arrogant, but it sets back our struggle by
several decades each and every time this is done by outsiders.
In South Africa the secret police take advantage of these divisions to entrench Black disunity. People who give financial
assistance for liberation must rather keep their funds if their
funds are to be used only to escalate Black disunity and self-
destructive internecine strife."[5] I mention that his critics claim
that his real grievance is that the outside money is not going

to Inkatha and its development projects, but he denies that. "Of course there is so much we could do if we had the funds," he says, "but honestly I have become very skeptical about money from the outside. It is a very rare thing, a very rare thing indeed, that anybody gives money without wanting to control it and advance their own purposes. That is why Inkatha relies upon the dues of its members. It's the only way that poor people can have real self-determination."

Buthelezi's detractors respond that, while Inkatha may not receive funds directly from the Kwazulu administration, it would not exist without the Kwazulu administration—and that administration is totally dependent for funding upon Pretoria. As one church leader remarked, "Buthelezi talks a lot about being realistic and derides what he calls the moral purists. But the fact is that Buthelezi puts on the purity act when it comes to funding and that doesn't wash. We may have moral problems with money from Bonn and Geneva, but he gets his money from the apartheid government!" Such a response may not be convincing, since it implies only a reiteration of the claim that Buthelezi should step out of the leadership of Kwazulu, but it does underscore the inescapable ambiguity of Buthelezi's position—an ambiguity which, I have come to believe, Buthelezi understands much more clearly than do his detractors.

Gatsha Buthelezi is a man of high principle forced to be a man of fast footwork. Some detect signs of paranoia, but one is again reminded that paranoids can have enemies too. Buthelezi has many enemies among whites and blacks in South Africa. Perhaps serenity is too much to look for in a man in his position. There is a redeeming dimension of humor, however, even self-deprecating humor. And he seems centered and confident when he speaks about Zulu nationhood, about the coming of a democratic South Africa, and most of all, about his Christian faith. He evokes the memory of Martin Luther King, Jr., for whom he has unbounded admiration, when he speaks about martyrdom. He does not seek it, he does not want it, but he does not fear it.

The struggle, he asserts, is much greater than himself, and that is why Kwazulu and Inkatha must be built up as an "impregnable" base. His constant theme is endurance, the long distance, the need for discipline. In the rhetoric of Inkatha, "discipline" is always cropping up. Some references to the need for solidarity and the control of dissent are chilling to those of liberal democratic sensibilities. His critics complain about the use of "strong arm tactics" and "goons" in Inkatha. An English political activist explains at length why she has misgivings about Buthelezi and Inkatha, concluding, "I suppose it all comes down to the fact that I don't like organizations that march children around in military uniforms." It is a well-founded dislike, but Buthelezi answers that such discipline is necessary during the period of struggle. The goal, he declares with feeling, is democracy—a bill of rights, an independent judiciary, economic freedom (although not "unfettered capitalism"), and all that is prized by Western civilization. Many leaders have said that undemocratic means must be accepted temporarily for a period of emergency, only to conclude later that the "period of emergency" would be endless. Buthelezi knows that and insists that he is not one of those leaders.

Believe him or not, Buthelezi is there, and the position he has built will likely be there after he is gone. There may never be a final dispensation in South Africa, but any dispensation that at last includes all South Africans will depend upon an agreement between the two largest population groups—the Afrikaner and the Zulu. The basic definition of the South African dilemma is, of course, to be understood in terms of black and white—but some whites and some blacks are more equal than others. To be sure, it is not the way it ought to be. But, since it is the way it is, it is probably a piece of good fortune that in the leadership of the black side of inequalities is a figure as seemingly thoughtful, humane, and determined as Chief Gatsha Buthelezi of the Zulus.

CHAPTER ELEVEN
THE REVOLUTIONARY OPTION

I N December 1982, the newspapers carried the story of a fourteen-year-old goatherd in Kwazulu who had been attacked by a python measuring five feet in length. The snake's teeth became embedded in the head of the knobkerrie, a small club, the boy was carrying but its coils gripped him tightly, threatening to squeeze him to death. By turning his own head the boy managed to sink his teeth into the python's neck and chewed out its throat until the snake was dead. The story is suggestive for thinking about violent revolution in South Africa.

No one in his right mind would doubt that the killing of the python was morally justified, indeed imperative, in terms of self-defense. Much less clear is the case for justified revolution in South Africa today.[1] The Afrikaners, however, are in an awkward position to insist that blacks are morally bound to "obey the powers that be." There was, after all, their violent rebellion against the English. And in 1914, when many Afrikaners opposed entry into World War I, the Dutch Reformed church declared that "no one may revolt against lawful authority other than for carefully considered and well-grounded reasons based on the word of God and a conscience enlightened by the Word of God."[2] Many blacks proposing revolution in South Africa today believe that their reasons are well-grounded and their consciences enlightened, also by the word of God.

Yet others seem to have endorsed revolution in principle, throwing caution to the wind. There are stories from the past of tribal chieftains who told their people that the gods had granted them immunity from bullets and then led thousands to their deaths before European gunfire. The Xhosas were a problem to the British until, in 1857, the seer Mhlakaza prophesied that the whites could be defeated if the Xhosas raised their great warriors from the dead. To do this, all Xhosa crops and cattle must be destroyed and then the warriors would arise and, with the help of a hurricane, drive the whites into the sea. Mhlakaza's counsel was followed and 25,000 Xhosa died of starvation, 30,000 were driven south in search of food, and the Xhosas were no longer an obstacle to British control. According to some critics, the proponents of violent revolution today reflect a death wish. According to more, they are possessed by a "Jericho complex," believing that the walls will collapse if only they shout loud enough.

Arthur Suzman is among those who think it a great mistake to assume that revolution would necessarily be black and from the left. Now seventy-seven, Suzman is an advocate who still calls himself "Queen's Counsel," although the term went out of use when South Africa left the commonwealth. He is also the brother-in-law of parliamentarian Helen Suzman and is head of the Jewish Board of Deputies in South Africa. There are more than 100,000 Jews in the country. They are among the most prosperous members of the society and, Suzman tells me, "have a peculiar view of affairs, a view trained by historical suffering." Because they understandably pay particular attention to evidences of anti-Semitism, they are particularly aware of the present and potential influence of the far right. "The anti-Semitism of the left does not escape our attention, however, especially as it touches upon Israel," says Suzman.

Military details are shrouded in deep secrecy, but no one disputes the many reports of a close and growing military cooperation between South Africa and Israel. Not only militarily but also diplomatically, exchanges and cooperative efforts have become routine and a matter of public knowledge. As Suzman and others explain, there is nothing surprising about this. Both countries are "pariah nations" in international forums such as the United Nations. Both are bordered by nations which have declared their eternal enmity and intention to destroy them. In addition, there is between the Israeli and the Afrikaner in particular a sense of peoplehood and destiny, no matter how diluted by secularization. "There is an old right here," explains Suzman, "and it is irrevocably opposed to the government's relations with Israel and even to the rights of Jews in South Africa. They still talk about a worldwide capitalist conspiracy of the Jewish moneylenders. They circulate *The Protocols of Zion* and other such obscenities."

He acknowledges that rightist anti-Semitism is on the decline and he is generally satisfied with the government's condemnation of it, "but we Jews know better than to be sanguine; oversensitivity is a lesser risk than complacency. . . . It is too simple to talk about right and left here. The anti-Semitism of what is called the left has troubling similarities with the old right, and we can all too well imagine circumstances in which the old right could become the new right. . . . I can tell you, there is a propensity toward the politics of extremes. Both talk about violent change. One wants to secure white supremacy and the other wants black domination. In either case there are scores to settle and both extremes want to shoot it out." As we have seen and will see again, talk about violent reaction by whites opposed to any form of power sharing with others is a staple in discussions of South Africa's future. It is in the background, but it is firmly there, as we turn our attention to the prospect of revolution leading to black rule.

The question of the moral justification of revolution does not need to be forced in these discussions. Moral language, even explicitly religious language, comes naturally to most black leaders. Observers have noted that most black leaders in Africa have been trained in missionary schools and many are deeply committed Christians. Julius Nyerere of Tanzania and Robert Mugabe of Zimbabwe are devout Catholics, while Kenneth Kaunda of Zambia promotes his version of "African humanism" in terms of Christian discipleship. As President Nyerere explained to me in an interview in 1971: "The European [meaning Western] fear of communism is understandable because you experienced a communism that was anti-Christian. It had to be, because in the last century and much of this century religion was allied with oppression. But that is not our experience in Africa. Here Christianity is a revolutionary force for change and can make common cause with all other progressive forces." These leaders of the "frontline states" committed to the armed struggle against South Africa, like those churches in the West that are similarly committed, make much of the fact that Christians are prominent in the leadership of groups such as the African National Congress and the South West Africa People's Organization. "If it comes to revolution," a black priest of the Anglican church tells me, "the Christians will be the first ones to be put up against the wall and shot, and it makes no difference to me that a Christian pulls the trigger." But his is a dissenting voice. Apparently it makes a considerable difference to others who articulate a moral justification for violent revolution.

Among whites in South Africa there has also been moral agonizing about the revolutionary prospect. The public agonizing crops up chiefly in connection with conscientious objection to military service. Conscription makes white males subject to two years service, then another two years spread out over twelve years, and they are still liable to being called up until age fifty-five. The English churches have long and adamantly called for laws protecting conscientious objectors. The government has been most reluctant, at least in part because calls for the protection of conscientious objectors have often been combined with the claim that South Africa is involved in a "civil war." The government, of course, is inclined to view military service as a patriotic duty in defense of one's country against the total onslaught by external enemies.

In April, 1983, a "depoliticized" form of conscientious objector status was allowed for anyone who, on religious grounds, objected to all war and refused to bear arms for anybody anywhere. As in the U.S., no provision is made for "selective conscientious objection." Unlike the U.S., the new status was made less attractive by joining it to the requirement that those exempted fulfill six years of alternative service under government direction. According to the military, three to four thousand young whites fail to show up for service each year. It is assumed that most of them have left the country in order to escape the draft. There may be other good reasons for avoiding military service, but opponents of the government interpret these figures as an indication of the moral turmoil experienced by young white South Africans who recognize that the black revolution that they are being asked to fight is in fact morally justified. "There are," Bishop Tutu says, "young white men of conscience who do not want to have to answer to God for being on the wrong side of the struggle."

In the minds of many the moral question commingles with notions of historical inevitability. It seems a long time ago that British Prime Minister Harold Macmillan spoke about "the winds of change" sweeping Africa, but that sense of irresistible movement is still present. It was at a fever pitch in the sixties and seventies when nations to the north were becoming independent one after another and, as a black schoolteacher told me, "We woke up every day thinking, 'We are next. We are next!' " While no one in South Africa (or almost anywhere else in the world) can legally advocate violent revolution, Bishop Tutu does express this feeling of historical certitude: "The liberation and freedom of the blacks in this land are inevitable." Whites, he says, scurry to protect their separate privileges, but "they have little time to enjoy them as they check the burglar proofing, the alarm system, the gun under the pillow and the viciousness of the watch-dog." He cites the American and French revolutions, the American civil rights movement, "the emergence out of co-lonial bondage of the so-called Dark Continent. Then there was the extraordinary resistance of the peasant people of Viet-nam ... who made [the U.S.] bite the dust in this struggle for the right to self-determination of a small people." Even the Afrikaners, who "believed themselves to be victims of British exploitation ... triumphed so that today they are at the pinnacle of their power." What is to be learned from all this? "It seems, therefore, to be a universal law that when a people decide to become free then absolutely nothing will eventually prevent them from reaching their goal. Why should it be thought that we blacks in South Africa will prove the exceptions to this rule?"[3]

RELIGION scholar John de Gruchy of the University of Cape Town says that change through violent revolution is the "trick card" in all discussions about South Africa. "No matter how careful you try to be in talking about the prog-nosis for change in South Africa, you always hear in the back of your mind the objection, 'But what if there's a revolution?' If there is, it relativizes everything else you might say, of course. But I think we cannot allow ourselves to be intimi-dated by that objection, because then we would simply stop thinking and talking about alternatives to violent change, and that would be tragic." Reflecting on his own experience, he says, "When I was away doing graduate work at the University of Chicago in the sixties, I thought then and I said then that South Africa had no more than five years before there would be revolutionary change." Fifteen years later de Gruchy is more appreciative of the oft heard remark that in South Africa the clock has been stuck at five minutes to midnight for thirty years. And yet he, being a very sensible person, does not deny the possibility that it actually is five minutes to midnight.

Ed Huenemann of Morningside Heights in New York is an interpreter of matters South African for liberal Protestants in the U.S. He is in close communication with South Africans plugged into the World Council of Churches orbit and on that basis is convinced that "of course there will be revolution, much sooner than anyone expects." "The only question," he says, "is how bloody it will be, and that depends on whether the superpowers stay out." The U.S. is already there, he explains, in the form of Israel which is "the U.S. tool for keeping the lid on in South Africa." Thus it is hypocritical of Pretoria to play up "the myth of the communist threat" as though that were the main outside interference. He quotes a black clergy colleague in South Africa who says, "Of course the Russians are involved, just as the C.I.A. is involved, but we'll only turn to the Russians if we have to— but then we will." Another South African friend tells him, "Our chief concern cannot be whether the revolution is successful. We are making the revolution and the result is in the hands of God. Our chief concern is whether we will be remembered as Bonhoeffer or as Hitler."

A political scientist in South Africa who describes himself as a Marxist and supporter of ANC, and who asks to go unnamed, tells me that the inevitability and the morality of revolution are for all practical purposes the same question. "You Christians say we should 'read the signs of the times' to see what God might be doing in history, but even if a man is not a Christian he can agree that you cannot set moral judgment over against history." (I do not argue this rendering of what it means to read the signs of the times.) The professor acknowledges that the heady days of belief in the inevitability of the winds of change blowing over the continent have been dealt severe setbacks. "But then hope was powerfully revived by Mugabe's triumph in Zimbabwe. I know people say there is no analogy between Zimbabwe and here, that the English there had the option of coming to South Africa and, if revolution comes here, have the second option of going to the U.K. But the crucial analogy is still there in the fact that black revolutionary force overthrew an oppressive white regime." The Afrikaners' claim that they have no option of going elsewhere and will therefore stay and fight to the end is, he believes, "vastly overrated."

"Revolutions are always unpredictable," he tells me. He cites the instance of the Belgians who, only months before surrendering the Congo to Patrice Lumumba, were confidently drawing up a fifty-year development plan for the colony. Only a little while before Angola and Mozambique gained their independence through armed struggle, Henry Kissinger was saying that the Portuguese were "in Africa to stay." And two years before he was forced out, Ian Smith declared that "never in a thousand years" would there be black rule in Rhodesia. "So I advise you not to listen to people who give you wise-sounding reasons about why there will not be revolution here. Revolution is not something you calculate, it's something you smell, and I can smell it in the air."

There are revolutions and then there are revolutions. The government and those to the right of it are inclined to declare that a person is advocating revolutionary armed struggle (and, of course, communism) if he simply ponders in public the likelihood of "evolutionary violence." Thus, for instance, Dr. Motlana of Soweto was briefly banned and is routinely under suspicion. There is a considerable distance, however, between advocating revolutionary armed struggle and encouraging deep social and political change that is accompanied, perhaps of necessity, by intermittent violence.

Motlana wants it understood that it is not for moral reasons but for purely practical reasons that he has concluded that the "hard revolutionary change" of armed struggle is "out of the question." His own call is for negotiations without any preconditions, "as long as it is understood that we are drawing up a constitution for the one land of South Africa." He has an appealingly simple idea of what might come from such negotiations. "Just take the present constitution of the country and delete from it all reference to race. Period. In other words, all race laws must go. Basically we have a beautiful constitution. I have no objections to this constitution, except where it refers to race." In view of the fears that groups have of one another—fears both within and across the color lines—and in view of the need to protect minority rights, Motlana's proposal may be too simple. But it might be a place to start. His call for unconditional negotiations is not too different from Gatsha Buthelezi's insistence upon a national convention to determine the future of the country, although Motlana is highly critical of Buthelezi.[4]

Dr. Motlana does not criticize the African National Congress by name but he has little use for the proposition that armed struggle is the only or the chief hope for change. "You have to have a sense of history," he says. "The Bolsheviks were able to do it because of the breakdown of the regime, because they had their people riddled throughout the civil service, the army, and so forth. Here blacks are outside all significant power. Our victory depends in part upon sustained guerilla action, urban and rural, but then blacks have to be in positions to capitalize on the fears they generate." He believes the Afrikaner is already more terrified than he admits. "There is a great depopulation along the borders. Whites are leaving. North of here there are vast farms that have been abandoned. They try to hide it, but they are suffering, and most of all they are suffering a loss of confidence. That uncertainty, that insecurity, is going to increase. Do not forget that the whole system depends upon black muscle, upon labor, and that's the Achilles heel. The labor action is just beginning and it's going to become more political, much more political."

Motlana says he wants to be realistic. "All the actions so far are only a kind of yeast, and the yeast is not yet working in the larger loaf." He says he understands those who talk about some grand international strategy to overthrow the apartheid regime, but that is only a dream. "It's a mistake to depend upon outside countries to do what we must make happen here. I remember many years ago, when John F. Kennedy became president and Harold Wilson became prime minister, then many of us thought this would make a big difference. But it didn't. Americans overestimate their importance. I say frankly, Americans are often a pain in the neck, even the ones who want to be on our side." He quickly adds, however, that he is not anti-American, that he is at least as skeptical of the Soviet Union and its surrogates. "The brutal fact is that countries act in their own self-interest, and blacks here must act in their self-interest." At the same time, however, Motlana insists that American foundations and labor organizations are critical in supporting progressive change in South Africa.

"We need money from the Ford Foundation and multinationals and trade unions for the simple reason blacks don't have the resources here. That's the only way we're going to get blacks in positions of power, in positions which make it realistic to talk about revolution or, better still, about unconditional negotiation which makes revolution unnecessary." He knows some militants disagree with him. "When I was in prison some chaps were very upset when I said that revolutions are made by the middle class. 'Oh, you have bourgeois ideas!' they said." He laughs and remarks that his own son has a B.A., and "he can quote Marx to me, and he does all the time, at great length and very eloquently, but I am afraid I am not persuaded."

Others appear to be persuaded, however, and their chief voice and vehicle is the African National Congress. Established in 1912 by self-consciously moderate leadership (which of course looked very radical to most whites), the African Native National Congress, as it was then called, distanced itself from the beginnings of communism which had cropped up in the mining areas and was concentrated on the "white proletariat." In the early twenties, the sundry socialist leagues and Marxist clubs joined to form the South Africa Communist Party (SACP), an orthodox, pro-Moscow organization that was promptly admitted to the Third International which Lenin had established in 1919. White-black conflict on the left erupted in 1928 when Moscow declared that ANC should become "the sole representative of the oppressed masses of South Africa," thus seemingly consigning the overwhelmingly white SACP to a back seat. Most whites in SACP opposed the directive, and soon SACP, which at one point had nearly two thousand members, was down to less than two hundred. But the faithful remnant set about trying to educate ANC to Marxist-Leninist orthodoxy.

By 1947 the SACP activists had a number of leadership positions in ANC, although, I am told, by no means "the complete control" of ANC, as Pretoria would have us believe. In the following years Moscow became increasingly specific about the usefulness of ANC in its global struggle against capitalist imperialism. Such blatant assertions by Moscow suggesting that it controlled ANC were too much for many blacks in South Africa who did not want their revolution to be a pawn in somebody else's game. In 1959 they formed the Pan African Congress (PAC). PAC's protest was also against ANC's reliance on white leadership and alleged alienation from the African masses. In 1960 the government banned all three organizations—ANC, PAC, and SACP—and since then ANC, albeit in exile, has been the most internationally recognized instrument of revolutionary change in South Africa. Today the United Democratic Front, of which both Boesak and Tutu are patrons, is generally assumed to "represent" the ANC viewpoint within South Africa.

PRETORIA keeps a voluminous file of Soviet and SACP literature which regularly and explicitly states that ANC and SACP are intimately coordinated as the instrument of armed struggle in South Africa. In this literature no secret is made of the fact that the struggle is aimed at a victory in which a monopoly of power will be exercised by the revolutionary proletariat. The government delights in quoting from this material in order to substantiate its claims about a communist-led "total onslaught." Such propaganda, however, does not disturb the revolutionary sangfroid of the ANC. They respond that, while Moscow and SACP may say what they want about controlling ANC, ANC speaks and acts for itself. Statements by both Moscow and Pretoria are sometimes resented by ANC leaders because both are seen to be implying that blacks are not capable of revolutionary action except under white tutelage. In response to the claim that military and financial aid from the Soviet Union makes ANC a puppet of Moscow, it is said that more money comes from Sweden than from the USSR. In addition, millions of dollars are received from other countries, from the United Nations and its specialized agencies, and from a network of churches in the West. As one ANC spokesman told me, "It is our policy to receive support from a wide range of sources so that we will not become too dependent on one party. But that does not mean that we do not know which are the progressive forces in the world and which are the forces of oppression."

That ANC has come a long way from its moderate beginnings in 1912 nobody denies. Until it formally allied itself with the thoroughly "Stalinized" SACP after World War II, ANC embraced goals well within, for example, the vision of the U.S. civil rights movement. Today the focus is on armed struggle and sabotage within South Africa. ANC is officially headquartered in Lusaka, Zambia, and has a formal "presence" in the neighboring countries of Angola, Botswana, Zimbabwe, Mozambique, and Tanzania. Its operations from these countries, as well as from Lesotho and Swaziland (which are surrounded by South African territory), have been increasingly restricted, however, by lethal raids and harassments conducted by Pretoria's defense forces. In 1984 Pretoria applied economic and other pressures that sharply reduced, and in some cases eliminated, ANC's capacity to operate from neighboring countries. The effective leadership of the organization operates mainly out of the ANC office in London.

It is sometimes said that, among Soviet-backed liberationist armies around the world, ANC is not yet fully blooded. In the world of revolutionisms, it is somewhat embarrassed by its early history in which it espoused nonviolence. But in recent years ANC has tried to make up for lost time. Until 1981 its sporadic acts of sabotage within South Africa were relatively small and aimed clearly at military targets, taking care to avoid loss of life to civilians. But now revolutionary actions are becoming, as it were, more impressive. ANC has taken credit for a number of explosions in urban centers and for a spectacular attack on the heavily guarded nuclear plant of Koeberg, near Cape Town. The most lethal action to date is the May 1983 bomb attack outside Air Force Headquarters in the heart of Pretoria. Nineteen people were killed, nine of them black, and more than 200 were injured. The python was beginning to sense an enemy presence at its throat.

The "frontline states" which have harbored ANC are more and more putting a short leash on its operations. Not only are these states vulnerable to South African military action, but they are overwhelmingly dependent upon South Africa in almost every aspect of their economies. Therefore ANC is forced to move its training camps and other belligerent operations farther north. Thomas Karis, an Africanist at City University in New York, and other experts agree that much of the training is done by East Germans with heavy financial backing from the Soviet Union, Libya, and, as mentioned earlier, the United Nations. According to U.S. intelligence estimates which most experts find credible, ANC has one to two thousand people in military training outside South Africa and two to three thousand secret members inside South Africa. The figures offered by ANC spokesmen are, as might be expected, much higher. In any event, says William Foltz of Yale University, "What is of interest is not the number of armed people they have. It is the number of people building networks and building cell structures in South Africa."[5]

Joseph Lelyveld of the *New York Times* has provided some of the most perceptive reporting from South Africa. He has talked with Oliver Tambo, the former law partner of Nelson Mandela and now president of ANC in exile. Speaking at his home in London, Tambo expressed satisfaction with the rising struggle inside South Africa and the military reaction of Pretoria against ANC bases. "When they do that," he said, "we feel that the struggle is proceeding, it's advancing, it's reaching more heights. We have accepted that it's going to be very bitter, brutal and savage. We think it's got to be. You can't talk the system out of existence."

Lelyveld notes that the ANC "shows different faces in different forums." At the 1983 Vancouver assembly of the World Council of Churches it described itself as "a community of love and justice on a pilgrim road to freedom." At about the same time, at an East German celebration of the Karl Marx centenary, it spoke of its "natural alliance with the Soviet Union and the world socialist system as a whole." Lelyveld, like others, is impressed by the secretiveness of the ANC leadership. It keeps any anxieties about contradictions to itself, thus permitting it to make antithetical public statements in a quite unruffled manner. Also like others, Lelyveld's talks with ANC leadership make him wonder whether so many years in exile have not taken their toll. Apparently sincere ANC statements about what is happening inside South Africa are frequently tinged by romantic exaggeration and are sometimes manifestly contrary to fact.[6]

In interviews with Western correspondents, Oliver Tambo routinely presses three lines. The first is that ANC is the sole representative of the liberation struggle in South Africa. Movements such as the Pan African Congress and the late Steve Biko's "black consciousness" movement are distractions. On black consciousness: "It's a product of white consciousness, a reaction." Second, U.S. policy over the years and the Reagan administration in particular are the enemy of liberation. Washington, he says, has declared South Africa to be "a very reliable, beloved ally." Third, ANC is not the puppet of Moscow. He acknowledges the military and other aid from the Soviets, but explains, "There would be no independence for anyone without those weapons. . . . Where would we be without that assistance? Could we go to Washington?" But Tambo insists, "It is not correct to say that the ANC is Communist-oriented. We are a liberation movement and our direction is socialist. It's got to be. . . . It couldn't be anything else, otherwise you sit down and accept the status quo. But as for the idea that the ANC is controlled by Communists, or is Communist-oriented, I reject it outright."[7]

It is suggested to me by one black student in Soweto that Pretoria is responsible for making communism fashionable among some young blacks. "If the government is so much against it, it must be very good," he said with a smile. A freedom song sung by some young blacks goes, "We shall follow our Slovo. Even if we are detained. Even if we are hung." The reference is to Joe Slovo, a white lawyer from Johannesburg and leader of SACP, who is now in exile and is frequently pictured as the brain behind ANC attacks inside South Africa.

That ANC is overwhelmingly dependent upon the Soviet bloc and, by its own frequent admission, allied with Soviet purposes in the world is not seriously in dispute. What one makes of the fact is something else. Dr. Motlana again: "Most of us think we should have some form of socialism, some state intervention." He mentions "democratic socialism, like in Sweden." "But I am not a Marxist. Back in my ANC days, we resented communist influence on our organization, an influence that continues to this day. Discussion of the struggle—the African nationalist versus the Communist Party—took place in my consulting rooms. I didn't agree with the breakaway group that became the Pan-Africanist Congress, though I shared their political views. They should have stayed to get rid of the communists and fight from within."[8] Motlana cannot say it in so many words, but the implication is that ANC is somehow still the chief instrument of the struggle. He knows that it is hard to say how anyone in South African can "fight from within" to change an exile leadership thousands of miles away.

Other blacks inside South Africa are still looking for alternatives to ANC. Recent stirrings of the Azanian People's Organization (AZAPO) bid to revive the black consciousness movement that went into decline following Biko's death in 1977. (Azania is the preferred name for South Africa among many black nationalists.) It is commonly believed that ANC counts among its own supporters in South Africa numerous young people who in fact identify with AZAPO and other nationalist movements. Some political actors in the West hold out little hope for change in ANC and use the communist influence within ANC as a club with which to beat all liberationist efforts. An example is a document titled "Soviet, East German and Cuban Involvement in Fomenting Terrorism in Southern Africa," which comes out of hearings by a U.S. Senate subcommittee chaired by the very conservative Jeremiah Denton of Alabama.[9]

Among students of African affairs in the U.S., a fairly typical response to items such as the Denton report is that of Ross K. Baker of Rutgers University. His point is not so much that Denton and others are wrong about the facts, but that they do not understand the policy implications. "Imagine," says Baker, "how much staff time, witness fees, travel expenses, and printing costs were expended on the effort to establish links between South African liberation movements and the European Communist states and Cuba! Had they given me, or anyone else who reads a newspaper, the cab fare to go over to the senate, I could have told them that these movements receive military, financial and moral support from the Communists. Where *are* they going to turn? To the Reagan administration?"

274

According to Baker, "The best that can be hoped for, in some future administration, is that the United States may resume its role as broker and reestablish some credibility with the liberation movements and their supporters in the front-line states."[10] The use of "liberation movements" in the plural suggests a fluidity in the ways of pursuing liberation that ANC adamantly rejects as both nonexistent and impossible. In one international meeting after another, the ANC leadership has demonstrated great skill in opposing other claimants and capturing sole control of the South African liberationist banner. Moreover, there is scant historical evidence that U.S. sympathy for movements that have declared themselves for the Soviet side will wean them away from that commitment, even if some within those movements might want to be weaned away. In sum, the situation poses severe problems for liberals in the West who cannot endorse Marxism-Leninism and who have learned from past experience the dangers of viewing incipient totalitarians as gentle agrarian reformers.

Many of us resist the "intrusion" of East-West power politics into liberationist struggles that are thought to be essentially North-South in character. South Africa, with its peculiar view of itself as both a Third World and First World country, makes the connections in a different way. When he came to power in 1948, Daniel Malan made a bid for membership in NATO, but the Western alliance declined to so extend its southern flank. South Africa would prefer to be a regional superpower allied with the West, but, if that is not possible, it is prepared to be such a power on its own. As P. W. Botha says, he is for the most cordial relations with surrounding countries "as long as we all accept the basic principles of stability, maintaining civilized standards and maintaining economic responsibility."[11] For the neighboring countries, of course, those code terms are tantamount to the hegemony of South Africa in southern Africa. South Africa's idea of forming a "constellation of states" is, Pretoria believes, in competition with the Soviet Union's similar idea.

A scholar close to the government points out to me, for example, this passage in a Politburo journal published in Moscow: "If we have the imagination to look at the continent as a potential economic region, we must take into account the area which does have a massive industrial base, a numerous and experienced working class, and the possibility— given its early emancipation—of acting in relations to most of the continent in the role developed Russia played towards the more underdeveloped parts of the Soviet Union."[12] Some observers, including many critics of Pretoria, believe that the modus operandi for the building of such a continental Soviet-controlled empire around the "emancipation" of South Africa is already in place. The military dimension of the plan is evident, they say, in a division of labor between the USSR, East Germany, and Cuba. The Soviets supply the higher strategic direction, logistic support, and arms; East Germany supplies experts, technicians, and instructors (especially for training intelligence agents and the secret police); and Cuba is responsible for the bulk of the combat force.[13] It is noted that this is the division of labor which has proved very effective in, for instance, Ethiopia at the northern end of the alleged empire-to-be. Closer to the South African home, the division of labor is evident also in Angola.

Hennie Serfontein, an affable antigovernment free lance journalist who serves as a stringer for European and American publications, tells me the above version of reality is "preposterous." "The government can't have it both ways," he says. "On the one hand, they talk about total onslaught and the threat of South Africa being wrecked by apocalyptic violence. On the other hand, they say ANC is the instrument of Soviet empire building. If the Soviets want to have an empire in Africa, they don't want South Africa destroyed, they want it to be in good shape. And no liberation struggle wants to triumph only to rule over a country that's been decimated.

So it's obviously in the interest of ANC, the Soviets, and everybody else to bring about change without destroying the country." If, he adds, a black-ruled South Africa ends up being closer to the Soviets than to the West, that is "only natural." "After all, who would the revolution have to thank for its success?" Like many others, he tells me that too much is made of the West's strategic dependence upon South Africa's minerals and other resources. "Even if South Africa is in the so-called Eastern bloc after liberation, there's nothing to stop East-West trade; it's going on all the time and I think that's a good thing. Anyway, the West would probably have easier access to resources after liberation. A black government would be easier to manipulate than the Afrikaners who are always sure to strike a hard bargain." I refrain from mentioning that some people might detect a trace of racism in the last remark.

The concern that ANC may be captive to Moscow's direction is real and widespread. Repeatedly I am told by non-Marxist blacks, however, that that concern must be weighed against the fact that alternatives to ANC are too beholden to Pretoria and its ties to the West. "One way or other," a black university student at Wits tells me, "our struggle will be distorted by the struggle between the superpowers." In any event, just as it is said that there is no way of getting around Gatsha Buthelezi, so it is acknowledged that there is no way of getting around ANC. It is not acknowledged by everyone, of course, but by everyone who thinks about change through violent revolution. Although the leadership has been in jail or exile for more than twenty years and may well be out of touch, and although it is admitted that the small membership inside South Africa is thoroughly infiltrated by the security forces, ANC is for most politically conscious blacks the symbolic bearer of the struggle for justice.

Despite his frequent strictures about ANC this seems to be recognized also by Chief Buthelezi. As we have seen, he is outspokenly critical of ANC's dependence upon Moscow. He also opposes the ANC line that things must get worse before they get better, that any turmoil and increase of fear inside South Africa is a revolutionary step forward. Unlike ANC, Buthelezi has not been enthusiastic, for example, about much of the student agitation inside South Africa. "There is something spiritually sick about the way in which school protests have been conducted. We all respect the mettle of a young man or woman who feels constrained to do something about the inferiority of their educational system. That respect, however, turns sour in our mouths when it becomes clear there is no real commitment to the struggle but only a boastful ego trip." Again unlike ANC, Buthelezi does not measure the development of the black community only in terms of the political utility of agitation: "Teenager thuggery is a phenomenon the world over in every society. Every generation of teenagers produces its own brand of thuggery. We can do without a contribution of our own teenage thugs in our struggle for liberation."

Buthelezi disagrees with the proposition that liberation is to be pursued "by any means necessary." Only democratic opposition, he says, holds the promise of a better future. "Victory over apartheid without democratic opposition as an essential and central strategy will only be the victory of one totalitarianism over another," according to Buthelezi. Yet he hedges his bets, suspecting that at some point, in an unpredictable future, collaboration between ANC and Inkatha will be almost inevitable. Much of his criticism of ANC is directed at its posturing as the only representative of the liberation struggle. "The ANC attempts to reduce Inkatha to just another organization on the same level as any other black organization in this country. The ANC in exile jealously guards the label given to it by the OAU [Organization of African Unity] and other states that it is the authentic representative of the black people of South Africa. I say bluntly that if this is the label the ANC accept, that label will be its epitaph."

Buthelezi's conversation suggests that he does not seek

to displace ANC but does demand a clearer recognition by its leadership that Inkatha is both legitimate and essential. With a presumed constituency of millions of blacks within South Africa and a track record of effective opposition to Pretoria, he and his organization, he suggests, should be acknowledged as an equal (at least) partner in the liberation struggle. "To say that you cannot fight apartheid from within South Africa is to say that you cannot fight it at all. And equally, to say that you can only fight it from within is to say that you cannot fight it at all."[14]

A particularly revealing evidence of ambivalence toward ANC is a position paper issued by Inkatha and carrying the heavy title, "No Successful Revolution Can Take Place in South Africa Without the Co-operation of Chief Buthelezi." While being careful to say that the revolutionary option is not on for the foreseeable future, and while strongly urging alternatives to violent change, the paper goes on to explain why, if violent revolution ever does take place, it cannot succeed without Inkatha and most certainly cannot succeed against Inkatha. Implicit in the argument, of course, is that to proceed without Inkatha is to proceed against Inkatha.

Keeping in mind the caution that revolutions are declared impossible before they happen and inevitable after they happen, one is forced to admit that talk about revolutionary change in South Africa is, more often than not, passionately romantic or abstractly ideological. Twenty years ago Martin Spring, who now publishes a newsletter in South Africa, was South African correspondent for *Newsweek* magazine. "I found it impossible to convince my New York editors," he says, "that South Africa was not on the brink of a violent revolution that would see the black majority sweep the white minority into the sea." He continues, "Even if the circumstances of South African blacks were as bad as the most extreme critics say, this would not in itself constitute a revolutionary climate."

Spring lists the "prerequisites" for successful revolution

"in any country or any time," without all or most of which revolution cannot happen. There must be a weakening of a traditionally strong government; the emergence of an alternative ruling elite in the form of a frustrated middle class; major participation by that elite in the power structure; the acquiescence or support of significant sectors of the traditional elite; and secure bases inside or outside the country. "Not one of those circumstances is to be found in South Africa," Spring concludes. He thus agrees with many scholars inside and outside South Africa who say that, no matter how odious the present order may be, and no matter how skeptical one may be about the government's willingness to change toward greater justice, the South African state is not about to be overthrown by violence.[15]

People who argue against the revolutionary option (and also against the status quo) tick off other reasons why, as they say, revolution is not on. They note that much of the black political elite in opposition movements are professional politicians, essentially rhetoricians with no other base in the society. Unlike, for example the Algerian revolution, or even the IRA in Northern Ireland, the small black underground has not established even the beginnings of an alternative government capable of dealing with community problems of crime, education, unemployment, and so forth. Unlike the Vietcong in South Vietnam, guerrillas in South Africa can count on no support from an effective regular army. As noted earlier, the "frontline states" have no such armies and, under military and economic pressure from Pretoria, are increasingly reluctant even to let ANC maintain a presence within their borders.

Unlike the Portuguese experience, there is no notable disaffection within the "metropolis" of the ruling group, and the South African army is a demonstrably effective and cohesive force. Soldiers are fighting at home (well, right around home), not overseas, and for their own survival, not for other people's property. The army, especially at command levels, is thought to be a liberalizing influence among whites in South Africa, but liberalization in no way means overthrowing the government. And so one is offered a long list of reasons why revolution is, if not impossible, at least so remote a possibility as to be beyond the pale of immediate consideration.[16]

Alan Cowell reports for the *New York Times* on a meeting in Lesotho of delegates from African nations who call for the revolutionary overthrow of South Africa. The meeting is held, he notes, a few weeks after Pretoria invaded Lesotho and effectively "cleaned out" the ANC presence. Lesotho could do nothing about the South African action and may well have colluded in it, but that is not mentioned at the meeting. Cowell observes, "It was a major irony of the conference that to reach Lesotho by air all routes led through Johannesburg." He concludes, "Faced with South Africa's military might, the main weapon of response available to black-ruled Africa and its outside supporters is oratory. . . . Western military analysts share the judgment among Western businessmen that their enormous investments in South Africa are safe for a long while."[17]

Nevertheless. . . . Many white South Africans express the fear that too much confidence is being placed in military might. Military leaders themselves have remarked that the struggle is 80 percent political and only 20 percent military. With major troop commitments in Namibia, plus an army thinly spread out to guard a border that spreads across the continent, plus the soldiers needed for growing interdictions in neighboring states, a manpower problem develops that could have devastating impact on the economy. General Magnus Malan has publicly stated that South Africa cannot do what Rhodesia did for so many years. White Rhodesians ended up spending six months of the year fighting in the bush. A comparable development in South Africa might lead to a South Africa that many whites would no longer want to defend. True, the proportion of whites in South Africa is five times greater than it was in Rhodesia, and the military recruitment base could be supplemented by the inclusion of coloureds and Indians, but for those who are thinking twenty and fifty years ahead the manpower prospect is still worrying.

In addition, were South Africa to continue on the course of moving the homelands toward independence, there is no guarantee that these "sovereign states" would always be compliant. And with each new independent homeland the amount of border that needs protecting is greatly expanded. Then too, if another hope of Pretoria is actualized—the hope to be the economic engine for a prosperous "constellation of states" in southern Africa—South Africa will find itself bordered by nations with a greatly increased military potential and no decrease in their dissatisfaction with South Africa's exclusion of blacks from the full rights of citizenship. Countering the proposition that South Africa is already a garrison state, I am told that the percentage of the GNP spent on defense is less than it is in the United States, and that the total of the police and security forces is smaller than the New York City police department. The figures may be accurate, but they do not speak to the psychology of a country that feels it is under siege. Official pronouncements alternate between alarmism about "total onslaught" and smug self-assurance, bordering on braggadocio, about South Africa's economic and military superiority. The impression conveyed is one of deep uncertainty, and it is not entirely discouraging to those who have embraced the revolutionary option.

For Mfanafuthi Makatini, better known as Johnny Makatini, the revolution is not an option, it is the certain future. I mention that I am thinking of possible subtitles for a book I might do, perhaps "The Futures of South Africa." "No," he says, "that would not be accurate. There are no *futures* of South Africa, there is only one future and that future is ours." The very personable and articulate Makatini was as a young man in the fifties a teacher in Natal. Together with other young teachers he became actively involved with ANC, and he and his fellows were forced to resign. He says he received four hours' notice from the ANC leadership to leave everything and give his life to the struggle. He has never looked back. Today he heads the ANC's observer mission at the United Nations, serves on its executive committee, and is said by some to be one of the two or three most important black leaders in the struggle for the liberation of South Africa. The opinion is widely shared that he would likely be South Africa's foreign minister if ANC took over.

We meet for lunch on New York's East Side, and the nonstop conversation goes on for more than three hours. He is eager that ANC be understood correctly. His years in New York tell. The conversation begins with apartment talk. He is having trouble with his sublet in Stuyvesant Town and wonders if I have any leads. As a single man he doesn't need anything "very grand." I'm afraid I have none. That Manhattan ritual attended to, he launches into a brief description of the world and of South Africa in particular. He is, in turns, didactic, pensive, whimsical, and occasionally belligerent. Throughout our conversation he nurses one martini on the rocks. Yes, he says, he is always glad to talk with someone about South Africa. The years of exile take their toll, and it is possible to get out of touch with what is happening there. "But we receive reports all the time, and we talk with people coming from home, and almost all the time what they say confirms our analysis."

The United States, he says, is key, and sometimes he imagines what he would say in a meeting with President Reagan. " 'Mr. President,' I would say very respectfully, 'you misunderstand if you think we are against you. We admire the United States, but you are on the wrong side of our struggle for freedom.' I would tell him that what we are doing is exactly the struggle of America against Britain. Americans should understand that. I would ask him why, if America and the Soviet Union could be allies to defeat Hitler, they cannot cooperate in defeating apartheid. 'Mr. President,' I say to him, 'the revolution is coming. There is not much time, but there is still time enough for the U.S. to get on the right side.' "

"Everything is playing into our hands," Makatini says at several points. In line with this he says that Reagan, even with his "obsessive fear of communism," is good for the struggle. Better than Carter? I ask. "Oh, Carter," he responds, smiling and shrugging his shoulders dismissively. "Carter and Andy Young," he continues in the same tone, "they were supposed to do so much for human rights in South Africa. But poor Andy, people thought he might help but then we discover him in South Africa talking with the government about how to promote neocolonialism." I indicate some surprise at that. "No, you must understand, that is all Andy was doing, telling them how to take the brutal edge off apartheid so it would look better to people in the West."

Throughout our conversation the cantus firmus is that the worse things get the better things are for the revolutionary prospect. Everything else is a variation on that. That is the way it is with historical inevitabilities. "Whatever happens, we win. If the regime becomes more repressive, the people become more radical. If the regime relaxes, then the expectations of the people rise. And so also with the economy, whether it goes up or down. In fact it's better for us if there's more prosperity; then the people are more angry about the disparities between rich and poor. So you see, whatever happens, we win. We win even when it looks like we are losing." The Rockefeller Commission got it wrong when they titled their report *Time Running Out.* "Time ran out a long time ago. Maybe in the 1950s you might say 'Time running out,' but now it is past time. In the fifties revolution seemed like a bold idea, but now it is the natural thing. Our people have seen it happen all over the continent and they ask, 'Why not us?' Now *not* having a revolution is the unnatural thing."

Employing the familiar Marxist terminology, Makatini says that South Africa is now in a prerevolutionary situation.

"Until now there has been much talk," he says with intensity, his eyes narrowing, "but pretty soon now, very soon, you will see, there will be more fight than talk. The talking is over." Makatini is well aware that in international liberationist circles some people refer derisively to ANC's earlier adherence to nonviolence. He says that now ANC has definitely taken its place within the world scene. At the UN its status is "one step below the status of the PLO," and the ANC's recognition as the sole representative of the oppressed people of South Africa is only prevented by a "remnant" of Pan African Congress influence in the Organization of African Unity.

"There is no alternative to armed struggle," he says. He is adamant on this, repeating the point several times. "We have the world record on trying nonviolent means. Nobody can say we did not give nonviolence a chance. Even when people laughed at us, we said we were nonviolent. Nobody laughs at us now." Back in the fifties maybe there were alternatives to armed struggle—negotiations, a national convention, other things. "But they [Pretoria] said No to everything. Maybe negotiations would have been successful then, but frankly I'm glad they said No. Any agreement that was possible then would have fixed blacks into subservience. Today there would be a much bigger black bourgeoisie, but the people would still be oppressed and there would have been no revolutionary potential." To every peaceful proposal for change, no matter how unlikely, Makatini responds with a firm "It's too late." "You must understand that we're not going back, never! All the talk about nonviolence and negotiations, all this talk is old, it's tired, we've been there, it doesn't work. We have no illusions about that. There is no alternative to armed struggle."

Then the obligatory question of how long. "I don't like to answer the question of how long it will take. But I can say this, within ten years, and I personally think five years might be closer to the fact." He talks about the combination of armed struggle and external pressures such as international boycotts. He also believes that union organizing ("the labor struggle") among blacks will become more political and more important. He quotes the great Albert Luthuli who once said that victory would come within his lifetime. "When I heard that, I thought I would go one more than Luthuli, so I said 'Victory before I get married!' And maybe I am wanting to get married pretty soon," he laughs. Turning somber, "You must understand that nothing can stop us. Nothing. If they assassinate me, if they assassinate other leaders, that is good. Our prestige rises and the revolution grows. It is just like the Palestinians and Israel. The more the oppressor wins, the more he loses." He is not discouraged because he knows that the victory of the armed struggle is inevitable. "When it comes, we cannot say. We are often surprised by events, it is true, we are caught with our pants down. So exactly when the struggle triumphs and exactly how, I think it will catch all of us, the enemy and us, with our pants down once again," he says with a broad smile.

We discuss the human costs of revolution, and I mention General van den Bergh's estimate that 3 million or more blacks would die in an all-out armed struggle. "That interests me," Makatini says, "I had never heard before what figures they use." He pauses for reflection and says, "Yes, that is reasonable, 3 or 4 million. That is close to our experience in Algeria." He explains that he was for some years ANC's man in Algeria and that in the Algerian revolution 1.2 million died out of a population of 12 million. "Yes, considering the number of people, 3 or 4 million may be correct for our situation." I wonder if such a prospect is not inhibiting. "No, of course not, why should it be? Of course death is very sad, you would have to be a fanatic like Khomeini to deny that. But you look at revolution with your eyes open." He becomes quite animated as he asserts, "Of course there may be millions of deaths, but is that worse than millions of people dying from the slow genocide that is happening now? Is it better to die slowly? No, it's better to get it over with. I know how our people think, especially the young people now. If you tell a rally in Soweto about the costs of revolution, about how many people will die et cetera, they'll say, 'To hell with that! Get on with it!' " Makatini avers that the important thing is that South Africa be free. "If there were only 4 million of us left after the revolution, that would be better than the present situation."

He explains that ANC is not morally insensitive. "We have signed the Geneva conventions on humane warfare and we have invited the regime to sign too, but they refuse. So you can see who cares about morality." He observes also that until now the ANC has been hitting only "hard targets" such as police stations, trying to avoid civilian casualties. "We would have the right to shoot people in their houses because they are all belligerents, they all receive military training, but we have chosen not to do that." The self-restraint of revolutionaries is not unlimited, however, and Makatini emphasizes that the regime's refusal to agree on humane warfare may well force ANC to be less sentimental in the way it presses the battle. "They will scream about international terrorism, but, if we are forced to these measures, it will be nothing compared with the terrorism they practice all the time," he explains.

"Our mission on the continent of Africa is to demonstrate the possibility of a nonracial democratic state," he asserts with an evident feeling of pride. There will be no confederation, no consociation, no qualified franchise, "nothing like that." Must it be one person, one vote? "Not necessarily. But these are all details that will be decided collectively. The important thing is that there will be a unitary state, a common citizenship, one South Africa." Somewhat surprisingly, since this is not usual in ANC literature, he says it could be a multiparty state. "Well, the whites, for example, are going to need their own party," he says. I note that there are few multiparty states in Africa. Yes, he knows that, probably no more than five. He includes Tanzania in his count and seems a bit miffed when I point out that Tanzania is a one-party state. "Never mind," he says somewhat defensively, "if democracy is a rare thing in Africa, then that's part of our revolutionary challenge." Evidently economic details will also have to await a collective decision. "My own contribution to the decision would be that it should be a mixed economy, something like Sweden or China."

Is he concerned at all about who would be making these collective decisions? "If the decision is collective," he responds, "you can see that the 'who' does not matter." "Personalities are not important," he continues. "The revolution is bigger than I am, it is something you give yourself to. Mandela, for example, is important but he is not critically important. He would be offered the leadership after the revolution, but I know he would decline it, and that's because he believes in collective decisions."

To qualify for a part in the collective decision making the chief requirement is that a person recognizes now that "there is no alternative to armed struggle." "After the revolution the decisions will be made by those who came to that recognition before the revolution," Makatini elucidates. People who cooperate with so-called alternatives to the armed struggle, such as P. W. Botha's new dispensation, "belong in the dustbin." I mention Allan Hendrickse and am assured that Hendrickse will not be so stupid as to participate in the government's constitutional reforms. (This was shortly before Hendrickse and the Labour Party announced they would take full part in the election to the coloured chamber of parliament.) "Why should anybody abdicate their part in making the decisions of the future?" he asks. "We are the main force, we are the only force. I can tell you that every so-called alternative is just another version of the Oppenheimer option that the English speakers like so much. It is a way of making blacks a little more comfortable in their slavery. At the very most it's semislavery. Do you see any reason why people who support slavery now should be making decisions when South Africa is free?" The counterrevolutionary sin is to suggest that any kind of dialogue is possible between opponents in this armed struggle. "I agree with the Afrikaner who said that proposing dialogue between them and us is like dialogue between a whale and an elephant; there is no point of meeting," Makatini says with a smile. (It presumably was another Afrikaner who said to me, "To dialogue with the ANC is like sitting down to negotiate the arrangements for your own hanging.")

Makatini becomes more cautious in talking about Gatsha Buthelezi. He says Buthelezi is a friend, "but he is sitting on the fence. I do not understand what he is doing. The danger is that he may try to be a third force, and that would be a big mistake. As you know, he is advised by rabid anticommunists." The last factor, he says, perhaps explains Buthelezi's criticisms of ANC, which Makatini says he had not heard about before. "But there is no doubt that Gatsha is important; we recognize that he is the leader of the largest group in the country." In addition, says Makatini, who is himself a Zulu, the Zulus are the most formidable fighting force. "You must understand the Zulu mind. The Zulus are like the Germans— they believe in the leadership principle. The leader just points them toward the enemy and tells them to fight, and they follow orders without questioning." He pauses and there is a slightly apologetic smile, "I hope you don't think there is anything racist in what I said." I assure him that I understand.

But I am still curious about his respectful attitude toward Buthelezi in light of Buthelezi's vigorous pursuit of alternatives to the armed struggle. "Yes, I know, he wants a national convention. I do not think we can rule that out under any circumstances whatsoever. *If* the regime would legalize all organizations, including ANC, if they released everybody from detention, if they lifted all bans and restrictions, if they repealed the pass laws and the Group Areas Act, if they repudiated the whole Bantustan idea, if, if—then maybe there could be a national convention. But you know and Gatsha knows that they're not going to do these things." I suspected that by the time Makatini finished his list of preconditions there would be very little for such a convention to deliberate.

A more conciliatory note is struck in talking about what happens after the revolution. The subject is no longer the necessary death of millions or the consignment of collaborators to the dustbin of history. "We need the whites. Not as much as they need us, but we need them. . . . The great task then will be national reconciliation, I think about that all the time," he says in an almost melancholy manner. "I have dreamt about this, toward the end of the revolution and the victory is ours and thousands and thousands of whites are on the boats running away. How then can we have a multiracial society?" So what is the answer? "They'll come back when they see they have no reason to be afraid. They came back in Algeria." Makatini draws a sharp distinction between the Afrikaner and the English speakers. He does not say so, but one gets the impression that he would not be excessively downcast if the English stayed away. The Afrikaner is different. He is a true African. "The Afrikaner is one of us. He came from Europe before the industrial revolution, before everything that has made Europe the way it is today. After the revolution I truly believe we could start over again with the Afrikaner, the way it should have been from the beginning."

There is an element of poignancy in Makatini's reflections on black-white relations. He tells about meeting a white woman from South Africa in London. In a moment of whimsy he told her that he was from Toga, had a Ph.D. in economics and political science, and was in London with a diplomatic mission. "She was amazed and explained to me in a most respectful manner that she had never had the opportunity of talking to a refined black man before. She said that in South Africa all the blacks were very different, they were illiterate and violent and had the most terrible manners. I decided not to tell her who I really was. It probably would have been too great a shock to her." In such moments Makatini speaks about "acceptance" in a way that is quite moving. "They think we hate them. We do not. They think we are barbarians. We are not. But how can they know better? We do not talk to one another. We cannot." Then, abruptly, "They are captive to their myths of racial superiority; the whole exploitative system depends upon maintaining those myths. On that I think they'll never change until they're forced to change."

There is also an evident ambivalence when the discussion turns to ANC and its alleged captivity by Moscow. Makatini does not deny the facts about ANC's alignments or the involvement in its leadership of whites who are communist. "But that does not mean we are dependent upon the Soviet Union in the sense of being controlled by them. Remember that the ANC is older than the Russian revolution." He also cites as evidence of independence that ANC is sending a delegation to China without consulting the Soviets or asking for their approval. And, yes, people like Joe Slovo make an important contribution, "But they are not involved in the day by day decisions."

Like others with whom we have spoken. Makatini says that anxieties about Soviet influence are deliberately nurtured by racists who exploit the prejudice that blacks could not run their own show. "It is absurd that people make such a worry about the Soviets. Are they going to send troops into Africa? No, they are our friends, but they are different." Then again a trace of poignancy, "Our ties are with you. Our people do not speak Russian or Bulgarian, or whatever they speak over there. We are part of you—socially, culturally, economically, in every way. I almost weep that Americans can't understand that." And indeed he seems on the verge of tears. But, almost visibly, he shakes himself out of it. "I'm not surprised of course. The U.S. has always been shortsighted. Their fear of communism prevents them from seeing who their friends are. If they're determined to be our enemies, well, that's their look out."

These, then, are facets of what is called the revolutionary option. In Johannesburg, Lusaka, London, and New York it is the subject of interminable debate, engaging the most remarkable questions of geopolitical balancings of power, of revolutionary theory and praxis, of the meaning of justice in a disordered world. And all the while I keep thinking about that goatherd and the python.

CHAPTER TWELVE

NO FINAL DISPENSATION

FROM Carel Boshoff to Johnny Makatini. From the Broederbond and the South African Bureau of Racial Affairs
to the African National Congress. There, one might think,
we have surveyed the full spectrum of South African viewpoints on the future of South Africa. There is some truth in
that, but I have come to believe it is far from the whole truth.
The parties, passions, and paranoias of South Africa drive in
confusedly different directions that cannot be accommodated
by the image of a simple spectrum running from left to right.
From the Boshoffs to the Makatinis—that is the way the conflict and the choice is routinely presented to the world. They
are the "extremes" and on some "middle ground" between
them moderation and wisdom is to be sought. Perhaps. But
I think it more likely that wisdom, and reason for tempered
hope, is to be found not on middle ground but on quite different ground. No lasting dispensation can be established by
splitting the difference between the white oppression of blacks
and the black oppression of whites.

A different image was suggested one afternoon in conversation with Ian Player, the brother of championship golfer
Gary Player. Ian Player runs a nature preserve in Natal and
has also concerned himself with the preservation of Zulu
culture. He considers himself nonpolitical, but ruminating
on the state of South Africa he said this: "Here is where we
are, I think. We are like a huge herd of cattle that have rushed
into a ravine and then discover that it is dead-ended. They
mill about and churn about in a frenzy, and finally some of

them try to go backwards, while others try to find a way out of the ravine." Apartheid is the ravine and the confused churning is the last thirty years of Afrikaner history. The Boshoffs are pushing to go backwards, the P. W. Bothas are looking for another way out. Like all such images, it is limited, but it is suggestive.

Gerrit Viljoen, minister of education and a member of the "inner cabinet," tells me that apartheid is a thing of the past and separate development is "an interim policy." Does this mean that the homelands idea may be abandoned? "Yes, it may well be. Why not? We are a government of change." Denis Worrall, who chaired the constitutional committee of the President's Council, tells me that there will be an effort to create one or two more "independent" homelands, but then the "interim policy" will have run its course. "No one in a responsible position today, certainly not the prime minister, believes that the answer is the political accommodation of blacks in their own national states," he says. This is exactly what the Boshoffs fear is the government's intention. The homelands idea is the very heart of grand apartheid, and its abandonment means the certain end of the Verwoerdian dream.

The nature of the ravine from which the government seeks to extricate the country is described succinctly in these lines from the first report of the constitutional committee: "It is true, of course, that perceptions of interest may change, so that interests which conflict at one point in time may cease to do so at another. But in foreseeable circumstances in South Africa, the perceived interests of Whites and Blacks are hardly likely to change *so as to persuade either population group that its vital interests would be sufficiently protected and promoted by the other*" (emphasis added). The last sentence bears a careful second reading. Note that it could be agreed to by almost everyone in South Africa. It is, I believe, indisputably accurate. Note also the flexibility of language—"foreseeable circumstances," "perceived interests." It is subject to change.

And it is changing all the time. In September 1985 a delegation of foreign ministers from the European Economic Community came to Johannesburg to press for more rapid change. This was at the time that the EEC was getting ready to adopt more rigorous sanctions against South Africa, and President Reagan, also ordering rather mild sanctions, was announcing that "constructive engagement" should now be understood as "*active* constructive engagement." On September 1, in response to the EEC delegation, Pretoria issued this formal statement: "If by 'apartheid' is meant, 1) Political domination by any one community of any other, 2) The exclusion of any community from the political decision-making process, 3) Injustice or inequality in the opportunities available for any community, 4) Racial discrimination and impairment of human dignity, [then] the South African Government shares in the rejection of that concept."

The statement went on to make a number of other pledges, including "political participation of all communities at all levels in matters of national or common concern," and the establishment of structures to carry out these goals "through negotiations between the leaders of all the communities." Of course such a statement leaves a great deal undefined. It does not specify who are "the leaders of all the communities," and, as of this writing, there is no indication that this means negotiation with, for example, a freed Nelson Mandela. In sum, the statement is still a long way from the unconditional negotiation called for by Chief Gatsha Buthelezi and the Progressive Federal Party in their newly formed "Convention Alliance."

What does the government really intend, and will it be able to do what it intends? There are two questions there, and the safe answer to both, which happens also to be the honest answer, is that I do not know. It is also a thoroughly unsatisfactory answer. The first question—what does the government really intend?—is somewhat more answerable than the second. Somewhat. If one pesters and probes up to and perhaps a little beyond the bounds of civility, answers begin to emerge, some more plausible than others. In the preceding chapters we have listened to a wide array of answers to a wide array of questions: Is the limited inclusion of coloureds and Indians a step toward the inclusion of blacks or a dam against their inclusion? Is the distinction between urban and rural blacks a design to empower or to further divide and weaken the blacks of South Africa? Is the homelands idea a permanent factor in policy, or will it be abandoned, or will it be replaced by some other scheme of partition between black and white? In sum, is this a genuinely reformist government that is at least moving in the direction of political equality and economic opportunity for all people within a democratic South Africa?

Denis Worrall should know about as well as anyone. More than anyone he has been at the center of the constitutional conceptualization of the new dispensation. The nth time I came back at him with these questions, indicating my dissatisfaction with his responses, he appeared resigned and a bit impatient. "Listen," he said, "there are some things we cannot say because we do not know, and there are some things we simply cannot say. You've read Huntington. That's it. That's the Scripture. Not necessarily in the specific details, but that's the spirit and the substance of what this government is trying to do. That's it."

The Huntington analysis is much discussed inside and outside of government circles. It is titled "Reform and Stability in a Modernizing, Multi-Ethnic Society," and was prepared for the Political Science Association of South Africa. Samuel P. Huntington, director of the Center for International Affairs at Harvard University, is acclaimed or reviled as the guru of the new dispensation. His analysis, prescription, and very tentative prognosis warrant the closest attention. If there is a hidden agenda, this could be the key to it.[1]

By "ethnicity" Huntington means primarily the four principal racial groups in South Africa. In other societies, ethnicity may have more to do with language, nationality, or religion. There are in the world, Huntington says, multiethnic societies that are "vertical or hierarchical" and other multiethnic societies that are "horizontal or parallel." To put it differently, in some societies the ethnic distinctions are up and down and in others they are side by side. South Africa is the first kind. Race determines your place in the pecking order. That is too bad in Huntington's view, because in side-by-side multiethnic societies it is easier to resolve conflicts. (Even there it's hard enough, as witness Sri Lanka, Cyprus, Lebanon, and Nigeria.) Where communities that have their own internal up-and-down hierarchies live side by side in a society, it is possible to develop something called "consociational democracy."

But in vertical multiethnic societies, change becomes a zero-sum process. One community's gain is at the price of another community's loss. This is especially true when an ethnic minority is on top. That group then exploits and oppresses the majority group that it views as inherently inferior. Among the societies that have been or are like that in our time are Rwanda, Liberia, Rhodesia, Burundi, Guatemala—and South Africa. Such vertical multiethnic societies are not good insurance risks. They are regularly being overthrown, often in a very bloody manner. That is because they have a very unstable method of social stratification—of determining how people arrive at or get assigned their place in society. The reason it is unstable is that stratification based upon race is "ideologically obsolete." It goes against the grain of the way we moderns think things ought to be. Because political scientists prefer the "value-free" language of the laboratory, Huntington doesn't put it this way, but the point is that "vertical" multiracial orders are judged to be morally repugnant, and South Africans must face the fact that they are not going to argue the modern world out of that moral judgment. The further fact is that the ruling groups in South Africa are increasingly part of that world and agree with that moral judgment.

There are some societies where minorities dominate majorities and may get away with it for an indefinite period. Saudi Arabia is one, South Africa may be another. Those who take this view point out that the whites, especially the Afrikaners, are unified in being determined to maintain their privileges. In addition, there is no doubt about white superiority in the military and other means to fight enemies both internal and external. Finally, the black opposition is divided, and important black leadership can be co-opted by the government.

Against this notion that South Africa can go on as it is for an indefinite period, however, Huntington places some other considerations. No matter who is in office in Washington and London, South Africa is going to come under increasing international criticism. Second, for the South African economy an increasing number of skilled black workers is more important than surplus numbers of unskilled workers. And third, blacks will become increasingly effective in opposing a system that excludes them from political power.

Huntington does not think revolution is around the corner, but "revolutionary violence does not have to be successful to be effective." All that is required to be effective is to create divisions within the ruling group over how to deal with the violence. "At some point in the next decade or two, some combination of black mobilization, economic trouble, and external threat are likely to create a crisis within the South African political system that will only be resolved by fundamental change of that system," this analysis asserts. The government's challenge, then, is to try to shape events in advance rather than to be caught in the position of merely reacting to crisis.

The political system of South Africa was out of synch with its social reality. That is, a four-race society has had a one-race political system. Almost everyone in South Africa recognizes that this is a very unstable arrangement. What to do about it is another question. In descending order of the scope of change involved, there are four familiar proposals for reconstituting the society or the political system, or both. First, says Huntington, is violent revolution in which whites, coloureds, and Indians would be expelled, thus creating a one-race society with a one-race polity. "While such a solution may seem far-fetched at present, it could become more conceivable after a prolonged period of racial polarization, guerrilla warfare, and revolutionary conflict." This proposal would likely involve "a greater or lesser degree of genocide." A historical example is the way the multiethnic Ottoman Empire became the uniethnic Turkish republic through the slaughter and expulsion of Armenians and Greeks.

A second possibility would be to get really serious about the homelands and remove the blacks from "white-coloured-Indian" South Africa. Then South Africa proper would have a three-by-three arrangement, a three-race society and a three-race polity. But that doesn't work if black labor is to play an increasing role in the South African economy. Such a "solution" is three-by-three in theory but, with all those black workers in South Africa, four-by-three in actual fact. Anyway, if one accepts a three-by-three arrangement, the inexorable logic suggests moving on to a four-by-four set up.

A third direction is to abolish race as a category and have a one person, one vote system. "The key issue here is whether South Africa is a society of individuals or a society of racial communities. The record would suggest that it is far more the latter than the former," according to this analysis. "In addition, if fully implemented, a non-racial polity would seriously injure the interests of all four racial groups. Without some form of concurrent majority, Whites, Coloureds, and Asians would feel threatened in the political sphere by the automatic black majorities produced by a one-person one-vote system. Without some form of affirmative action and compensatory benefits, blacks would feel severely disadvantaged in the economic system by the application of strictly meritocratic criteria for employment, promotion, and wages."

This leads to the fourth possibility, which is genuine power sharing between all four groups. It means moving from apartheid's four-by-one formula to a four-by-four arrangement, bringing society and polity into synch. "This type of change is fundamental but not revolutionary, the most basic type of reform." Here is where the idea of consociational democracy comes in. It is built upon a "grand coalition" of the leaders of each group, and requires both cooperation among leaders and their ability to control their own followers. According to Huntington, "What the theorists have labeled 'consociational democracy' is nothing of the sort; it is more appropriately designated 'consociational oligarchy.' " It excludes democratic competition within groups and therefore cannot accommodate the emergence of new leaders who might challenge the arrangement agreed upon by today's leaders. In addition, consociational systems require that the elites of one community recognize the elites of other communities as equals. That is not the case in vertical multiethnic societies such as South Africa. But Huntington thinks it possible that, through "a unique and extraordinarily difficult effort at reform," the preconditions for consociational institutions just might be created.

Perhaps the most intriguing and astonishingly candid part of the Huntington work is its treatment of "the politics of reform." He starts out with the somewhat obvious: movements for fundamental change have analytical, prescriptive, and strategic components. The analytical says what's wrong now, the prescriptive says where we should be going, and the strategic says how we might get there. Not so obviously, he says that in moving toward a postapartheid political system the strategic may be more important than the prescriptive. "At this point, to know precisely where one is going is perhaps less important than to know clearly how one can get there." The key word there is "precisely." Fundamental change in South Africa is "waiting for its Lenin." Not that Huntington favors Lenin's tactics, strategy, or goals. "I am suggesting the need . . . for intense attention to the strategy and tactics of reform comparable to that which Lenin devoted to the strategy and tactics of revolution."

Surveying historical and current examples of societies undergoing fundamental change, Huntington latches on to Brazil as a suggestive example. The key concept there in the movement from a closed military government to a more open polity is *distensao* or "decompression." The government does not say where, precisely, it is moving, but it is moving. "Most importantly, the commitment of the government has been to a political process not to a political system." This strategy keeps options open for the government while avoiding divisive and damaging debates among reformers. It is the strategy adopted in part by P. W. Botha in the 1983 campaign for constitutional reform. He and his colleagues constantly reiterated that a Yes vote was a vote for an open-ended process. At the same time, however, in order to win support for the process he had to appear to be closing off some options, such as the full inclusion of blacks in the new dispensation. But, as we shall see, deliberate deception is not off limits in the Huntington strategy.

Six factors, we are told, are key to the reform process: political leadership; strategy and tactics; timing; power; issue selection and sequence; and reform coalitions. It might be argued that all these come under "political leadership," but we are reporting Huntington's analysis, not rewriting it. Political leadership for reform is a tripartite process "with the reform leader fighting a two-front war against both stand-patters and revolutionaries while at the same time attempting to divide and confuse his enemies." With the help of the Conservative Party and its allies, on the one side, and the African National Congress and its, on the other, P. W. Botha finds himself positioned to be a reform leader. That does not mean he is a reform leader in fact. "Whether efforts are made to utilize that opportunity only history can tell for sure because it is of the essence of the reformer that he must employ ambiguity, concealment, and deception concerning his goals." In other words, only in retrospect will we be able to say with certainty whether or not this is a reform government.

It is much harder, says Huntington, to be a reformer than to be a revolutionary. The reformer must have "the political ability and adaptability to engage in log-rolling and back-scratching, to shift allies and enemies from one issue to the next, to convey different messages to different audiences, to sense the eddies and tides of public opinion and time his actions accordingly, and to hide his ultimate purposes behind his immediate rhetoric." Huntington believes that "successful reform is rare if only because such talents are rare."

The reformer must employ "a combination of Fabian strategy and blitzkrieg tactics." The strategy is step-by-step, but each move is prepared in relative secrecy "and then, at the appropriate moment, it is dramatically unveiled, political support for it galvanized, and the reform enacted quickly before its opponents can effectively mobilize and organize themselves to stop it." Huntington believes that in 1978 and 1979, when Botha and others were going about declaring "adapt or die," the government had things backwards. It was using a blitzkrieg strategy with Fabian tactics, scaring off support by proclaiming fundamental change and then looking weak in its follow through. Timing is critically important. The government must appear to have the initiative and never appear to be acting from a position of weakness. That, says Huntington, is why the last minute reforms of the Shah in Iran turned out to be such a dismal failure. Time also requires having enough time for initiatives taken to be solidly implemented. South Africa may be running short of time, but "the later the process is started, the more difficult it becomes to carry it through successfully."

The power component is a big problem because at present it is so concentrated in South Africa, and those who have it have so much to lose. The fears of whites in South Africa are much more intense than were the fears among the elite during "the gradual incorporation of the middle classes and working classes into European polities in the nineteenth century." Fears born from self-interest and racial prejudice may make it difficult to undertake change democratically. Therefore, "the route from a limited uni-racial democracy to a broader multi-racial democracy could run through some form of autocracy." This is the much discussed "de Gaulle" option. In the form finally adopted, the constitutional reform has a presidency more along the American than the French model. But among its designers there appears to have been considerable sympathy for Huntington's suggestion that an "enlightened despotism" might be required for a time in order to move South Africa toward greater democracy.

Reform, be it understood, is not necessarily the alternative to violence. In fact, paraphrasing Marx, violence may be necessary as the midwife to reform. But the government must be in a position to control and use violence even while it is repressing counterviolence. "Within limits reform and repression may proceed hand-in-hand. Effective repression may enhance the appeal of reform to radicals by increasing the costs and risks of revolution, and to stand-patters by reassuring them of the government's ability to maintain order." Violence on the left and right must not be permitted to get out of hand, however, as it has in several Latin American republics. "When this happens, the outlook for both political order and social reform is dismal. The government that is too weak to monopolize counterrevolutionary repression is also too weak to inaugurate counterrevolutionary reform."

The process of reform cannot appear to be neat and logical. It is "usually tedious, inconsistent, and most unsatisfactory for almost everyone involved." The appearance of continuity is important, even while fundamental change is underway. "If new institutions are to be introduced, they need to be legitimated in terms of old values." This requires "substantial elements of duplicity, deceit, faulty assumptions, and purposeful blindness." In Huntington's analysis we are instructed as to why it was essential for the government to insist that the homelands policy was still in place when it was campaigning for the new dispensation in 1983. Had the government not so insisted, it would have greatly reduced support, "with the conservative Afrikaners seeing political representation for coloureds and Asians inevitably leading to black representation also."

While going ahead with reform, the government has much other business to attend to. Some of that business can get in the way of the business of reform. Huntington cites the question of Namibia. The government "was under heavy pressure from the United States and the other Western powers to arrive at a prompt resolution of the latter issue. If a Namibian settlement, however, involved a perceived set-back for South Africa and an immediate or prospective victory for SWAPO (South West Africa People's Organization), the ability of the South African government to reinvigorate the process of domestic reform would be significantly weakened for a substantial period of time." And in truth, in South Africa during the months prior to the 1983 referendum, discussions about Namibia focused much more on its possible impact upon the referendum than upon the danger of Cubans in Angola, which was the official reason for delaying a settlement in Namibia.

Finally, says Huntington, there is the need to build coalitions. "A multi-racial polity can only come into existence as the result of a multi-racial process. . . . One senses that the elements of a great coalition may well be present in South African society waiting for the leaders to engage them in a process of peaceful change." Potential recruits to such a coalition include members of all the population groups, some elements of the civil service, and the military establishment, while the coalition could find external allies in the governments of the United States and the United Kingdom. Opposed to such a coalition for reform would be the entrenched pro-apartheid bureaucracy installed by Verwoerd. But most of them are reaching retirement age. More effective opposition might come from radical black leaders who, through positive appeals and coercive threats, might "undermine the credibility" of moderate leaders willing to be part of such a coalition. The government's strategy might be one not of "divide and rule" but of "divide and reform." Given the rivalry among black leaders, it is conceivable that "at some point strong black leadership will be necessary to negotiate meaningful agreements with white leaders and to induce its constituency to support those agreements. Just as democracy among whites may hamper reform, so also may fragmentation among blacks."

The goal, then, is fundamental change that will bring society and political system into synch—a four-race society and a four-race polity. Consociational democracy (or, as Huntington prefers, consociational oligarchy) has never been achieved in an up-and-down, vertical, multiethnic society. But it is a challenge that could be attempted "with skillful political leaders cagily employing the right combination of Fabian strategy and blitzkrieg tactics, with a sense of timing exploiting positions of strength, concocting the proper mixture of reform, reassurance and repression, sliding two steps forward and dodging one step backward, where necessary playing on fear and employing deception, disaggregating issues so as to minimize opposition, capitalizing on the potentialities to create one or more reform coalitions, isolating revolutionaries on the one hand and stand-patters on the other, and through such a process eventually bringing into existence a new system of political institutions and thus giving renewed life to their country. Such a relatively happy outcome requires some small amount of luck and a large amount of political talent. It could indeed be ironic—and tragic—if a land that has so much of everything else should be lacking in these."

I T is hard to know what a plan really is when a stated component of the plan is deception. Is the government now moving toward a four-race, four-polity model along consociational lines? And, if so, does that movement offer reasonable promise of a political order that approximates our democratic idea of justice? The second question is easier to answer than the first. I believe the answer is yes. Within the limits and discontents of politics, such an order could conceivably accommodate the legitimate aspirations of all parties better than do the great majority of nations in the world today. To the first question, whether the government is in fact moving in this direction, there can be no certain answer. At this point no amount of additional information would change that reality, for it has to do both with the intentions of those in power and with their ability to do what they intend. As to their intentions, if they intend to pursue the course outlined above, they then cannot *say* what they intend. As to their ability to do it, that will only be known in the retrospect of history.

Now it can be said that many of the most astute observers, both inside and outside South Africa, think the government has, in spirit and substance, accepted the analysis, prescription, and strategy proposed by Samuel Huntington. Some high level officials in the government obliquely say this is the case. But of course, in accord with the Huntington strategy, they may be lying. It also can be said that many of the public statements by the government *are consistent with* the Huntington proposal. This is most clearly the case with the statements of the constitutional committee of the President's Council, the committee that was chiefly responsible for conceptualizing the new dispensation. But here again one runs into the rather esoteric dialectic by which their statements may mean the opposite of what they seem to say. Perhaps most persuasively, it can be said that the government's actions over the last several years *are consistent with* the design proposed. At very considerable political risk, P. W.

Botha and his colleagues have done what they would have done *if* their purpose was to advance this design. As politicians say elsewhere, so government politicians in South Africa say, "Watch what we do, not what we say." This deserves to be met by robust skepticism, since too often such politicians end up neither saying nor doing the right thing.

The right thing, if there is one right thing, may never get done in South Africa. In the course of our exploration we have encountered people advocating many things as the right thing: a white self-sustaining nation separate from and not dependent upon black labor; a revival of the apartheid ideal in its Verwoerdian purity; unconditional negotiations in a national convention; armed struggle leading to a nonracial (or multiracial or uniracial) socialist society; an individual-based one person, one vote liberal democracy; peaceful partition into nations confederally related; and variations on all of the above. It is reasonable to believe that the present government is working toward a consociational order that will include all population groups in South Africa. It is certain that no order will be lasting if it is designed and advanced by whites alone. Ultimately there will have to be negotiations toward a polity in which black influence is commensurate with black numbers and black interests. The most hopeful reading of the present government is that it is working to create the preconditions for such negotiations.

Among the most assiduous of South Africa watchers is the British journal, the *Economist*. In its finely nuanced editorial judgment of late 1983, "The motor of political reform in South Africa has just three speeds: slow, stop and reverse. The present proposals are no advance but Mr Botha has boxed himself into a position where their rejection would be considered a reverse—which is why the far right opposes them. They have therefore become a precondition for advance." And again: "Some will say this is merely polishing the crockery on the Titanic. Yet they have been saying so for two decades, during which the white regime has become ever more secure (and independent of the rest of the world in its security) and the oppressed non-whites have gained nothing from the support of their liberal friends abroad. Mr Botha's neo-apartheid has proved startlingly effective in preventing revolution, by keeping the country relatively prosperous . . . and by sweeping its opponents into death or oblivion. People genuinely concerned with human rights and the stability of southern Africa should examine each change on its merits, not merely on its contribution to revolutionary potential. Mr Botha is undeniably seeking to widen the pluralism of South Africa's previously all-white democracy, and thus broaden the basis for consent. It is a paltry step from which he may yet pull back. But it is a step."

Even such severely guarded hopefulness has been reduced by the fall of 1985. Then the *Economist* wrote that there are basically two believable scenarios for South Africa: "degenerative collapse" or "state of siege." Degenerative collápse is very bad news for everyone concerned. State of siege is hardly good news, according to the editors, but at least offers room for pragmatic maneuvering toward a now unforeseeable future dispensation. "For 300 years, Afrikaners have clung to their African foothold by such pragmatism. A State of Siege regime may prove more authoritarian than classical apartheid. It would also be less dogmatic. . . . It could be far more acceptable to the outside world. Authoritarian regimes are unpleasant. They are not ostracized for being so, and can continue in power for a long time."

The government of South Africa insists there is another scenario, namely, the new dispensation, whatever that may turn out to be. Pretoria tells the world that it is taking steps, but that a serious misstep could bring the real reactionaries into power, such as Treurnicht and his Conservative Party. This line of argument has now worn very thin. The split in Afrikanerdom has taken place. Botha precipitated it, and the responding blow from the defenders of classical apartheid was hardly fatal. Political analysts in South Africa believe it is extremely unlikely that under the present electoral system the Conservative Party and its splintered allies to the right could displace the present government. On the other hand, were the Botha government to move more directly toward genuine negotiations, it would almost certainly have the support of large sectors of the population that now oppose it. That, at least, is the view that has gained ascendancy among observers who are convinced that continued white domination is indefensible and the prospect of violent revolution is, as they say, too ghastly to contemplate.

The urgent need is for hope that is beyond illusion. Here is where the churches—black, Afrikaner, and English, but mainly black and Afrikaner—are utterly indispensable. They are the institutional bearers of the transcendent symbols and moral values by which most South Africans claim to order their lives. The people in charge of the new dispensation are, for the most part, technocrats. As technocrats they are, whether they want to or not, advancing secularization. Where pragmatism and rational calculation are the order of the day, the world becomes, to use Max Weber's term, "disenchanted," freed from transcendent meanings. The technocrat says that fundamental change must be presented in terms of old values. But his reference to values is in passing, and usually only in connection with tactics. This reflects a grave limitation of the technocratic mindset.

Culture is not so plastic that it can be readily manipulated to serve the tactician's desires. The ideas by which people live cannot be taken apart and rearranged like pieces in a tinker toy set. And people—at least some people—are not so stupid that they cannot detect the fraud of disguising the new as the old. It may be, as we have heard some suggest, that the Afrikaner needs a strong dose of secularization. The civil religion of Afrikanerdom must perhaps go through a period of what might be called metaphysical decompression. But no people can live entirely bereft of a sense of higher purpose, even of destiny. A bad dream must be replaced by a better dream, for no people can live without a dream. Much attention is being given to a political reconstruction, but I believe no political design will endure unless it is accompanied and legitimated by a cultural reconstruction. A lasting dispensation will not be simply a pragmatic accommodation to reality, although that is no doubt an essential part of it. A lasting dispensation will also offer a morally compelling vision of the reality that might be.

The Afrikaner's understanding of the old covenant was grievously flawed on many scores, and fatally flawed by racialism. Perhaps now the intellectual and moral energies of black and white together can articulate a new and inclusive covenant. Such a covenant would have to speak both of judgment and of hope, of sin and of forgiveness, of endings and of beginnings. I see Allan Boesak among those signing the new covenant, and Desmond Tutu leading the service of national reconsecration. Beyers Naudé has a place of honor, and beside him stands Mfanafuthi Makatini representing the new ANC. Bobby Godsell is there for Anglo-American, along with Jayaram Reddy, who is still putting in a word for keeping the economic engine ahead of the political caboose. Luci Mbuvelo, who has become a kind of patron saint of labor, heads the huge delegation of workers. There is Johan Heyns, cautiously assenting to a new and better mythology, and Gerrit Olivier, who managed to get into the text some of the language of Madison and Hamilton. And there, in the center, are Gatsha Buthelezi and P. W. Botha. It may be that all of these, and the many others present, are not-too-distant successors to today's actors. But there they are, together commending their agreement to the higher authority that all profess to serve. The ceremony of the new covenant takes place, of course, at Blood River.

But I am dreaming, and the time for such a dream may have run out.

Or its time, please God, may still be coming.

NOTES

Notes to Chapter One

1. Unless otherwise noted, the conversations recorded took place in South Africa or with South Africans in the U.S. and Europe between 1970 and 1985. Public figures will ordinarily be identified fully. In some instances confidentiality was a condition for our conversation and, with few exceptions, the promise of anonymity was rewarded by greater candor.

2. Quoted in Hans Morgenthau, *Politics among Nations* (New York: Knopf, 1978), p. 134.

3. On the first use of the term "African," see L. H. Gann and Peter Duignan, *Why South Africa Will Survive* (Cape Town: Tafelberg, 1981), p. 7.

4. *South Africa: Time Running Out,* The Report of the Study Commission on U.S. Policy toward Southern Africa (Berkeley: University of California Press, 1981), p. 28.

5. *First Report of the Constitutional Committee of the President's Council* (1982), p. 30.

6. On the religious factor in Afrikaner self-consciousness, see, for example, T. Dunbar Moodie, *The Rise of Afrikanerdom* (Berkeley: University of California Press, 1975).

7. For a discussion of the flirtation with nazism, see Gann and Duignan, *Why South Africa Will Survive,* p. 92.

8. For a lively telling of the Blood River legend and its continuing importance, see Barbara Villet, *Blood River* (London: Everest, 1982).

9. *Mafeking Road* (Cape Town: Human & Rousseau, 1981), p. 63.

10. On the Trek, see Villet, *Blood River,* p. 72.

Notes to Chapter Two

1. Villet, *Blood River,* p. 96.
2. Ibid., p. 97.
3. Ibid., p. 53.

Notes to Chapter Three

1. Quoted in *Time Running Out,* p. 41.

Notes to Chapter Four

1. Quoted in E. Digby Baltzell, *The Protestant Establishment* (New York: Random House, 1963), p. vi.
2. Anton Rupert, *Priorities for Coexistence* (Cape Town: Tafelberg, 1981), p. 26.
3. Villet, *Blood River,* p. 137.

Notes to Chapter Five

1. Isaiah Berlin, *Four Essays on Liberty* (New York: Oxford University Press, 1969), p. 172.
2. Peter Walshe, *Church versus State in South Africa* (Maryknoll, N.Y.: Orbis, 1983), p. 147.
3. For a favorable interpretation of the Program to Combat Racism, see Marjorie Hope and James Young, *The South African Churches in a Revolutionary Situation* (Maryknoll, N.Y.: Orbis, 1981), pp. 84ff.
4. Walshe, *Church versus State,* p. 141.
5. Ibid., p. 153.
6. Nadine Gordimer, "Living in the Interregnum," *The New York Review of Books,* Jan. 20, 1983.
7. Walshe, *Church versus State,* p. 212.

Notes to Chapter Six

1. Desmond Tutu, *Crying in the Wilderness* (Grand Rapids: Eerdmans, 1982), pp. 113–14.
2. Ibid., p. 36.
3. Religious News Service report, Sept. 1, 1983.
4. Tutu, *Crying in the Wilderness,* p. 82.

Notes to Chapter Seven

1. The Bosch testimony was reported by the Ecumenical News Service, no. 83.03.58.
2. Etienne Leroux, *Seven Days at the Silbersteins* (New York: Houghton Mifflin, 1967), pp. 141–42.
3. Hurley's views on disinvestment were reported in the *Financial Mail,* Dec. 14, 1979.
4. The exchange between the government and the independent churches quoted here was reported in the *Citizen,* Aug. 29, 1981.

Notes to Chapter Eight

1. The *Sunday Times*, July 10, 1983.
2. *New York Times Book Review*, June 13, 1982.
3. Allan Boesak, *Farewell to Innocence* (Maryknoll, N.Y.: Orbis, 1977).
4. *Time*, Jan. 1, 1979.

Notes to Chapter Nine

1. J. M. Coetzee, *Waiting for the Barbarians* (New York: Penguin, 1982), p. 135.

Notes to Chapter Ten

1. This quote draws details from a quotation in Hope and Young, *The South African Churches*, p. 209.
2. For some polling results and an example of the way they are employed by the President's Council, see *First Report of the Constitutional Committee of the President's Council*, pp. 41ff.
3. The interview with Dr. Motlana draws also on Robert I. Totberg and John Barratt, *Conflict and Compromise in South Africa* (Lexington, Mass.: Lexington Books, 1980), pp. 31ff.
4. Quoted in Hope and Young, *The South African Churches*, p. 111.
5. Buthelezi's presidential addresses are published in *Inkatha*, the movement's journal.

Notes to Chapter Eleven

1. For a discussion of "justified revolution" in a manner analogous to "justified war," see my "The Compleat Revolutionary" in Peter Berger and Richard John Neuhaus, *Movement and Revolution* (New York: Doubleday, 1969).
2. Quoted in John de Gruchy, *The Church Struggle in South Africa* (Grand Rapids: Eerdmans, 1979), p. 225.
3. Tutu, *Crying in the Wilderness*, pp. 87–89.
4. For a more detailed description of Motlana's views, see Totberg and Barratt, *Conflict and Compromise*, pp. 38ff.
5. Data on ANC numbers is drawn from David Winder, "Waging a War of Sabotage in South Africa," *Christian Science Monitor*, Sept. 16, 1983.
6. Lelyveld's report on the ANC leadership is in "Black Challenge to Pretoria," *New York Times*, Oct. 12, 1983.
7. Tambo quoted in "Interview with Oliver Tambo," *New York Times*, Feb. 7, 1982, and "A Talk with Oliver Tambo," *The New Leader*, Jan. 24, 1983.

8. Motlana on communism and ANC quoted in Hope and Young, *The South African Churches,* p. 204.

9. The Denton report is available from the Subcommittee on Security and Terrorism, U.S. Senate.

10. Quoted in "Son of HUAC," *Worldview.*

11. Interview with P. W. Botha, *South African Digest,* Sept. 23, 1983.

12. Quoted in *Southern Crucible* (Pretoria: Africa Institute of South Africa, 1980), p. 49

13. This division of labor is described in Gann and Duignan, *Why South Africa Will Survive,* pp. 240ff.

14. Quoted in *Inkatha,* July 1978, p. 4.

15. For further elaboration of the argument, see "Prospects for Revolutionary Violence," *Martin Spring's South African Newsletter,* Nov. 1981.

16. For a thorough statement of the near impossibility of revolution, see Gann and Duignan, *Why South Africa Will Survive.*

17. Alan Cowell, "South Africa's Neighbors: The Chains Won't Break," *New York Times,* Jan. 31, 1983.

Notes to Chapter Twelve

1. The complete text of the Huntington analysis is published in *Politikon,* the journal of the Political Science Association of South Africa, Dec. 1981.

INDEX OF NAMES